Understanding Therapy

Understanding Therapy

How Different Approaches Solve Real-World Problems

Rudy Nydegger

An Imprint of ABC-CLIO, LLC
Santa Barbara, California • Denver, Colorado

Library of Congress Cataloging-in-Publication Data

Names: Nydegger, Rudy V., 1943– author.
Title: Understanding therapy : how different approaches solve real-world problems / Rudy Nydegger.
Description: Santa Barbara, California : Greenwood, [2019] | Includes bibliographical references and index.
Identifiers: LCCN 2019025659 (print) | LCCN 2019025660 (ebook) | ISBN 9781440865084 (hardback) | ISBN 9781440865091 (ebook)
Subjects: LCSH: Psychotherapy.
Classification: LCC RC475 .N93 2019 (print) | LCC RC475 (ebook) | DDC 616.89/14—dc23
LC record available at https://lccn.loc.gov/2019025659
LC ebook record available at https://lccn.loc.gov/2019025660

ISBN: 978-1-4408-6508-4 (print)
978-1-4408-6509-1 (ebook)

23 22 21 20 19 1 2 3 4 5

This book is also available as an eBook.

Greenwood
An Imprint of ABC-CLIO, LLC

ABC-CLIO, LLC
147 Castilian Drive
Santa Barbara, California 93117
www.abc-clio.com

This book is printed on acid-free paper ∞

Manufactured in the United States of America

This book discusses treatments (including types of medication and mental health therapies), diagnostic tests for various symptoms and mental health disorders, and organizations. The authors have made every effort to present accurate and up-to-date information. However, the information in this book is not intended to recommend or endorse particular treatments or organizations, or substitute for the care or medical advice of a qualified health professional, or used to alter any medical therapy without a medical doctor's advice. Specific situations may require specific therapeutic approaches not included in this book. For those reasons, we recommend that readers follow the advice of qualified health care professionals directly involved in their care. Readers who suspect they may have specific medical problems should consult a physician about any suggestions made in this book.

This book is dedicated to the people over the years whom it has been my privilege and pleasure to work with in psychotherapy. What I have gained from working with them, learning from them, and becoming a part of their lives during challenging times has made my life fuller and richer. To all these people I owe sincere thanks and an appreciation for what they have brought to my life.

Contents

Preface

Most people would acknowledge that they know what psychotherapy is and feel that they have some idea how it works. Many of us have seen examples or stories about therapy in movies, books, or TV shows and have even known people who have been in therapy. Even for those who have been in therapy themselves, the knowledge of what therapy is, who can do it, and what it does is still often a mystery.

Psychotherapy is a relatively new treatment modality, although there have been advisors, physicians, healers, counselors, clergy, and many others who have been sought for their wisdom, advice, and support throughout all human history. Most people will seek therapy if they have problems in their lives that they do not seem to be able to manage themselves, symptoms or issues that do not seem to respond to other approaches or treatments, or just because they do not know where else to go to get help that they feel that they need. Of course, it is also true that many people will seek out therapy because a significant person in their life (parent, spouse, friend, etc.) encourages or even insists that they get help for their problems.

Psychotherapy can mean many different things, but basically it involves psychological techniques that are designed to help people more effectively manage their lives and deal with their problems. These techniques do not rely on medical practices like medication, surgery, or other physical types of treatments and usually involve verbal and/or behavioral approaches to help people accomplish their treatment goals. Some approaches to therapy are very directive and involve the therapist telling the patient or client things that they should do or think to help make the changes they want and need. Other therapeutic techniques are more nondirective, and in these approaches the therapist does less directing and more listening and supporting. In this form of therapy, the assumption is that the patient or client has the resources within themselves to deal with their own problems, and the therapist will try to provide the setting and support to help the person arrive at their own solutions.

The fact that psychotherapy involves nonmedical approaches does not mean that alternatives like medication cannot be used to help treat psychological difficulties, but those approaches are within the realm of medicine and are therefore provided by physicians or other medical specialists. However, some medical providers are also trained to do psychotherapy, and some psychologists are also trained to prescribe medications, so these lines can be somewhat "fuzzy." More typically, psychotherapists will work together with medical providers so that the patient can get appropriate medication or other medical treatment *and* get psychotherapy from their therapist, and often this type of coordinated treatment is helpful for the patient.

This book is designed to be an introduction to psychotherapy and to present and explain therapy, how it works, and who does it. In Part I of the book, we will explore what psychotherapy is and will define and explain the various concepts and terms that are related to it. We will also delve into the background and history of therapy, where it came from, and how it evolved. Because there are often misconceptions about therapy and what it does, one chapter will address the myths and misconceptions about psychotherapy and explore them in detail. Biases, fears, and faulty expectations about psychotherapy will also be discussed.

The last chapter in Part I will discuss the different kinds of professionals who conduct psychotherapy, the kinds of training that they have, how they practice, the kinds of therapeutic services that they provide, and where they are likely to practice. "Psychotherapy" or "therapy" is not a profession by itself but involves techniques that are used by trained professionals to provide treatment for their clients or patients.

You may have noticed that the term "patient" is used to describe the recipient of therapy, and sometimes the term "client" is used. In the 1960s and 1970s there was a movement to remove the "disease" misconception about psychological problems, and many felt that the traditional medical model of disease did not fit most of the "problems of living" issues that brought most people into psychotherapy. It was strongly argued that most of the people seeking help were not sick, did not have a disease, and therefore were not truly patients. Thus, they felt that these people seeking care would be better called "clients." Today we know more than we did a few decades ago; we know that some psychological problems do have underlying physical issues (e.g., genetic predisposition for some types of problems), and while most psychological issues for which people seek help do not have an underlying medical problem that causes their difficulties, they are still people coming to a professional to be treated and to have their difficulties dealt with and hopefully eliminated or minimized. Today, people are usually less touchy about the "patient"/"client" issue, and most professionals will use the terms almost interchangeably depending on what they are talking about or who they might be addressing.

It will also be obvious to the reader that the terms "psychotherapy" and "therapy" are used as if they both mean the same. Clearly, "therapy" is a generic term that describes a method used to treat a problem. For example, a lip balm for chapped lips is also a type of lip therapy. However, in the context of this book, the "therapy" that we will be discussing is almost always going to be "psychotherapy," and therefore, these terms will be used interchangeably.

In Part II of the book, we will describe and discuss the many and various types of psychotherapy starting with the psychodynamic approaches beginning with Freud and looking at some of the other and newer approaches from this school of thought. These approaches begin with the assumption that psychological difficulties derive from conflicts *inside* of our minds, and therapy involves techniques for dealing with these underlying issues, and two chapters look at these types of theories.

The next chapter examines the humanistic and existential types of therapies. These approaches are similar in some ways to the psychodynamic approaches, but they tend to focus more on conscious thought and decisions and do not deal as much with material from the unconscious parts of our mind. The following chapter looks at the cognitive approaches to therapy, and very much like the humanistic and existential therapies, the cognitive techniques focus primarily on conscious thoughts and other mental activities; they, too, tend to avoid the unconscious materials.

The behavioral approaches comprise the next section of the book, which looks historically and more recently at the behavioral approaches to therapy. These methods work primarily with overt behavior and do not deal with subconscious materials at all. Further, they work more with behavior than thoughts and feelings, although some of the more recent approaches do involve work with cognitive and emotional issues.

Although this book addresses psychotherapeutic approaches to treatment, we will at least touch on some of the more medical types of treatments since they are frequently practices that psychotherapy patients might also be involved with. The most common form of treatment for psychological issues is medication, and we will briefly describe the types of medications that are used to treat psychological/emotional problems. In addition, we will discuss electroshock therapy and some of the more recent experimental medical approaches to treatment. Finally, we will examine other more physical types of treatments that are being used instead of or in combination with psychotherapeutic treatment.

The last chapter in Part II of this book will look at some of the other forms of psychotherapy that are being used and will examine some of the group and family approaches to treatment. In addition, some of the newer technological innovations like teletherapy will be explored. We will also explore some of the adjunctive types of treatments like art therapy, dance therapy, and drama therapy. Some formal programs that claim to work better than psychotherapy are available to the public and are intended to replace medication and psychotherapy as methods of treatment for psychological difficulties. Although controversial, we will examine some of these programs as well.

In Part III of the book we will present a few case studies that involve a significant variety of psychological problems and show how they might be treated. This part does not involve "proving" which approaches are best but rather how different approaches might be used to deal with specific types of problems.

After having read this book, the reader will be conversant in the main forms of psychotherapy, who practices it, what they try to do, and how they work. The case studies will give each person some insight into how the various types of psychotherapy might be employed to address some of the typical issues that bring people into therapy.

Acknowledgments

A book like this depends on a lifetime of education, knowledge, and experience. There are some people whose influence in my life was certainly significant and occasionally profound. I will start with the person who had more to do with my becoming a psychologist than anyone else—the late professor Robert Knapp from Wichita State University. I had no interest in psychology as a field and certainly was not drawn to psychology as a profession. As a chemistry and math double major who had to take a psychology course for my distribution requirements, I reluctantly signed up for introduction to psychology, and since I was in the honors program I had a small class taught by the chair of the department and found it to be somewhat interesting. I then decided to take another psychology class and signed up for experimental psychology because I wanted to see what science would be like studying people instead of physical substances in test tubes and complex equations. Professor Knapp was teaching this class, and although several students warned me that this was a difficult and boring class, I decided to take it anyway. Initially, Professor Knapp was very interested in having a student from the hard sciences sign up for his class, and as we got to know one another he was excited about my interest in the science of psychology, and he got me involved with some original research and even let me design and execute my own study. I was so excited about this that I decided that I wanted to study animals and people, and although I loved chemistry and math, I was passionate about applying science to understanding and helping people. I later got even more interested in working with people and took my scientific knowledge and approaches to working directly with and helping people using clinical psychology. Without that course and the devoted mentorship of Bob Knapp, I am quite sure I would never have become a psychologist. His friendship and wisdom were a part of my life until his recent death, and his memory is still very important to me personally and professionally.

One of the other people who had a major influence on my academic and scholarly decisions was the dean of students at Wichita State University—Dr. James Rhatigan (now retired as the former vice president of student affairs). Dr. Rhatigan, who came from a counseling psychology background, was a wonderful role model who showed me how a professional person can take their knowledge, education, and training and use this background to make a positive difference in people's lives. I have known few people who have touched more people and had a more positive influence on the lives of students, alumni, and staff of the university. Further, his impact on the values and culture of the university and higher education, in general, has been monumental.

Of course, there are many others in my background, education, and training who have had a positive impact on my professional and personal life, but these two men need to be singled out as most important in how I have spent my life and the things I have tried to do professionally.

Writing a book is a time-consuming and intense undertaking that is challenging, fun, hard work, and fulfilling. It does, however, take one away from the other things in life that one wants and needs to do. My wife Karen; my kids Ashley, Morgen, Colby, Liesl, and Austin; my grandsons Lucas and Sam; and all my other family and friends have continued to be my foundation and support and have made the effort well worth the trouble. Further, I once again must recognize and thank my editor Maxine Taylor whose support and help over the years have made me a better author, and her influence has certainly improved my books.

Thanks to all of you.

PART 1

Introduction to Psychotherapy

CHAPTER ONE

What Is Psychotherapy?

Originally, the term "psychotherapy" came from two words in ancient Greek—*psyche*, meaning breath, spirit, or soul, and *therapeia*, meaning healing or medical treatment, but today it is defined as "the treatment of the mind, personality, emotions, and behavior using psychological methods." The American Psychological Association adopted a resolution in 2012 that was written by John C. Norcross: "Psychotherapy is the informed and intentional application of *clinical methods* and *interpersonal stances* derived from established psychological principles for assisting people to modify their behaviors, cognitions, emotions, and/or other personal characteristics in directions that the participants deem desirable."

The intention of psychotherapy is to help people make changes that they identify and agree with to improve the quality of their life. Psychotherapy is an interpersonal process that involves a psychotherapist who provides services, and (a) patient(s) or client(s) who asks for help dealing with their identified issues. What makes psychotherapy somewhat unusual as a professional service is that by listening, supporting, making suggestions, and giving advice, the psychotherapist is doing much of the same things that a person's friends or family would do to provide help. In fact, many people will avoid going into therapy because they assume that they can get the help that they need from friends or family, and therefore see no reason to have an appointment with a professional. However, there are several differences between a professional psychotherapist and a well-meaning family member or friend. First, the professional has academic and clinical training to equip them with the knowledge and skills needed to provide appropriate, meaningful, effective, and ethical treatment. Second, the professional therapist will be more objective. Third, the therapist will have no emotional connection with the patient or client, and therefore has no emotional investment in the outcome of the treatment.

There are often misconceptions about the similarity or differences between counseling and psychotherapy, and there is quite a bit of overlap between the two. Typically, "counseling" usually involves guidance and advice about "everyday" problems in specific areas and is usually of a short duration. For example, a school counselor would advise and guide students regarding academic and school-related issues, or a clergy person may counsel a member of their congregation on spiritual, moral, or ethical issues. However, it is certainly possible, that during psychotherapy there might well be some counseling used for specific issues. Some counselors (e.g., counseling psychologists) may also be trained in psychotherapy, but not all would be. Therefore, psychotherapists would be trained to provide counseling as part of their services, but not all counselors are trained to provide psychotherapy. We will discuss the various forms of treatment methods and providers in a later chapter and make it clearer as to where and with whom people should ask for and receive the psychotherapeutic help they need.

Historical Developments

Psychology as an academic and scientific field is relatively recent (somewhat over 100 years old), and the use of psychotherapy by trained professionals is also recent by historical time. However, throughout human history there have been people who have used psychological methods to treat others for mental or even physical problems even if they did not have the professional training that we expect today. Whether it was clergy, rulers, family members, physicians, philosophers, or others, there seem to always have been members of society who others would seek out for help, advice, and support. Something resembling psychotherapy was probably first developed in the Middle East during the ninth century by the Persian physician and psychological thinker, Rhazes, who had been the chief physician at the Bagdad Psychiatric Hospital. In the West, however, the treatment of the insane was usually nonexistent, cruel, or blatantly harmful. By the 19th century in Western Europe and North America, there was a movement toward "moral treatment" of the insane that utilized noninvasive and non-restraint forms of treatment. Providing a comfortable place to live and sleep; having adequate nutrition, minimal if any restraint; and more humane ways of treating the mentally ill were now the more accepted ways of providing care for the insane.

During the 18th and 19th centuries in the West, there were professionals and researchers who were trying to find more scientific and physical ways to explain and treat psychological issues. Phrenology, as developed by Franz Josef Gall (a respected anatomist), tried to understand human psychology by examining and measuring the skull. This was based on the unfortunately wrong assumption that bumps on the skull were related to more-developed areas of the brain, and that indentations in the skull were related to less-developed areas of the brain. By using these measurements, Gall felt that he could explain why certain people had weaknesses or flaws in their psychological functioning. Of course, this did not result in any meaningful treatment, but it was used primarily as a diagnostic and research tool.

Similarly, the study of physiognomy was popular in the 19th century and was an approach to psychology that tried to understand human psychology by examining individual's facial characteristics. Once again, this approach was for investigative purposes and did not involve any form of treatment. William Sheldon also tried to explain human personality by looking at body types and relating different body types to personality characteristics. This approach was not used for treatment but did result in a significant amount of research; however, it was soon found to be invalid.

One approach in the 18th and 19th centuries that did involve treatment was introduced by Franz Anton Mesmer and is called "mesmerism" or "hypnosis," and is still used occasionally today. Mesmer believed that by tapping into "animal magnetism" people could be placed in a trance, and some of their psychological problems could be treated with this technique. The use of noninvasive and non-medication treatment for mental conditions aroused considerable influence and resulted in some significant research and clinical investigation in several laboratories including one in Nancy in France. The Nancy psychopathologists (people studying abnormal psychology) included Jean-Martin Charcot, Pierre Janet, Ambroise-Auguste Liebeault, and others, and were part of such an influential school that even Sigmund Freud went there to learn from these revolutionary practitioners.

When Freud came back to Vienna and started working with his colleague Josef Breuer to become a consulting neurologist, he learned some new ideas and techniques from his mentor. Breuer was treating patients (usually women) who suffered from what they called "hysteria" that involved a person experiencing physical symptoms with no identifiable medical reason. One of Breuer's patients had a very serious case of "hysteria," and Breuer found that simply having her talk about her symptoms and what was going on in her life resulted in some relief from her symptoms, even if only temporary; in fact, his patient described this approach as the "talking cure." We will discuss Freud in more detail in Chapter 4, but the historical reality is that Freud took this basic approach and idea and developed the most complete theory and form of treatment that had ever been developed before.

At about the same time as Freud was working with Breuer and the Nancy group, American psychologists were starting to do research on humans and animals that investigated the behavioral basis of psychology. This approach did not deal with non-observable phenomena like thoughts, feelings, or the unconscious, but only dealt with observable behavior and other measurable phenomena. One American behaviorist (as they became known), John

Watson and his students, even showed that abnormal behavior could be acquired by learning, and that abnormal behavior could be changed with new learning. This laid the groundwork for the later emergence of behavior therapy and behavior modification.

Another American psychologist working in the late 19th century established the first psychological clinic. Lightner Witmer was a professor of psychology at the University of Pennsylvania and organized a clinic to treat children with learning disabilities. He was also the person credited with naming this new field clinical psychology. Historically, Witmer is very important—he started the first clinic established to treat psychological problems, he named the field, and he made the important connection (as did the behaviorists) between research and treatment.

Another interesting development in the 19th century in the United States involved the approach to trying to understand and treat mentally ill patients with psychological techniques. Most people who were using psychological treatment methods were not dealing with the seriously mentally ill, and these more severely disturbed people were generally treated by psychiatrists and neurologist, that is, if they were treated at all. However, there were a few people who were trying to understand and treat the mentally ill with nonmedical approaches. It was felt that when a person became mentally ill they became "alienated" from their true self, and those who tried to work with and understand them were called "alienists." Although this term has been used more recently in books, movies, and TV shows, it has not been used much at all since the early 20th century. Interestingly, the alienists were often used to determine a person's competence to stand trial because of their mental condition. Today, the professionals who often specialize in these types of issues are called forensic psychologists or forensic psychiatrists.

Prior to World War II, psychologists were primarily involved in academic pursuits like teaching and doing research, and clinically, they largely conducted psychological assessments and evaluations. Few psychologists were involved in psychotherapy, and most of this type of therapy was conducted by psychiatrists, most of whom were trained psychoanalysts in the Freudian tradition. There were some nonmedical psychoanalysts (called lay analysts), but that was the clear exception. However, when the soldiers, sailors, and marines started returning from World War II, it was obvious that many of them needed psychological care, and there were not enough psychiatrists or psychoanalysts to meet the need. That is when the Department of Defense went to the universities and the American Psychological Association and expressed the need and desire to have psychologists trained to provide psychotherapeutic care for returning service people. Training programs were designed and implemented on the "Scientist-Practitioner" model, and the guidelines for the training of clinical psychologists were accepted. Therefore, today psychotherapy is practiced by other professionals besides psychiatrists, and it is true that few psychiatrists today practice psychotherapy, and they do not spend as much time in their training on nonmedical forms of treatment.

After the introduction of psychoanalysis, most of the psychotherapy that was used came from this tradition and involved in-depth treatment that was usually lengthy and expensive. Consequently, mental health treatment was usually not available to those who could not afford it, health insurance did not cover it, and psychotherapy was not felt to be effective in the treatment of severe mental illness. Therefore, most people who had needs for mental health treatment did not receive any treatment at all, and those patients with severe psychopathology (mental illness) were usually hospitalized and treated with rudimentary and usually ineffective medical treatments, and therefore their "treatment" was usually just custodial care.

Particularly in the United States, there were ideas coming out of the universities that were leading to new theories and new possibilities for treatment methods. Starting around the beginning of the 20th century but really gaining popularity were the behavioral approaches that were based on good research and were scientifically sound and held distinct possibilities for the development of effective methods of treatment. At the same time, other scholars were working on theories and methods based on cognitive processes that were also strongly supported by research and experimentation. These newer approaches were seen as being distinctly different from psychodynamic approaches like psychoanalysis because they were dealing with observable and quantifiable data that did not depend on ideas like "unconscious" that could not be observed or measured. Many felt that these more scientifically sound approaches were superior and offered significant hope for the future.

Between World War I and World War II, there was also a movement that was developing as an alternative to the unconsciously based psychodynamic approaches and the laboratory-based behavioral and cognitive methods that were coming largely out of the universities. Some practitioners were finding alternative ideas from the field of philosophy. For example, some European psychiatrists were interested in applying ideas from the philosophical field of existentialism to psychotherapy. Rather than focusing on the unconscious or only on observable behavior, they were more interested in looking at choices and decisions that people made and helping them find ways to be more "authentic," better balanced, and fully integrated in their psychological life. Another group, which came largely after World War II, was interested in applying the philosophical perspective of humanism to psychotherapy. These practitioners did not focus on the unconscious but preferred to concentrate primarily on observable behavior, and in this way, they had some similarities with the existential therapists. However, the humanists were basically focused on the ideal that each individual person is unique and valuable in their own way, and that therapy should be primarily focused on helping persons become the best individuals they were capable of being in their own personal and unique way. This approach became very popular among the public and with many psychologists and was a major influence in psychology and psychotherapy in the 1960s and 1970s.

Today, the mental health professions are not as rigidly tied to specific methods and theories as they used to be. Few practitioners will limit themselves to only one form of treatment but will learn several different types of treatment strategies, and then apply the best strategy to each specific individual client or patient depending on their needs and goals. There has been a movement in recent years in the fields of medicine, psychology, and even social work that emphasizes the importance of using treatment methods that have been validated experimentally, and there is increasing evidence that certain treatment methods are most likely to be successful with certain disorders. While this is an important and valuable approach, some risks are associated with it as well. For example, some patients may not like or be suited for a treatment even if it is experimentally validated. Thus, there needs to be some flexibility as to the choice of treatment strategy based on the experience and expertise of the provider of the service. Further, there is also the risk of insurance and managed care companies using the ideal of empirically validated treatment to dictate treatment type even when it might not be best for the patient, or to use this as a basis to avoid paying for legitimate treatment because the provider chose to use something other than a validated treatment. These are true risks, but the basic idea of empirically validated treatments is sound but must be employed with sensitivity and flexibility respecting the wisdom and experience of the trained and credentialed professionals and keeping in mind the best interests of the patients.

Needs and Issues

There are many different opinions about the needs and necessity of psychotherapy ranging from those who feel that everyone should have therapy to those who feel it is a ridiculous waste of time and money and no one should bother having therapy. Of course, as in many cases made from a "right-wrong," or "good-bad" perspective, the reality is probably someplace in that middle "gray" area. Most research and professional perspectives would suggest that psychotherapy is a vitally important treatment modality. In fact, reliable research finds that psychotherapeutic treatment is valuable and an empirically supported form of mental health intervention.

Many people take advantage of mental health treatment, including psychotherapy, and in a survey done in 2004, 27% of all adults received mental health treatment in the United States. Of these, 47% reported a history of medication but no therapy, 34% reported that they had had medication and psychotherapy, and 19% reported psychotherapy but no medication. What is particularly interesting about this survey is that most psychological and medical literature demonstrates that medication alone is rarely a fully appropriate treatment for mental health conditions. In fact, medical as well as psychological research has consistently found that medication is simply not an adequate treatment for most mental health conditions alone, and that in most cases psychotherapy alone or psychotherapy with medication is more effective and less likely to result in relapse. One study showed that 80% of depressed people can be significantly helped by an appropriate mental health treatment, but only 20% of depressed patients received the appropriate treatment. Thus, if we have 100 depressed persons, only 20 of them are likely to receive the appropriate treatment, and of those, 80% or 16 of them would likely benefit from the treatment, which means that today, we can expect only 16% of people with depression will benefit from the *appropriate* treatment for depression.

One might ask why people are so unlikely to receive psychotherapeutic treatment for mental health conditions. The reasons for this are concerning and not likely to change quickly. First, there is still a stigma associated with mental health treatment, and many people will not go into treatment because of this concern. Further, medication may have a quicker treatment response than psychotherapy, but the problem with medication-alone treatment is that when the medication is stopped, the condition typically resurfaces. However, if a person is experiencing mental health symptoms purely because of some temporary stressful change in his or her life, then medication alone might be entirely appropriate; however, this is not the case in most mental health conditions. Medication is typically the first line of treatment for most patients for several reasons. Many people are looking for a "quick fix" for their problems, and asking their primary care physician (PCP) for something to help them feel better is an easy place to start. Although we are doing a better job of educating physicians about mental health conditions and treatments, they still do not have a lot of information about different kinds of treatments, but they do have frequent visits from representatives from the drug companies who will give them information and samples of new medications.

Today many communities are underserved by psychiatry, and there just are not enough psychiatrists to meet the need. This has been helped by the availability of sub-doctoral providers like psychiatric nurse practitioners (NPPs) and physician's assistants (PAs). It is also true that in some states doctoral-level psychologists with additional medical training can be licensed to prescribe psychotropic medications. However, most prescriptions (80+%) of psychotropic medications are written by non-psychiatric physicians, including PCPs, pediatricians, and obstetricians/gynecologists (OB/GYN).

These providers are usually treating the patient primarily for other conditions, and given the difficulty in getting appointments with a psychiatrist and his or her lack of knowledge about other forms of treatment, these physicians will often prescribe medications as one way to try to provide some help for their patients.

It is also true today that drug companies are permitted to provide advertising on TV, radio, print media, and online that tries to sell the idea that medication is a valuable and "adequate" treatment for many/most mental health conditions. Of course, medication does play a role in mental health treatment, but the drug companies do not provide education and information about other more valid types of treatment besides medications. Thus, the public gets the perspective that "drugs are the answer to their problems." Further, the insurance and managed care companies encourage physicians to prescribe psychotropic medications and make it sometimes difficult for patients to receive psychotherapeutic forms of treatment. Particularly when physicians can prescribe psychotropic medications to patients, they are already treating for something else; this saves the insurance companies money (at least in the short run). Even if patients only see a psychiatrist for medication, it seems that this is cheaper than psychotherapy. By grossly underpaying for psychotherapeutic services, the insurance companies discourage providers for even wanting to provide psychotherapy that has resulted in many doctoral-level mental health professionals getting involved with other professional activities that pay them better than psychotherapy. This means that many people are having to go to clinics or master's-level providers for psychotherapy, and while this may be quite appropriate for some situations, these providers neither have the education/training nor provide the range of services that doctoral-level professionals do, and some patients are discouraged by this and may not even pursue treatment.

Status Today

Although many things are discouraging about the availability and utilization of psychotherapy today, the research and experience is strongly supportive of the importance of psychotherapy as a valid and useful form of treatment for mental health conditions. There are significant challenges for the mental health professions in making sure that appropriate treatment is available for patients who need or want it. For example, insurance reimbursement for professionals providing mental health services is woefully inadequate (many hairdressers and mechanics make more money per hour than a doctoral-level mental health professional), and thus fewer people are going into professions like clinical psychology and psychiatry, which makes the problem even worse. It is also true that there is far less money available for training, and thus fewer people can afford to get the training and education necessary to become mental health professionals.

Another major impediment in the provision of mental health services is the difficulty that many people have in getting the care that they need. Many, perhaps most, of the people who need mental health treatment are not able to access the appropriate treatment and often do not get any care at all; as the number of uninsured citizens increases, this problem will only get worse. The solution to this issue is political, but until the voters give a strong message to the politicians that mental health education and treatment is important, they will continue to pay lip service to the idea that health and mental health services are important, and they will simply not vote for anything that will cost more money—even if it is the right and most cost-effective thing to do, a sad state of affairs, but reality nonetheless.

CHAPTER TWO

Common Misconceptions about Psychotherapy

Most people have some ideas about psychotherapy; however, it is also true that many people's ideas about psychotherapy are simplistic, misconceived, or just wrong. Because knowledge about psychotherapy is readily available, people tend to think it is easy to understand and have expectations and ideas that are not well grounded. For example, there is not one type of therapy, nor is there one type of therapist. There are many forms and models of psychotherapy, and there are several different professions that prepare practitioners to conduct psychotherapy. We explore in depth the basic different types of therapy and the various professions that provide psychotherapeutic services.

In this chapter we explore some of the misconceptions and biases about psychotherapy and how they affect both practitioners and patients/clients who might receive therapy. Some of the basic myths about psychotherapy include the following.

Myths and Misconceptions

Myth 1: People who go into therapy must be crazy and must have "mental" treatment.

Reality: Patients who avail themselves of psychotherapy range from truly and severely mentally ill people to the "worried well" who simply want someone to talk to about some difficulties they are experiencing in their lives. In most psychotherapeutic practices, a majority of the patients will fall someplace between those extremes, but very few practices in the outpatient sector (not hospitalized patients) will primarily treat patients with severe mental illnesses but are most likely to have active patients who may have psychological difficulties like anxiety and depression and will have an appropriate diagnosis but are able to function outside of a hospital setting.

It is certainly *not* true that most people who go into psychotherapy for treatment are “crazy” and have severe mental illness. However, research and experience does indicate that while people with serious mental illness usually will primarily have medical forms of treatment (e.g., medication) and may even have to be hospitalized, these patients will often benefit from psychotherapy in addition to their medical forms of treatment. Further, it is also true that many people with less-severe psychological problems who may seek out psychotherapy may also be taking medication, but this is usually to help them function more effectively, and for these types of patients, medication alone is rarely adequate treatment by itself without accompanying psychotherapy.

The conclusion is that most people who receive psychotherapy are not crazy but are pretty “normal” people who are having some specific difficulties with their lives, relationships, work, and so on and who just need some help figuring out how to deal with their difficulties. However, people with severe psychological difficulties can usually benefit from psychotherapy as part of their total treatment program. It is also true that sometimes people without a psychological diagnosis will need to talk to an objective “outsider” who might be able to help them sort through some difficult conflicts or situations, and therefore, a perfectly normal person might also find a reason to engage in psychotherapeutic treatment.

Myth 2: Talking to friends or family is better than talking to a therapist who is a stranger and does not know you at all.

This almost sounds like it makes sense, but it is clearly wrong. That is very much like saying that you do not need to go to a doctor because you have a friend who reads a lot of medical stuff on the Internet. While it is positive to have friends and family who are good to talk with, who know you well, and whom you trust, you cannot expect them to have the knowledge, experience, and training to deal with some of the complex issues that are the source of difficulties from which a person is suffering. Further, you cannot expect that a person who knows you well and to whom you are close to will be objective and unbiased. They might be sympathetic and supportive and understand what is bothering you, but they cannot have the same expertise and knowledge as a professional, nor can they easily sort out their own feelings and be objective about someone they know. For this reason, most professional therapists would never treat a friend or family member themselves but would refer this person to another professional for treatment.

While it may be tempting to talk to someone you know and who knows you well, it is true that their knowledge also involves expectations and past experiences that will color their advice and understanding of your problem, and therefore, their intervention will not be objective or unbiased. While talking to friends and family is good, you can never use them as mental health professionals any more than you could reliably use them as lawyers, physicians, dentists, and so on. Even if your friend or family member is a professional person, they would never pretend to be objective about someone with whom they had a relationship.

The best advice is to use your friends and family in the roles that are most important for them to fulfill and use professionals (including psychotherapists) to fulfill the roles they are trained to fill. For example, you should not expect your health or mental health professional to be your friend, and you should not expect your friends or family to be your professionals. You can be friendly with and even like your professionals, but their role is to treat and care for you and not to be your buddy.

Myth 3: If you just work on getting a more positive attitude about your problems, you do not need to get psychotherapy.

Most people who have struggled with problems like anxiety and depression have had others advise them to "Just don't think about it—think about all of the good things in your life and just forget about the problems and they will go away"; if it were only that easy! Most problems that lead people to seek out psychotherapy are much more complex and serious than something you can just put out of your mind and go on with your life. Of course, all of us will have the occasional minor issue that is not a big deal and is something we should just put aside and go on. The two best rules for stress management are as follows: Rule 1: Don't sweat the small stuff; and Rule 2: Most of it is small stuff. A lot of the time we get worried and upset about issues that are not that big a deal or something we cannot do anything about anyway; under these circumstances learning to "let it go and let it be" is a good thing to do. However, when it is not that easy, and when it is bothering us to the point where it is interfering with our life, then we need to consider the possibility that professional help might be warranted.

Having a positive attitude about life can certainly be good and can even help us cope more effectively with many of life's problems. However, a positive attitude will not change all the things that trouble us, and it will not erase the difficulties and symptoms that may result from our having a psychological problem or disorder. Knowing when to "just let it go" and when to seek help is an important distinction and one worth remembering.

Myth 4: Psychotherapy is just about letting people "vent" and get things off their chests.

Sometimes, having someone to listen to us when we need to "vent" really helps. In fact, in therapy we refer to "catharsis" when a person can talk about something that is upsetting to them; experience the emotion associated with the issue; and have someone listening who will not judge us, will not just laugh at us, or will not make fun of us for feeling badly; this can be helpful. However, therapy is never as simple as just getting something off your chest; even when this is helpful, it does not resolve the underlying problem, nor does it prepare us to avoid or change the situation(s) that led to the situation that made us feel as badly as it did.

Being able to vent is sometimes something that friends or family can help us with, but this expectation comes with some considerations. First, if you are venting about the same thing time after time, others get tired of hearing about it and will stop wanting to listen to you. Second, if the same issue keeps coming up, venting alone has not helped the problem. Finally, if venting to friends or family has not changed anything, perhaps expressing the issues to a professional might result in some outcomes that might be helpful.

Myth 5: Psychotherapy is usually just about talking about your childhood and blaming your parents for your problems.

In the past, psychotherapy did focus heavily on childhood experiences, and it was assumed that all adult problems had their roots in childhood. While some adult problems are linked to experiences in childhood (e.g., abuse), it is true that many problems result totally or primarily from experiences in our adult life. Very few psychotherapists will focus only or even primarily on childhood experiences to try to understand an adult's difficulties, nor will many therapists blame *only* a person's parents for their difficulties. There are, unfortunately, situations where a person had a very traumatic and difficult childhood, and that reality would certainly be a focus for treatment, and when a person's parents were the source of the trauma, this reality must be dealt with in therapy as well. However, in most cases, a patient's parents might not have been perfect and might have made some mistakes, but simply blaming the parents does not help the person make changes that will improve the quality of their life; they must learn how to deal with their history, make changes in their personal life, learn new skills and perspectives, and try to live a life that is better than their history might have laid out for them. If we are honest with ourselves, we would admit that none of our parents are or were perfect and most of them made plenty of mistakes; however, most of them did the best they could do under the circumstances, and as adults we need to learn to accept that fact, forgive them, accept them, and live our lives as things are today. Of course, when childhood trauma involves abuse and/or neglect, forgiveness is a more complex issue and might have to take a slightly different perspective; these types of situations might need professional assistance to work through them.

Myth 6: Psychotherapy takes a long time, and many people are in therapy at least once per week for most of their lives.

Certainly, when Freud first started doing psychotherapy, it was a lengthy process and took many visits and frequently many years to complete therapy. More recently, people have developed much more efficient modes of therapy, and insurance companies will not pay for lengthy treatment when more efficient and effective types of therapy are available. Although some patients require longer and sometimes "maintenance" forms of treatment because of chronic conditions, most psychotherapy is measured in a matter of months rather than weeks or years. Of course, this depends on the type of problem being dealt with and the type of treatment being used. However, a small minority of patients are in treatment for many years on a frequent basis. Sometimes, a patient with a chronic condition will have their case file kept open in case they need to come back in or need maintenance type of treatment, but even then, they might come in only one to three times per year for checkups, and this is after the main part of psychotherapy has been concluded.

Myth 7: Psychotherapy is expensive, and insurance companies usually do not pay for it. Even if the insurance pays for therapy, this means that your company will know that you are being treated and what your problems are.

These common misconceptions are usually not true at all or are considerably exaggerated. While insurance companies would rather not have to pay for services, most policies do provide for some type of mental health treatment. Depending on the state in which one lives and the insurance laws of that state, mental health services might have some type of limitation on the number of visits that are allowed, or what types of mental health problems are covered, but if someone has a question, they can call the insurance company in question to ask about the coverage and the providers who are available under its policy. It is always a good idea to have your policy in front of you when you call the company to make sure that you are getting the most accurate information.

The Health Insurance Portability and Accountability Act (HIPAA) of 1996 protects health information and makes it illegal for someone to release information to anyone who is not permitted to see the information, and the patient has the right to know who can see their health data. The employer rarely has the right to confidential health information except under specific circumstances of which the employee is aware and has given permission.

If a person does not have health insurance, they have a few options if they want to receive care. They can pay for psychotherapy privately out of their own pocket, and while that can get expensive, many therapists will have a sliding scale and adjust their fees for those who cannot afford care otherwise. Also, clinics are available for those patients who do not have insurance and who cannot afford to pay for treatment themselves. Some clinics also will have sliding scales so that patients are changed based only on what they can afford to pay.

Cultural and Gender Biases in Psychotherapy

One of the factors that may be a problem in providing appropriate psychotherapy for patients who need care is that a therapist may not be available from their own background or gender, and the patient may feel that the therapist will not likely fully understand them or the problems that they are experiencing. It is true that when the therapist and the client are from different cultural backgrounds, this can be an issue. In recent years, a significant effort has been put into helping therapists be more comfortable working with people from different cultural backgrounds, but this is still a concern. We have found that with a little sensitivity, empathy, and extra training, most therapists can become quite comfortable and effective working with people from other cultures, but it is important that they have the appropriate training and not just good intentions.

In a similar vein, some clients feel more comfortable working with a therapist of a specific gender. While there is considerable evidence that the sex of the therapist ultimately does not make a difference in most therapy with most clients, it is always a good idea to respect the preferences of the patient unless it is impractical to do so. In recent years, in most of the mental health professions, we are seeing far more women coming into these fields than there were in the past. In fact, in some areas most new providers are women. There are many sociological, personal, professional, and financial reasons why this is the case, but it is only an issue if a specific client strongly prefers a male therapist and none is available in the area where the person is being treated.

When looking at cultural background and sex of patients, there is some interesting research on who and why some people in different groups will seek or avoid mental health treatment. In most underprivileged minority populations, the problem is usually the availability of care. These groups are typically underserved in the United States, and the fact that they are not being treated is not because of their cultural background but rather because of their socioeconomic status and the accessibility of appropriate mental health care. However, some groups are more likely than others to seek care.

For example, the main difficulty in getting appropriate care for African Americans is the access to care. Many times, they do not get care in time, and consequently, their problems are frequently more serious because they are not treated early. It is also true that like Caucasian patients, African American males are less likely to go for mental health treatment than females, and this is true even when treatment options are available. Latin American patients will usually not go into treatment primarily because of the lack of treatment opportunities. However, when treatment is available, they will usually access it and will be compliant with both medication and psychotherapy and will usually improve with treatment. Asians, on the other hand, may avoid mental health treatment because of the stigma and the fear that such treatment will bring disgrace to the family and make the patient a less-desirable marriage prospect. Pacific Islanders and Native Alaskans who are frequently underserved often do not have access to reasonable mental health services. It is also true that most mental health providers are white, middle-class and upper-middle-class professionals, and minority patients may feel that they will not be appreciated or understood by someone from a different group, and there is some truth to that concern; this also will make it less likely that people from minority groups will enter mental health treatment.

With respect to differences between men and women in mental health treatment, it is usually found that in most cultural groups, women are more likely to experience mental health difficulties like depression and anxiety than men are. However, this is also affected by the fact that at all ages, boys and men are less likely than girls and women to voluntarily access health services, including mental health services. Men, in general, tend to keep their feelings and their problems to themselves, and women are more likely to share and discuss their issues with friends and professionals. Consequently, males are typically less likely to enter psychotherapy than females. There are a few differences in some cultures, however; for example, in India men usually have more open access to health services than women, and this is true of mental health services as well.

Fears and Faulty Expectations

Many times, people are fearful of starting psychotherapy because they do not know what to expect. They might be afraid of discussing their difficulties because the fear that by "opening that box" they could find that there is something terribly wrong that might be very problematic and/or embarrassing.

People are also concerned that their problems are trivial and that a therapist would feel that treating them would be a waste of time. Fortunately, their problems are usually easily taken care of in the initial stages of psychotherapy, but we must get the patient into therapy before they can find that out.

People frequently have the expectation that talking about their problems will make the issues go away, and this is almost never the case. It is not talking about the problems that makes them go away but rather what a person is willing and able to do differently about their problems that makes them change for the better. Further, most of the difficulties that bring people into therapy have been building for years and will not go away quickly. Therapy usually involves helping a person make changes in the ways in which they act, think, and feel, and this may take some time. Clearly, if a person with problems keeps doing the same things with the same people and in the same situations, nothing will change. Therapy is about helping people make changes that will help them improve the quality of their life, and this is not a quick fix. Some patients feel that medication for psychological problems is better than therapy because it may work faster. While this might be true to an extent, it is also true that medication alone is almost never adequate treatment because when a person stops taking the medication the problems simply return. However, psychotherapy is usually a better way to make changes that will decrease the chance of relapse. That is why many providers like to use the combination of medication and psychotherapy. However, research evidence is clear that psychotherapy with or without medication is usually a more effective way to make psychological changes than medication alone.

Patients frequently expect that in therapy the provider will tell them what to do to make the people around them change. It is common for people to come into therapy with a list of things that a person or people around them are doing that is causing problems. Good therapy usually involves focusing on patient behavior and what the patient can do themselves to cope with and adapt to the people and situations around them. That does not mean that we sometimes have problems that are caused by the people around us, but we have no true control over other people's behavior, and focusing on how we can make them change will almost never work. Similarly, some will go into therapy expecting that the therapist will have answers to all the patients' problems and tell them exactly what to do. In most cases, the therapist will help the patient explore their options and then determine what will be the best course of action to take to improve their situation. Of course, many therapists will help generate options and explore outcomes, but they will always point out that the choices are up to the patient.

Sometimes, patients are not sure what to expect from a therapist and may feel that they do not "click" with a provider and may even bounce from one therapist to another trying to find the right fit. This might also be an example of therapeutic resistance where the person does not really want to get into therapy, and by bouncing from one therapist to another, they never really have to get into the issues that they do not want to truly confront. However, it is also true than no therapist can or will be effective with every single client, and sometimes when the client–therapist fit is not a good one, the responsible therapist will refer the client to another provider who might be more effective with this specific patient. It is usually good judgment for patients to plan to spend at least three or four visits with a therapist to determine if it is the right person for them. Further, if a patient does not feel that they are on the right track with a therapist, they should bring this up and discuss it. If the therapist is not willing to discuss this type of concern or is not willing to listen to the patient's concerns, then it is obviously time to find another therapist.

CHAPTER THREE

Types of Therapists: Where Do They Practice and How Are They Trained?

One fact that is confusing in trying to understand psychotherapy is that it is not a profession, but rather it is an activity. A person who engages in psychotherapy provides a service to someone who has expressed a need for help dealing with personal, emotional, behavioral, cognitive, or social issues that they have not been able to resolve on their own or with the resources at their disposal. There is not a profession or career as a psychotherapist although some professionals identify themselves in this way. There is no state or province in which a person can become licensed or certified as a psychotherapist; however, psychotherapy is usually (depending on the state) identified as a professional activity that can be performed only by certain licensed professionals. It is also true that only professionals for whom psychotherapy is within their "scope of practice" are permitted to conduct this activity. "Scope of practice" refers to the range of activities that a professional may engage in because of the license they hold. Thus, as psychologists, psychiatrists, or social workers would be able to conduct psychotherapy as permitted by their license, lawyers or dentists, although licensed professionals, would not be able to conduct psychotherapy because that is not an activity within their scope of practice.

In recent years, the range of professions permitted to conduct psychotherapy has increased, and this is primarily because of shortages in the traditional mental health professions and the increased need for services, including psychotherapy. While this makes the situation even more confusing for patients and clients, it is true that more options are available to meet these needs. However, trying to decide whether one needs psychotherapy, where one might get the therapy, and what type of professional to contact may be confusing to people who are not familiar with mental health services.

Some people feel that psychotherapy is a waste of time and largely unneeded and unnecessary, but others feel that everyone should have therapy. Like with many issues, the truth is probably somewhere in the middle. It should be obvious that when a person is suffering from symptoms of a psychological disorder (anxiety, depression, etc.), they should be a candidate for psychotherapy. Further, when someone feels that their life is out of control, and they are not able to deal with the issues confronting them, then psychotherapy might be warranted. People having trouble at work or school, at home, with relationships, socially, and with alcohol or drug abuse could probably benefit from psychotherapy. Another indicator for therapy is that when those people around an individual strongly recommend professional help, this should be a "red flag," suggesting that therapy might be a worthwhile option. The truth is that the "downside risk" of therapy is small; you might waste some time or a few dollars, but that is about all that is really being risked, and if therapy turns out to be helpful, then it was clearly worth the small risk.

When someone who might benefit from psychotherapy is resistant to try it, it might be suggested that they try therapy a couple of times, and if it does not appear to be helpful, then they can just stop going—no major risk at all. It is also important that when people are seeking psychotherapy they should not look specifically for a type of therapy, but rather, they need to look for the most appropriate and experienced therapist they can find. Even if the person has a friend who benefited from therapy X, that does not mean that the new therapy patient will benefit as much from that approach, and a different strategy might make more sense. The patient should discuss with the therapist what the problems and issues are, what they want and need from treatment, and what their expectations are. It is appropriate at this time to mention a treatment, and if the provider feels that this is reasonable and something that they are trained to provide, then they can proceed in that direction. If the provider feels a different approach would be better, they can mention and discuss that. However, if the provider agrees that "therapy X" would be helpful, but they are not trained to conduct that type of treatment, then they can refer the patient to another therapist who might better meet the patient's needs.

If someone decides that they might benefit from therapy, the next question is, where do you go and who do you see? Most people do not know how to access this type of service unless they know of someone who has had therapy and can ask about a referral. The next best place to ask is one's primary care physician (PCP), who will usually have some knowledge of the mental health providers in the area. It is also possible to contact professional societies like the State Psychological Association, the State Medical Association, the State Social Work Association, or other relevant professional societies. The Internet can be helpful, but if you do not know the professions you are dealing with, it is easy to get into websites that look very official but are just ways for a specific group of providers (sometimes not even appropriately trained) to get more referrals. One strong piece of advice is to never go into therapy with any professional who is not licensed by the state in which they practice. Having a state license does not mean that the person is the right one for you to see, but it does mean that the individual has met the minimum amount of education, training, and experience to practice; it also means that they are compliant with the ethical standards of their profession. Without license, there is no protection for the patient as a consumer and no guarantee that the provider is appropriately trained and ethical. With these concerns in mind, we examine the various mental health professions that frequently provide psychotherapeutic services and explore their training and the kinds of services they provide.

Psychologists

Among the various mental health specialties, psychologists have the most training in psychology, which is hardly surprising since that is the field in which they specialize, and to be licensed in psychology, one must have an appropriate doctoral degree from an accredited university in a psychological discipline and have met the minimum requirement for experience and training. Each state in the United States and provinces in Canada have licensing laws for psychologists, and these are coordinated by the American Psychological Association (APA) and the Canadian Psychological Association (CPA). Clearly, each state and province makes and enforces its own laws, but the APA and the CPA try to help provide guidelines that allow for reasonable similarity and coordination between states and provinces. If one wants to practice psychology, or even calls themselves a psychologist, they must be licensed in the state or province in which they want to practice. It is possible to be licensed in more than one jurisdiction if a person wishes to, but the person must comply with the requirements of each individual state or province and maintain the qualifications within that jurisdiction.

Psychology is a broad and varied field with numerous specialties and subspecialties. Those who are licensed usually practice in the areas of clinical, counseling, neuropsychology, forensic, school, and industrial/organizational psychology. It should be noticed that most school psychologists have a master's degree and are not licensed. However, they can practice under the auspices of the school system in which they work. A few school psychologists with doctoral degrees can be and frequently are licensed. States do not typically license specialties but usually will only license psychologists generically; therefore, any psychologist who meets the educational and training requirements is able to get licensed if they choose, but rarely will psychologists get licensed unless they are treating patients or clients, providing consultation to people or organizations, or otherwise being paid for providing psychological services. Health service types of psychologists are trained to diagnose, treat, and prevent mental health problems, and they are the only mental health specialty that is trained to administer and interpret psychological tests. Other professionals may use lower-level screening tests, but only psychologists are trained to deal with more sophisticated psychological assessment devices like tests.

To be recognized and to advertise oneself as a specialist in a specific field of psychology (e.g., clinical, counseling, neuropsychology), one must be board certified by the American Board of Professional Psychology, which will certify that a psychologist has met the professional/ethical requirements and take appropriate examinations in one or more areas to become a specialist. Other organizations provide board certification, but they are not recognized by the APA or CPA, nor are they recognized by the state or provincial associations.

To become a licensed psychologist, a person must have a doctoral degree (usually a PhD, PsyD, or EdD) in a primarily psychological area of specialty and granted by a university that is accredited by the state or province in question, and these programs are typically four years of full-time education and training; however, the average time to finish a doctoral degree in psychology is in the four- to six-year range. To get a doctoral degree, one must first have a four-year bachelor's degree, and one may also have a two-year master's degree. In addition, the candidate for licensure must document all their training and supervised experience and pass a rigorous examination. Their compliance with the legal and ethical requirements of the license is also investigated and must also be complied with. Most states require that a person providing psychological services have at least two years of supervised experience on a full-time basis before being licensed. Some psychologists will also have a one- to three-year postdoctoral fellowship that will give them the supervised experience and additional specialty training in the area in which they choose to practice.

Many states require that a psychologist fulfill a minimum number of continuing education credits per year, and even in the states that do not require this, it is usually true that the insurance and managed care companies that help pay for psychological services will require annual continuing education for psychologists. Most states require that continuing education be based on attending conferences and/or doing online courses, most of which require some examination following the activity. Other states, like Vermont, also allow people to gain continuing education credits by attending classes, documenting the reading of books and articles, and other types of continuing education activities. For any psychologist who is licensed, they must be re-credentialed occasionally and document their compliance with the educational/professional/ethical/legal requirements of their license.

Although psychology is not a medical specialty, some psychologists will study psychopharmacology (the use of psychiatric medications) following the completion of their doctoral degree. This additional area of study involves substantial coursework, supervised experience, and practice in prescribing psychiatric medications. Although this training provides an ample basis for prescribing, it is new and only a few states and the Department of Defense currently recognize psychologists as prescribers.

Psychiatrists

A psychiatrist is a medical doctor (MD, doctor of medicine; DO, doctor of osteopathy) who has gone to four years of medical school and then completed some additional training in the diagnosis, treatment, and prevention of mental/emotional/behavioral problems. Psychiatrists usually take training after medical school in a psychiatric residency where they take courses, learn how to provide treatment under supervision, and gain increasingly more independence in their professional capabilities. Psychopharmacology is a major focus of psychiatric training, and this involves learning about and using psychotropic medications in the treatment of mental health conditions. They are also trained to use other forms of medical and physical treatment, including electroshock therapy, but also some experimental treatments like deep magnetic stimulation, and other new types of treatment. They will also be exposed to psychotherapeutic forms of treatment and will learn some of the basic approaches in providing psychotherapy. In practice, psychiatrists usually do not engage in psychotherapy, although sometimes they do, and may use the combination of medical and psychotherapeutic treatments.

Psychiatrists are also trained to understand how certain medical conditions or problems can affect psychological functioning or perhaps how other medications might influence how a patient is functioning psychologically. It is not unusual for psychiatrists and psychologists to collaborate in their treatment of a patient, and when treatment is coordinated between the mental health providers and a patient's other health providers (e.g., PCP), this is almost always a significant advantage for the patient.

Social Workers

There are many different types of social workers and many different programs in which they can study. Primarily, social work is the mental health discipline that deals with individuals and families but also deals with the social, educational, legal, and political systems in which people function. Of course, all mental health providers will need to work in these environments as well, but the social worker deals most thoroughly with the social systems in communities that are involved with and impact the lives of clients and citizens. One can get a bachelor of social work degree, a four-year degree that will allow a person to work as a social worker although they cannot work independently and must perform their tasks under the auspices of an organization where they are supervised and monitored or under the supervision of a licensed mental health professional. Master of social work is usually a two-year (full-time) degree, and these practitioners may work independently if they had met the educational and training criteria specified by their state to become licensed and to be able to practice independently. There are several different types of master's degrees that a social worker might seek, and these would have to do with the type of work they want to do and the client base they want to serve. Social workers often work as administrators and function in a variety of roles in different types of organizations. They might work in schools, hospitals, mental health clinics, or other types of medical facilities. They may also work for the government or insurance companies or in other settings. A clinical social worker has training in dealing with mental health issues, and like psychologists and psychiatrists, they are trained to diagnose and treat certain mental health conditions. While they usually work in mental health or medical settings, they can be licensed to practice independently if they have the proper training and the years of supervised experience necessary to qualify for private practice.

Some social workers have doctorate degrees, and these are usually a PhD in social work or a DSW (doctor of social work). While these professionals might be licensed to practice clinical social work, many of the doctoral-level social workers see clients but also work in an academic environment where they might teach and do research like professors in other fields.

Counselors

This is a broad category that involves different professions in which people are trained to counsel others in a specific category of problems. For example, a school counselor will counsel students and parents regarding school-related issues; pastoral or clergy counselors will usually counsel people on religious, spiritual, moral, and ethical issues but may also provide some personal, relationship, family, or social support or counseling in areas where they are trained and competent to provide services. Marital and family counselors, substance abuse counselors, and other types of specific counselors may provide support and advice for people experiencing specific types of problems. Some counselors will go through a specific training program and get certified to provide specific types of counseling like career counseling or substance abuse counseling. In fields that require only a certificate and not a license, the practitioners are not usually required to have a college degree but only need to complete the certificate program. However, doctoral- and master's-level licensed professionals may also get certified in one or more of these counseling areas. It is common, for example, for a psychologist or social worker to also have training to be a substance abuse counselor.

In most states, counselors will not have or need a state license to practice, but their ability to provide services is limited. Some states do license master's-level counselors, and they can practice independently although their services are not always paid for by insurance. Counselors can be helpful, but they are best at working with specific problems that lie in their scope of practice—that is, the disciplines in which they are trained to provide services. Unless they have additional mental health professional training, their scope of practice is usually limited to a narrow range of issues where they can be of most help.

Medical Subspecialists

In recent years, it has become increasingly challenging to find appropriate mental health services, and this is particularly true in underserved areas like rural, inner city, remote, and small communities and areas that are not near larger medical and educational centers. Therefore, we have seen other professions emerge to help meet the needs of clients who are trying to find help for the difficulties they are experiencing. More people entering the ranks of masters-level counselors are available to provide some of the services provided by psychologists, psychiatrists, and social workers, although they cannot prescribe medications or conduct psychological testing without supervision, but they can provide counseling services in the areas within which they are trained to provide services.

There have been many problems providing psychiatric services to the people in need of mental health services because, as noted earlier, doctoral-level psychiatrists and clinical psychologists are not usually available in underserved areas. Further, some research suggests that over 80% of psychiatric prescriptions are written by nonpsychiatrists—PCPs, OB/GYNs, and pediatricians write quite a few of these because they are often on the front line treating people who need care but cannot find a psychiatric provider who can see them. In response to this need, we have seen some nondoctoral-level specialists emerge, and this has been helpful. A psychiatric nurse practitioner is someone who has been to college and nursing school and has received a registered nurse degree and certification and then to graduate school where they learn about prescribing psychotropic medications and are exposed to some basic approaches to counseling and psychotherapy. The family nurse practitioner who works in a primary care type of office will also have some training in psychopharmacology and provide some basic care in this area.

Physician's assistants (PAs) have been to college and then to graduate school to become a PA. They may choose to specialize in any of a variety of specialty areas including psychiatry and are trained primarily to diagnose problems and prescribe medications. They are exposed to psychotherapy but usually do not have much training in this area. Other types of graduate degrees in nursing may prepare people for providing some limited services in the psychiatric and psychological areas, and these can be helpful as well.

So Which Type of Provider Should You See?

This is a somewhat confusing and controversial issue and frequently leads to unfortunate referrals to providers who are not trained to provide the needed services. However, the first step is to make sure that you are being referred to a professional who holds a state license in the field in which you need treatment. Then you should consult with someone you trust; this could be your PCP, your clergy, another professional, a family member or friend who has some experience with mental health services, or a local professional society in psychology, medicine, or social work. Online services make referral suggestions to local providers, but unless you absolutely know that the site is legitimate and unbiased, you should stay away from the online referral services—there are too many that are not professionally credible, and it is hard for a lay person to know this.

After you have some names, it is usually good to start with the more highly trained specialists who can provide the broadest range of services, and if they feel that a subdoctoral provider would be appropriate, they can refer you to someone else. The good doctoral-level providers are usually so busy that referring to someone else is not an issue; if they think someone else could handle the problem effectively, they do not mind referring people out.

It is always better to see a more-experienced provider if one is available. Seeing a new provider is better than not seeing anyone, but the more-experienced professionals will usually have the most and quickest success. Clearly, the more-experienced and qualified professionals are also the most difficult to get to see, but they are also usually the best people to ask for the name of someone else who would be appropriate to consult with for the problem someone needs help with.

Finally, selecting the best provider is more important than trying to decide in advance which type of professional you need to see. That is why getting referral information from someone you trust, like your PCP, is usually the best place to start.

PART 2

Types of Psychotherapy

CHAPTER FOUR

Traditional Psychodynamic Therapies

In this chapter we examine some of the earlier and most influential theories from the psychodynamic heritage. Although this is a word that you may have heard before, "psychodynamic" is not a term that most people could accurately define. When we break the word down into its component parts, it is clear as to what the term means; "psyche" is from the classical Greek and means mind, soul, or spirit. "Dynamic" refers to change or progress within a system or process. Therefore, "psychodynamic" refers to the changes that occur within the mind, soul, or spirit, and these types of theories focus on changes and processes that are acting and interacting within the mind of a person, and these interactions determine a person's psychological functioning.

History and Development

Psychodynamic theories focus on the elements and processes within the unconscious or subconscious mind, and finding ways to deal with these aspects of a person's psychology is the focus of psychodynamic therapies. Psychodynamic therapy is often referred to as "depth psychology" because it focuses and deals with the deeper parts of a person's personality and not just the observable behaviors and conscious processes. Frequently, people use the terms "unconscious" and "subconscious" interchangeably, but they are not the same. "Unconscious" refers to things that are outside of consciousness or not a part of consciousness, while "subconscious" refers to things that are below the level of conscious thought or processes and not just outside of consciousness. However, this is a subtle difference, and for most purposes, either term could be used to describe most of the processes that we will be discussing.

The first of the major psychodynamic theories and therapies was psychoanalysis, which was developed by Sigmund Freud in the late 19th and early 20th centuries. However, Freud never claimed or believed that his theory was the first that ever mentioned subconscious processes, but his was the first major theory that was fundamentally based on the subconscious as the prime determinant of human behavior.

Throughout the history of philosophical thought, people have speculated about processes outside of consciousness that might influence or even determine behavior. The first attempt to systematically develop the principles of psychodynamics was in 1874 in the publication of the *Lectures on Physiology* by the German scientist Ernst Wilhelm von Brücke. He was interested in the recent developments in physics and chemistry with the introduction of thermodynamics and was committed to the idea that some of the concepts of physics and thermodynamics could be applied to living organisms. He was also supervising and teaching a first-year medical student by the name of Sigmund Freud, who started applying the concepts of "dynamic" physiology to his own theory of the human psyche. He felt that energy systems governed the psyche much like the physical systems underlying human physiology. It was his belief that the psychic energy systems originally derived from the physical energy system in the body, but after it emerged they became parallel but separate systems. He did feel that these dynamic systems and the energy that drove them behaved much the same as energy systems in other realms, for example physics and chemistry.

From this beginning, psychodynamic psychological theories and therapies started to emerge, and all of them (starting with Freud's psychoanalysis) were committed to understanding the dynamic psyche as a system with structure and energy; some of the most important elements of this system were found in a subconscious that was not only dynamic and active but also determinative of thoughts, feelings, and behaviors at the conscious level of functioning. Therefore, these underlying dynamics could result in conflicts or other maladaptive processes that would interfere with the normal functioning of the whole system, and that "therapy" or treatment for maladaptive psychological functioning must address the underlying, subconscious conflicts or problems if any true treatment or improvement of the whole functioning system could be achieved. Therapies that are based on psychodynamic theories usually rely on techniques like dream analysis, free association, interpretation, and working through painful memories and issues to arrive at an insight into and understanding of the nature of the underlying conflicts and buried memories so that true resolution of the difficulties arising from these underlying issues could be realized.

Key Individuals and Their Contributions

Some of the basic principles of psychodynamic types of psychotherapy include the following:

- An emphasis on the fundamental importance of intrapsychic (inside the mind) and unconscious conflicts and their role in shaping psychological development.
- Identifying and working with the psychological defenses that people use to avoid dealing with the painful memories and conflicts that are the basis of the symptoms that they experience.
- A belief that most psychological difficulties are based on experiences from a person's childhood.
- The idea that the psychic representations of our experiences (including those from childhood) are organized around social and interpersonal relations.
- The conviction that psychological issues and dynamics will emerge in psychoanalytic therapy symbolically through the client–therapist relationship in elements like "transference" (the way a patient reacts emotionally toward their therapist because the therapist symbolically represents someone emotionally important in the patient's background) or "countertransference," where the therapist reacts to a client in ways symbolically related to someone important in their own psychological history.
- The use of free association as a primary method for uncovering unconscious conflicts and problems; this is where the patient just relates whatever is going on in their mind without editing or thinking about it.
- Focus on interpretations of transference, defense mechanisms, and other techniques to discover the relationship between intrapsychic issues and the symptoms the patient is experiencing and working through the problems facing the patient.
- The belief that successful treatment is based on the importance of patient insight regarding their psychic history and issues.

In this section, we examine some of the earliest and most influential of the psychodynamic theories and explore some of the therapeutic implications of these approaches and how they have impacted psychotherapy today. While these first few theories may be somewhat familiar to many people, certainly most will have heard of Freud and psychoanalysis. The other two of the most fundamental and important of the early theories come from two of Freud's students who left the psychoanalytic fold and began their own novel and important psychodynamic approaches to theory and therapy: Carl Jung and Alfred Adler.

Sigmund Freud

Born in 1856 in Freiberg, Moravia, which was then part of the Austrian Empire and is now in the Czech Republic, Freud was Austrian and spent most of his professional life in Vienna. His father was a wool merchant, who had two older sons from a previous marriage, and after the death of his first two wives, he married a much younger woman, Amalia Nathanson, who later gave birth to Sigmund. Young Freud was a gifted student who graduated from a prominent high school with honors. He loved literature and history and was proficient in German, French, Italian, Spanish, English, Hebrew, Latin, and Greek. He entered the University of Vienna at 17 and had planned to study law but joined the medical school in the university and studied philosophy, physiology, and zoology. In 1881 he received his medical degree, and in 1882 he began his medical career at the Vienna General Hospital.

Freud was interested in physiology and was part of the research team that discovered the topical anesthetic qualities of cocaine and found that it could be used for oral (mouth) and ocular (eye) surgery. In fact, if you think of the names of medications used by dentists, surgeons, and pain specialists, you will notice that the word stem "-caine" shows up frequently, for example, Novocaine, Procaine, Lidocaine, Xylocaine, and these drugs are usually synthetically developed and are chemically like cocaine. He was interested in research in neurophysiology, and after his research was published, he became an unpaid lecturer in neuropathology at the University of Vienna. He was also interested in clinical work and had a position in a local asylum.

Ultimately, Freud found that unpaid research and lecturing positions did not allow him to afford a "normal" life with marriage and a family, and he started working in private practice in neurology and was mentored by a senior colleague, Josef Breuer, who had a successful practice treating "hysteria," which was a psychological disorder that manifested with anxiety and physical symptoms that appeared to be physical ailments but for which there was no underlying disease or physical cause. Breuer was the first to find that some hysteric patients would get temporary symptomatic relief by talking about their disorders and what was going on in their life. In fact, one of his patients referred to this as the "talking cure."

Freud got married and started a family and got more involved with treating patients suffering from hysteria. He even went to France to study with Charcot and others who were treating hysteria with new methods like hypnosis and were having some encouraging results. Freud also started writing about his emerging theory and his approach to treating these types of patients using what he called "psychoanalysis," which was the first of the well-developed and systematic psychodynamic approaches to treating what he and others were calling "neurosis," which was a group of disorders that involved anxiety and physical symptoms like those found in hysteria. His writings and lectures aroused interest but also outrage and criticism. At one point in his career, he was ostracized and removed from some of the medical societies because of his revolutionary concepts and treatment methods. However, his treatments, teaching, lectures, and writings became much more widely known and appreciated, and he was becoming the most influential psychotherapist in the world. Freud was a brilliant man with an imagination and creativity to match, he was literate and well educated, and his knowledge of the classics and history clearly had an impact on his thinking and theory. In addition to having some new and impressive ideas, he was a gifted writer and even won the Goethe Prize in literature.

Freud's theory was based on psychodynamic structures and processes that he felt were largely responsible for shaping human psychology. He postulated three levels of the psyche: the conscious, preconscious, and subconscious or unconscious. The conscious mind involves what we are thinking about or experiencing at any given point in time. The preconscious is material that we may not be thinking about but can easily be brought to consciousness by directed attention: for example, what did you have for dinner last night? Probably, you were not thinking about this until your attention was directed to the topic, but after it was mentioned, you could bring it to consciousness—this is the preconscious. The subconscious (sometimes called the unconscious) is material that we cannot normally bring to consciousness and is experienced only in distorted or secondary form. Freud believed that memories or events that were too traumatic to be experienced directly in the consciousness would be put into the unconscious, and since they were unresolved issues these unconscious factors would create the basis for all psychological problems. Therefore, psychoanalytic treatment depended on discovering these underlying conflicts and finding ways to bring them to consciousness so that they could be dealt with.

Freud also postulated three "organs" of the psyche: the id, ego, and superego. The id is the fundamental part of the psyche and is the only psychic structure we are born with. The id is the repository of all the basic instincts that comprise the dynamic energy system of human psychology. One of the most controversial elements of psychoanalysis is Freud's belief that the basic energy system underlying all human psychology is sexual energy. Later in his thinking, he also added aggressive instincts as part of the basic system, and in his theory, all human behavior, thoughts, and feelings are based on sexual and aggressive instincts. As an infant starts interacting with the environment and the people in it, they begin having various traumatic and difficult experiences that are too frightening or uncomfortable to think about, and these get stored in the subconscious with the sexual and aggressive instincts that are also troubling to think about consciously. As the id comes in contact with the environment, it becomes clear that all of the id's needs cannot be fulfilled immediately if at all, and a new organ of personality emerges to help the infant (and later the child or adult) meet the id's needs within the constraints of reality, and the personal conscience of the individual after that begins to develop. The ego is the adaptive organ of personality that helps the infant meet the needs of the id as best as it can within the constraints of reality and another emerging organ of personality—the superego. The child starts learning the rules and values of society through their contact and interaction with their parents and other important social figures in their lives. They start to internalize these rules and values, and this becomes an important part of the superego and is what we think of as the conscience—we now do not need people to punish us for doing wrong; now we can punish ourselves by feeling guilty. One other part of the superego is called the "superego ideal," and this is the internalized ideal self that we are always striving to become.

Psychoanalytic therapy generally involves techniques to uncover some of the intrapsychic conflicts (those inside the mind); the analyst interprets these, and then with work and discovery, the patient will arrive at insight into the basis of their psychological difficulties, and this insight will result in resolution of the conflict and a lessening or removal of the symptoms that were troubling the patient and that brought them into treatment. The techniques that psychoanalytic treatment utilizes to accomplish goals include dream analysis; free association; analysis of defenses, analysis of resistance; and analysis of transference.

Freud felt that the only way to tap into unconscious materials is when the ego is relaxed and lets part of the subconscious "leak" into the conscious mind but always in symbolic or distorted form. Freud referred to dreaming as "the royal road to the unconscious" because the ego is so relaxed during sleep that material from the subconscious can be experienced in some symbolic form. This is why dream analysis was so important in psychoanalysis. He also used a therapeutic technique called free association, and this is when the person lays down and relaxes on a couch with the psychoanalyst sitting at their head so that they are not in direct line of sight. This is because the analyst wants the patient to just say whatever comes to mind with little "editing" of their thoughts or feelings. With this relaxed atmosphere, Freud felt that subconscious material could emerge with less distortion that typically occurs in normal thought.

Freud also analyzed psychological defenses, and this was a major part of his psychotherapeutic strategy. He felt that whenever a person feared that unacceptable impulses or memories were struggling to come into consciousness, this would create anxiety; we would use psychological defenses to distort the impulses or memories to try to manage the anxiety and keep it at lower levels. For example, if we had impulses or memories trying to manifest consciously, we might just deny that those feelings or thoughts were there and ignore or pretend that they did not exist—this is the defense of denial.

Or, if the thoughts or impulses were so traumatic that we could not even deny them, we could push them back into the subconscious and keep them there—this is the defense of repression. Another fundamental and important defense is sublimation; this is when an unacceptable impulse (sexual or aggressive) is converted into a socially acceptable motive like achievement, and this allows for partial fulfillment of the underlying impulse but in a way that is not damaging to the person or to society. Analyzing and interpreting a person's psychological defenses would give the analyst some understanding of the underlying impulses or memories that were being kept in the subconscious.

Resistance is another form of human activity that is a way of responding to unwanted thoughts or needs, and the analyst would examine and interpret this as well. For example, suppose an analyst was starting to encourage the patient to discuss their relationship with their parents, but this was obviously a difficult topic for them to deal with. The analyst might say something like "This seems like it is very important, so we will pick up on this topic at our next session," but then the person forgets or cancels their next few appointments; this would likely be interpreted as resistance by the analyst, and he or she would feel that the patient was trying (consciously or unconsciously) to avoid dealing with their thoughts and feelings about their parents.

Transference is another topic that psychoanalysis addresses, and this has to do with the ways in which a patient will respond to their psychotherapist. Freud discovered that in the process of analysis, patients would frequently begin acting toward the therapist in ways like how they might act toward a person to whom they were emotionally connected, for example, their parent. This could obviously be important in understanding some of the bases for a person's difficulties and thoughts, and the analyst would likely observe and interpret the patient's behavior to help understand some of the subconscious reasons why dealing with this parent (or another significant person) was so difficult. It is also true that the trained psychoanalyst (or any other therapist for that matter) must be aware of their own issues and be careful about responding to or feeling about a patient like they might to someone significant in their own life (like their child or spouse), and this is called "countertransference." Clearly, the trained therapist must be aware of their own countertransference issues and never let them affect how they conduct therapy. However, being aware of and analyzing transference in a patient is an important part of psychoanalytic psychotherapy.

Freud's psychoanalysis is a theory of personality, a theory of psychological development, a theory of psychopathology (abnormal psychology), and a method of treatment. His approach to psychotherapy was the first well-developed and comprehensive approach to treatment that was firmly based on a coherent theory of personality and psychopathology. Although there are few people today who are practicing traditional psychoanalysis, it has influenced every approach that followed it in one way or another.

Carl Jung

Another one of the early psychodynamic thinkers was Carl Jung, a Swiss psychiatrist who did some of the early research on the use of the word "association test" as a way of studying human psychology. He also treated patients and did further research at the Burghölzli Clinic in Zurich, Switzerland. His research earned him significant recognition around the world, and he received many honors for his work.

Jung was a brilliant and creative thinker and was always looking for new ways to understand and study human psychology. He became aware of Freud's psychoanalysis, and in 1907 the two men met and talked for hours. In 1911, they founded the International Psychoanalytic Association, of which Jung was the first president. Freud and Jung met frequently, and in an era without telephones, e-mail, or texting, they were diligent in corresponding, and they wrote frequent letters to each other. Many of their colleagues believed that Freud considered Jung to be the heir apparent to psychoanalysis and fully expected him to carry on the mission and vision of psychoanalysis in the ways in which Freud had formed and molded it.

However, early in their relationship, Jung began to recognize that Freud was a somewhat jealous parent and did not value or even accept ideas that challenged his theory or methods. As a bright and industrious young man, Jung had his own ideas and was publishing his work very frequently. As Jung became more widely known, it was very clear that his ideas and theory departed from traditional Freudian psychoanalysis and were even critical of some of Freud's ideas. Given the fact that although Freud modified his theory during his lifetime, he did not appreciate others "tinkering" with it and was outspoken in his disapproval of his critics. Jung's departure from traditional Freudian ideas was not well received by Freud, and the two of them broke contact and never spoke or corresponded again throughout their long and productive lives.

Jung was starting to theoretically venture into some different areas, and he firmly believed (unlike most psychologists today) that research and experimentation using the scientific method was neither the only nor the best way to learn about and study human psychology. He began studying phenomena like dreams, myths, folklore, and culture as "empirical" evidence of what human nature and the psyche were about. He, too, believed in the importance of the unconscious although his view of it was different than Freud's. Jung felt that since the unconscious is truly "unconscious," there is no way to study it directly, and thus looking for indirect evidence of unconscious processes (dreams, myths, etc.) was the best way to study it.

The main difference between Jung's conception of the unconscious and that of Freud was that Jung believed that there were two basic parts of the unconscious: the personal unconscious and the collective unconscious. The personal unconscious was much like the unconscious as characterized by Freud. This is unique to each person and represents memories, trauma, instincts, and so on that are too painful or threatening to experience consciously, and are therefore buried in the unconscious where they are less troubling for us. The collective unconscious is a unique concept in psychological theory and is one of the most central and important of the elements of Jungian theory. He felt that the history of human experience is captured and stored in a collective unconscious that is shared by everyone and influences all of us. He uses evidence from anthropology and history to demonstrate common patterns, beliefs, myths, and cultural patterns as evidence that all humans share a common history that is genetically disbursed and influences all people and all cultures around the world. He also discusses the observation that all humans appear to share many ideas and beliefs, and this may be called "human nature" by many, but he saw this as evidence of a shared or collective unconscious.

Jung saw the "self" as the core and unifying element of personality, and this integrates material from the collective unconscious, individual experience, and other factors like perception and memory. The process by which each person strives to attain their true self is what he called "individuation" and is a lifelong quest that all people share. When there are inner conflicts among the personal unconscious, the collective unconscious, the self, and experience, these conflicts would result in neurosis, where the person is experiencing symptoms produced by the conflicts. If the conflicts are extreme, this may lead to a total breakdown of the self, and the person becomes significantly disturbed and suffers from a "psychosis."

Jung's fundamental concepts include the following:

Unconscious: This part of personality includes material from evolutionary memory, personal experience, trauma, and other memories or events that are too troubling to experience directly in consciousness.

Personal unconscious: Jung felt that this part of the unconscious is a potent—probably the most important—part of the human psyche. For a person to be whole and functioning, there need to be an interaction and communication between the unconscious (including the personal unconscious) and consciousness. While we may not recognize information or material from the unconscious directly, we must be able to understand dreams, symbols, myths, and other things as part of our psyche and not just incidental parts of our experience.

Collective unconscious: The collective unconscious reflects material from the totality of human experience and evolution. This shared unconsciousness is found in all members of the species and provides a basis for our ability to share and understand one another's experiences and lives. The collective unconscious comprises what Jung called "archetypes," and this is one of the most difficult of his concepts to fully understand. By "archetype," Jung refers to an innate, universal prototype for fundamental ideas that may be used to understand and interpret our observations and experiences. A group of memories and interpretations found within an archetype is called a complex. For example, Jung would assert that there is an archetype of "mother," and this would be a fundamental prototype common to all people that allows them to experience and understand what "mother" means to them (and to everyone else). That does not mean that all mothers are alike or seen as being alike but rather that all humans have the inborn capacity to experience what "mother" means. The "mother complex" includes all the memories and interpretations associated with the mother archetype.

It should also be noted that as important as archetypes are to the collective unconscious, we can form individual archetypes that include ideals that one wants to emulate (e.g., respect or altruism), and these guide behavior and understanding as well. Archetypes (individual and collective) influence the human psyche and behavior in many ways. We will see archetypes manifest in dreams, myths and stories, music, poetry, religion, laws, and other elements of culture.

Shadow: This is an unconscious complex that involves repressed (pushed into the unconscious), suppressed, or disowned elements of the conscious self that are not experienced directly by the conscious mind. Often, the shadow involves aggression or hostility that the person does not want to acknowledge or deal with, but it can also represent some of the individual's highest qualities that they are either not aware of or not willing to allow them to surface because of fear of failure or other negative factors that inhibit the highest parts of our being from being expressed.

Anima and animus: Jung felt (as did Freud) that all people have some masculine qualities and some feminine qualities (to greater or lesser extent). He saw the "anima" as the unconscious feminine component of men and the "animus" as the unconscious masculine element in women. Today most Jungian scholars and practitioners feel that every person has both an anima and animus, and to be a healthy and fully functioning person, one must have balance between their masculine and feminine qualities. Those men who are "hypermasculine" are denying the feminine side of their personality, and he would see stereotypic women as denying their masculine qualities. In these cases, the person will never fully individuate and experience their true self because they are denying that an important part of who they are even exists.

As you might expect, there are many archetypes and complexes in Jungian theory and practice, but these will give you some ideas as to how he formed his ideas and some of the central elements of his approach. Jung's model was a significant departure from traditional Freudian psychoanalysis, but Jung also acknowledged the value of Freud's approach and his importance in contributing to the understanding of the human psyche and the treatment of psychological difficulties. To set his ideas apart from Freud's, Jung called his approach "analytic psychology" to distinguish it from Freudian psychoanalysis.

Psychological types: Jung also distinguished human personalities as being based in part on different types of temperaments and by psychic functions. He felt that there were two basic temperaments: extrovert and introvert. Of course, these were not two separate categories because everyone generally tends toward one pole or the other, but it is also true that we may differ in these temperaments based on our life experiences and the situations in which we find ourselves. However, each of us, in general, tends to have a tendency toward one of these temperaments most of the time. In addition, he said that there are four different psychic functions that all people utilize, but each of us tends to rely more heavily on one type of function in most situations. These functions include thinking, feeling, sensing, and intuiting. For example, we could identify people by their temperament and their typical function; thus, someone might tend to be a "sensing introvert" or a "feeling extrovert." Although people are far more complex than these simple ways of categorizing individuals, many today still find this a helpful way to identify people. Unfortunately, while this was very forward thinking a century ago, we know today that trying to find a simple way to categorize people will always be inaccurate most of the time because of the complexity of individual personalities and the dynamics of the situations in which people must function.

Psychotherapy: Jung used analytic psychology as one of the basic foundations of his approach to psychotherapy, but particularly later in his career, he astutely observed that his methods did not fit the needs of many people who needed and/or sought psychotherapy. Although his approach to therapy differed from Freud's and Adler's (whom we will discuss next), Jung appreciated and valued these other approaches as helpful ones to therapy. In fact, he claimed that Jungian analytic psychotherapy was an appropriate type of treatment for about a third of the people he treated. He also said that he used more traditional Freudian psychoanalysis on another third of the patients he treated. Finally, he used Adlerian psychotherapy in the remaining third of the patients who were referred to him.

Summary of Jung: A brilliant and creative thinker, Jung has had a major impact on many people, and his influence is still felt today. Many of his writings are complex and difficult to understand, but if one can investigate and explore Jung's ideas, one will see how interesting and compelling his approach can be. Of course, we know far more today than was known when Jung was doing research and treating patients, and thus many of his ideas have been discarded for more modern theories based on a larger body of research and theory. However, that does not diminish the role Jung has played in, or the impact Jung has had on, the field of psychology.

Alfred Adler

Adler was born in a suburb of Vienna, and his father was a Hungarian Jew who was a grain merchant. Being the second oldest of seven children, he had a lot of family members to play with and take care of. He was very competitive with his older brother Sigmund but was generally an outgoing and popular child. When he was three years old, his younger brother died in the bed next to him, and this affected him deeply. Alfred was a sickly child and suffered from rickets that kept him from walking until he was four years old. At the age of four he developed pneumonia, and he overheard the doctor tell his father that "your boy is lost." From that point on, Alfred decided that he would devote his life to become a doctor. He was bright and popular in school but was just an average student. He did qualify to enter the University of Vienna and studied medicine. Originally, he studied to be an ophthalmologist (eye doctor) but then went on to study neurology and psychiatry. His first office was a general practice, but he was interested in psychological factors and started working primarily with psychiatric patients.

In 1902 Freud invited Adler to join their Wednesday evening group that comprised young men (mostly physicians) who were interested in Freud's work and wanted to study with him. This group was the actual beginning of the psychoanalytic movement, and over time it grew to include many people and some from other countries. A long-serving member of this group, Adler was elected president of the Vienna Psychoanalytic Society in 1910 and served until 1911 when he and some of his followers became discouraged with psychoanalysis and Freud's jealous control over the content and theory of the approach; thus, Adler and his followers were the first to leave psychoanalysis because of differences with Freud, and they left even before Jung did. Adler was a bright and ambitious young man who frequently challenged Freud and made a point of developing his own theory that was different from Freud's. While Freud and Jung had been close until Jung left psychoanalysis and started his own approach, Freud and Adler had never gotten along well and eventually actively disliked and spoke disparagingly of one another.

Adler founded the Society for Individual Psychology in 1912, and this "school" of psychology made a clean break with traditional psychoanalysis, and he attracted others who were more influenced by the philosopher Friedrich Nietzsche than by Freud. Although Adler disagreed with Freud on many issues, he did value Freud's ideas and theories about dreams and openly credited Freud for opening the door to the scientific study of sleep and dreams. The main point of departure from Freudian psychoanalysis in

Adler's theory was his reliance on the importance of social factors in emotional development and in understanding the human psyche. He felt that social dynamics were more important than sexual and aggressive instincts in understanding people.

After having broken from Freud's influence and approach, Adler started attracting many followers, and he was popular and influential as a speaker and teacher. He traveled all over the world spreading the word about his approach and practice. He had a large following in the United States and frequently lectured in this country. Even today there are still pockets of Adlerian therapists practicing his brand of psychodynamic psychotherapy, and his influence can be felt in many of the newer approaches to theory and therapy that emphasize the importance of social factors in understanding human psychology.

There is no doubt that Adler was influenced by Freud and by psychoanalysis, but he was also influenced by philosophers like Immanuel Kant and Nietzsche and by the political leader Jan Smuts who coined the term "holism" that Adler would rely on in his theory and in his approach to psychotherapy. Some of the more important of Adler's ideas include the following:

Holism: Adler deeply believed that human beings were more than the sum of their component parts—even psychologically. We were not simply unconscious instincts and wired-in developmental processes, nor are we a collection of learned stimulus–response patterns. He felt that the only way to truly understand people was to learn about and accept these component parts of their psyche, but to realize that each individual was a whole, complete, and unique entity that was creating itself in response to the factors in its life. By using its own composite reality to shape its emerging self and to even modify its own environment, the person would become a fully integrated and healthy individual. In Adler's theory, you could not understand an individual by only studying the components of its psyche but also by looking at the whole and fully integrated "self" that was always changing and always emerging. Each person is endowed with the urge for self-development and social meaning. We are meant to strive for completeness and to make sense of ourselves and our world with respect to our social and interpersonal reality. He also believed that each of us had an inner concept of belongingness, usefulness, and contribution to all of humanity—that is, the inner drive to complete ourselves and to better the world for humanity. Interestingly, he also believed in a "cosmic consciousness" that is reminiscent of Jung's concept of the "collective unconscious."

Compensation: Very much like Freud, Adler believed that psychological difficulties were due to the person trying to protect themselves from problems in their life that they were or are unable to deal with in a healthy and productive manner by using defensive strategies (usually in the unconscious) to distort or modify these unconscious problems in ways that allow them to cope. Unfortunately, these dysfunctional strategies end up causing neuroses or other pathological states that create problems for the individual, but because the underlying cause is not available in their conscious mind, they have no way to adaptively manage these difficulties. Children who come from families that are loving, accepting, and supportive can manage their lives without fear of failure, and can make mistakes and learn from them, whereas the neurotic individual has buried the causes of their difficulties because their families would not tolerate normal mistakes and imperfections and the person began learning to hide or cover up their frailties and were never able to learn how to overcome their problems.

The child from a more dysfunctional background has learned to hide their fears and weaknesses, and because of their sense of inferiority, they often learn to compensate, or often overcompensate, for these feelings of inferiority by acting as if they have no weaknesses and are extremely competent, strong, and capable. What this usually means is that the person is not as "great" as they pretend to be, and by compensating or overcompensating, they are covering up their weakness by acting as if they are something more and better than they are. Thus, Adler would say that most bullies are cowards who are acting like they are strong and "tough," but this is just an act. Another example would involve people who claim to be richer than they are; truly rich people do not have to announce and brag about how rich they are because they already know it and do not have to prove it to anyone. Or, a true genius does not have to go around bragging about how smart they are because it is obvious to everyone without the person having to brag about it.

Withdrawal: Sometimes if the underlying fears and trauma are too much to cope with, the person will construct a fantasy of superiority, but unlike overcompensating, these people with withdraw into a "secret" life that excludes all the things and people that the person is threatened by. This person becomes increasingly disengaged from the real world and retreats further into this protective cocoon of protection from "reality," and this becomes a psychological barrier that prevents the person from being able to interact and deal with life in the real world and with real people. Eventually, they become lost in this insular, protected, and fantasy world in which others have no role.

Of course, Adler had dozens of other concepts and ideas, but these will give you a sense of how he approaches human psychology. Taking his ideas and looking at how Adlerian psychotherapy would be used, it is an understandable and positive view of therapy. It was popular at the time and was a different approach than what Freud used, and different from Jung's as well. Adler believed that all humans share a "nature" and a universal sense of what it means to be human; basic values and ideas that underlie all cultures are examples of how he saw the basics of human nature. However, his approach was also positive and was based on the integrity and value of every person, and he felt that everyone was unique and special and had special gifts that were worth pursuing. His therapy was designed to help people get in touch with their true selves and explore the things that are fundamentally who they are as humans and as an individual person. He wanted people to explore their lives, to reach out to others, to help humanity and other people, and to find and use their unique talents to make themselves and the world better. He also sought to inform people about the importance of education and childhood development, with the goal of making education more positive and supportive of children and less doctrinaire and rigid in its approach. His ideas were popular, and he had a broad and enthusiastic audience in the United States and around the world. He was extremely influential in shaping some of the emerging and newer approaches to psychotherapy, and his impact is still felt today.

How Is This Utilized Today?

Traditional psychodynamic therapies are still practiced today but not nearly as much as in the past. There are still practitioners who consider themselves to be Freudian psychoanalysts as well as some who practice Jungian analytic psychotherapy and others who are Adlerian analysts. Further, there are training centers where people can be trained and treated in centers devoted to one of these three important psychodynamic theorists and therapists. However, most of the centers and practitioners are found in major cities like New York City, Chicago, St. Louis, and Los Angeles although practitioners may be in any city in the country or the world. Today, most psychotherapists are trained in other techniques as well and are more likely to use the techniques with which they are most comfortable, in which they have the most training, and which best meet the needs of the patient or client.

The professionals who consider themselves to be allied to the psychodynamic school of thought are not typically associated with only one type of theory or therapeutic technique and are more broadly trained that was common in the past. If someone is interested in having this type of therapy, one should look at the website of a potential psychotherapist (if one is available) and then call them and discuss the type of approach they will usually use. Any therapist who is not willing to spend a few minutes discussing their practice with a potential client is probably not a person with whom a patient will probably feel comfortable anyway, and this might be a good way of finding a therapist who will be easier to work with.

Concerns and Critiques

Freud, Jung, and Adler were brilliant men who had a significant and lasting impact on the field of psychotherapy. Their theories are all psychodynamic because they work with what happens inside the mind or psyche, and they look at the different interactions and conflicts that arise. Further, as different as their theories are, their fundamental ideas represent variations on some similar and important foundation issues that first came from Freud. Jung and Adler both ventured into new areas against the wishes and advice of Freud, and their newer approaches significantly broadened the psychodynamic approach, making it more accessible and meaningful for a wider range of patients who needed help, and this was clearly a positive influence on psychology and on psychotherapy.

Traditional psychodynamic psychotherapy is considered to be "depth" therapy because it deals with many of the deeper underlying elements of the psyche. Consequently, this type of therapy is typically lengthy because it takes time to get into these hidden and cloaked elements of personality that are never expressed directly. This means that therapy is time consuming and works with symbolic and indirect forms of information, for example, dreams, free association, and other complex information as the basis of psychotherapy. In this approach, the goal of therapy is to try to uncover the basic causes of an individual's problems, help the person recognize and accept them, gain insight into the nature of the original conflict or trauma, and then work through the fundamental issues resulting in a "cure" that helps the person move on from the problems that had underlaid their psychological difficulties. By looking at this type of strategic approach, it is easy to see why this would take considerable time to accomplish all these challenging and complicated issues.

Clearly, these approaches helped many people gain control over some of the things that were creating problems for them and progress with their life in a more positive and healthy manner. However, there were and are some concerns about these approaches that limited their effectiveness and led to them being less utilized today than in the past. First, none of these early approaches were appropriate for most people suffering from psychological difficulties. It was found they worked best for patients who were well educated, verbally competent, and insightful; who had a generally good psychological history, and who were able to function reasonably well in many situations. Further, as we have learned more about psychotherapy and found many other approaches to therapy that are even more successful for a broader range of patients, we have also found approaches to therapy that are much more time efficient and do not take nearly as long to conduct. In fact, most research has demonstrated that lengthy, in-depth therapy is rarely justifiable because there are approaches that have proven to be more effective and that are also less time consuming. Finally, as brilliant as these men were, and as impressive as their theories were, we have learned so much more about psychology and psychological theories in the past century that it is clear that most of the things that these earlier theories proposed are simply wrong or at least the ideas are so vague and nonspecific that they cannot be evaluated scientifically and therefore are not widely accepted by most of the professionals and scholars in the relevant fields that rely on the research and theory today. However, this is not intended to minimize the importance of their contributions. Science is cumulative and self-correcting; what this means is that continuing research finds out what is wrong with current theories and finds new explanations that improve our knowledge and lead to better and more helpful theories, and these will improve over time as research progresses and finds new "truths." However, we would not be where we are today were it not for the contributions of the giants who laid the foundations for what we know today; Freud, Jung, and Adler were certainly three of these figures, and their contributions were important for all the progress and improvements we have made in the fields of psychology and psychotherapy.

CHAPTER FIVE

Neo-Psychoanalytic Therapies

As Freudian psychoanalysis grew and became more important and influential, people from all over the world came to study with and be treated by Sigmund Freud. Obviously, there was no way that Freud could treat everyone, and he felt that educating and training new analysts was one of his primary responsibilities. Even as he got older and his health was failing, he continued to work until the end of his life. Writing, training, teaching, and seeing his own patients were activities that he was devoted to, and he committed his life to these goals.

As more people were learning about and being trained as psychoanalysts, it is not surprising that many of these people did not agree with Freud or his approach and were looking for new ways to conceptualize and conduct psychotherapy. Some chose to follow the one of the first two to leave the Freudian fold—Jung and Adler—but other new voices and new ideas began emerging as well. From all over the world forms of psychotherapy began to emerge, but most of these early advances primarily came from Europe and North America. In this chapter, we examine some of these new ideas and approaches. Of course, literally hundreds and even thousands of new psychotherapists and therapies were being tried and tested, but we examine some of the most well known and influential of these practitioners.

History and Development

"Neo-(new) Freudian" refers to the psychodynamic types of theorists and therapists who emerged after Freud had established psychoanalysis, and although they might have shared some or even much with Freud's ideas and methods, they all represented departures from the traditional approach advanced by Freud; sometimes these new practitioners were called neo-analytic therapists, but this term refers to the same people labeled neo-Freudian. Since he was a jealous parent, when it came to psychoanalysis, Freud did not permit people to modify his ideas and methods and continue to be in the Freudian psychoanalytic tradition—they were now considered outsiders. Clearly, Jung and Adler were among the first neo-Freudians, but because they left the fold so early and paved the way for those who followed, they are treated differently, and this chapter examines some those who followed them and developed their own ideas and approaches, all of which differed significantly from Freud.

All the neo-psychoanalytic approaches share several basic elements that are common to all psychodynamic approaches. First, they deal primarily with the processes that occur within the mind and the interrelationships among these processes. They all would allow for and examine subconscious processes as well, but most of the neo-psychoanalytic approaches do not focus on these to the same extent as did Freud. Thus, the newer approaches differ from Freud by examining other mental processes besides the subconscious. Like Freud, the neo-psychoanalytic theories and therapies pay attention to events that happen in the earlier stages of development (infancy and childhood), but most of them also look at the developmental stages following childhood with more interest and emphasis than did Freud. One major difference between Freud's approach and those that followed him later is that none of them concentrated on the sexual and aggressive bases for the psychic energy system and allowed for a broader range of human emotions including social and personal motives that did not have a sexual or aggressive foundation.

These neo-psychoanalytic approaches (including Jung and Adler) have continued to influence the theories and practices of psychotherapy even today. Continuing psychodynamic approaches are even newer but still rely on some of the basic ideas of their predecessors. These new approaches tend to be more socially based and are typically briefer and less depth oriented than traditional Freudian psychoanalysis or the earlier neo-psychoanalytic approaches including Jung, Adler, and all the neo-analysts covered in this chapter.

The neo-Freudian or neo-analytic models of psychotherapy are primarily found with practitioners in Europe and North America although there are people around the world who use these approaches, but often this is because of the training that they received in the United States, Canada, and Western Europe. Therefore, it is not surprising that these approaches often are reflective of the cultures from which they emerge. It is also interesting that in recent years increasing emphasis has been on integrating ideas and practices from Asian and Middle-Eastern religions and philosophies into the theories and practices of psychotherapy (including psychodynamic approaches); these influences will be discussed later in this book.

The psychotherapists whom we examine in this chapter were all influential and were known as teachers as much as psychotherapists, and their approaches all had a major impact on the practice and understanding of psychotherapy. Many new approaches are available today, but most of them have derived from these earlier models, and we begin examining these in some detail. These models have been chosen because each of them is one or two generations evolved from Freudian psychoanalysis, and each of them is distinctly different from Freud, Jung, and Adler, and they differ significantly from one another. Further, they continue to impact psychotherapy practice today because of their approaches and ideas, but also because of the many generations of practitioners and teachers that they influenced.

Key Individuals and Their Contributions

Karen Horney

As one of the first women to become actively involved with psychoanalysis, Karen Horney (née Danielson) was a pioneer and innovator in many ways. As an assertive and somewhat rebellious youngster, she was usually ignored or criticized by her father who was authoritarian, and as a sea captain he was frequently absent from her life. She became attached to her mother although her mother suffered from mental health issues and eventually left her husband taking Karen and her brother with her. There were several episodes in her life where she suffered from depression, and this would be an issue for her throughout her life. She was attached to her brother, but he was bothered by this and rejected and avoided her. Feeling unattractive and rejected by others, she compensated by focusing on her schooling, and she eventually decided to study medicine—much against the wishes of both of her parents. However, studying at several universities she did receive her medical degree from Berlin University and started to practice there. She met a business student, Oskar Horney; they got married, moved together to Berlin, and began a family.

Having given birth to one daughter, and losing both parents in the same year, she became depressed and decided to enter psychoanalysis to help her cope, and she worked with Karl Abraham who was a student of Freud's. She also received analysis from Hanns Sachs and began studying psychoanalysis herself. She became capable and respected for her abilities and helped found the Berlin Psychoanalytic Institute in which she became a teacher. After her husband's business failed and he became bitter and ill, her brother also died, and she entered another deep depressive episode. Eventually, she and her husband separated and then divorced, and she was invited to become the assistant to Franz Alexander at the Chicago Psychoanalytic Institute. She took her three children and moved to Chicago and then left after two years to move to Brooklyn where she felt that she would be more at home with a large Jewish community many of whom had fled the Nazis. She found that this was a good place for her since psychoanalysis was respected there and she found many colleagues with whom to work and socialize. In fact, she became friends with two other neo-Freudians, Harry Stack Sullivan and Erich Fromm. She and Fromm later developed an intense romantic relationship that was difficult for both, and it ended badly.

As Karen Horney's ideas began to blossom and emerge, she was becoming increasingly in conflict with Freud's doctrine and approaches, and she became much more consistent with the ideas of other neo-Freudians, including Adler. She eventually formally separated from the traditional Freudian psychoanalytic traditions and organizations and founded other groups and training programs that were advancing the ideas of the neo-Freudians and their followers. Like the others in this new wave, she objected to the idea that most human drives and motives were based on sexual and aggressive instincts, and she believed that social and developmental factors played a big part in the development of human personality; for Horney, the treatment of children by their parents established patterns that would shape a person's personality and modes of coping throughout their lives.

Horney focused much of her writing, therapy, and teaching on the idea of neurosis, which she looked at somewhat differently than did most of her other psychoanalytic and neo-analytic colleagues. Rather than simply being a disorder that developed from traumatic or difficult situations in a person's childhood, Horney saw neurosis as a continuous process developing over a person's lifetime, and rather than being a unitary disorder, it would be more of a coping style and a way of dealing with conflict and problems. At times during a person's life, these neurotic patterns could become more problematic because of factors in the individual's life, and then these neuroses would manifest as pathology that required treatment. At other times, these neurotic patterns might be problematic but would be a basic part of a person's personality and would simply shape how they approached problems and life itself.

Horney identified 10 different types of neurotic needs that might develop over a person's life and would shape how they dealt with issues that they faced. These 10 needs were grouped into three categories, and she wrote and taught about these at great length. These categories and neurotic needs are the following:

I. Category 1: Compliance needs
   A. Need for affection and approval
   B. Need for a partner, someone they can love and who will solve all their problems
   C. Need for power

II. Category 2: Expansion/aggression needs

  A. Need to exploit others
  B. Need for social recognition
  C. Need for personal admiration
  D. Need for personal achievement
  E. Need for self-sufficiency

III. Category 3: Detachment/withdrawal needs

  A. Need for perfection
  B. Need to restrict life practices to within narrow borders

By examining these needs and categories, you can see how, in some circumstances, most (probably all) of them could be healthy and adaptive, but if they would get more extreme or pronounced during difficult times or periods of conflict, then these needs could become more dominant and could become problematic. While all people will have each of these needs to some degree or another, during childhood, parenting practices and relationships would shape which neurotic needs might become more important and even dominant in each person's life and would shape their personality, coping mechanisms, and forms of pathology that might emerge during their lives.

Horney was one of the few women in the field of psychoanalysis and even neo-analysis. She always felt there was too much emphasis on male issues, identities, conflicts, and development in psychoanalysis, and she began to study, and is seen by many as the founder of, the area of feminine psychology. Prior to Horney, theorists and practitioners had written about women's issues and development, but it often seemed to be more of an afterthought than a foundation of the theories. She addressed issues of the psychology of women in a more direct and complete way than had been done by anyone prior to her theory. She not only brought women's concerns to the forefront of neo-analytic discussion but also legitimized this area as a foundation of psychological thinking in ways it had not been seen before. Although later in her career she did not write as much about feminine psychology as she had, and began focusing on other areas, she is still identified as the person who first systematically and seriously introduced the psychology of women as an important area of study, research, theory, and practice.

Toward the end of her career, she started focusing more on the self and on self-realization and found that she agreed with Abraham Maslow that self-actualization is one of the fundamental human drives and is one aspect of what it means to be a healthy person and to avoid some of the problems that result from neurotic adjustment and problematic childhood issues. It is fitting that she spent the latter part of her career focusing on health and transcendence having broken away from Freud's theory that conceived of human nature as being based primarily on subconscious factors that resulted from the sexual and aggressive instincts that were the bases of all human personality and development. One of the primary differences between Freud and the neo-Freudian analysts is that the newer models, like Horney's, had a much more positive and optimistic view of human nature and human psychology.

Harry Stack Sullivan

Sullivan was the son of Irish immigrants and grew up in the town of Norwich, New York, which was very Protestant and anti-Catholic. This unfriendly environment resulted in his being largely socially isolated, which probably spurred his interest in psychiatry and must have had an impact on his emphasis on the importance of social interaction in psychological development. Like many of the neo-Freudian theorists, Sullivan was much more interested in social and interpersonal dynamics than on an unconscious that was driven by sexual and aggressive instincts. He felt that cultural forces were largely responsible for mental illness and did not feel that "intrapsychic" factors were the prime cause of psychological difficulties. He also felt that "loneliness" was the most painful of all human emotions, and this is hardly surprising given his difficult and unhappy childhood.

Sullivan went to medical school and became interested in psychiatry as his primary field of study and practice. He was interested in social influences and human interaction patterns as they shaped and influenced personal development. He, like Horney and others, also focused on the "self," and he conceived of the notion of the "self-system," which is a configuration of the personality traits developed in childhood and reinforced by positive affirmation and the "security operations" developed in childhood to avoid anxiety and threats to self-esteem; this is much like Freud's ideas about psychological defenses, although Sullivan focused mainly on social and cultural factors and influences.

As Sullivan's ideas began to form and his theory started to mature, his approach became known as "interpersonal psychoanalysis," and he attracted many students and followers. He was also the first to coin the phrase "problems in living," which emphasized the fact that many of the difficulties that people suffer are not due to mental disease but rather to issues they confront in their social and cultural lives. In later years, other psychiatrists, and psychologists (e.g., Thomas Szasz, Carl Rogers), noticed this idea and tried to help people see that having psychological concerns did not necessarily mean that a patient or client was "sick" or "diseased" just because they needed help. In fact, one psychiatrist, R. D. Laing, asserted that mental illness was simply a sane way of dealing with insane situations. While today we might see this approach as somewhat overstated, it is true that Sullivan was one of the first to try to look at psychological difficulties as being a part of being human and did not mean that a person seeking help was sick or different.

Sullivan was influential during his career and was active as a teacher and practitioner and was instrumental in helping to found several important psychiatric organizations and scholarly journals. Although he did not publish many articles or books, he influenced many scholars and practitioners, and much of what we know about his theory comes from collections of his lectures that his students put together in his name and published after Sullivan's death.

During his career he was also a consultant to the Selective Service and helped develop approaches to screening and evaluating draftees for the military. In fact, he even stated that homosexuality was not a valid reason for eliminating someone from the draft and that homosexuality played a minimal role in causing mental illness. He went on to say that homosexual soldiers should be accepted and then left alone. As modern and important as this approach was, too many people were threatened by the idea of homosexuals in the military, and this approach was not accepted. Although many think that we are past those misguided ideas about homosexuality being a "disease" and that it is a risk to other healthy parts of society, these archaic notions are still guiding the views of many people and organizations.

Sullivan never married, nor did he have any children, although he did have a 22-year relationship with a young man (Jimmie), who was 20 years his junior. Although they were never open about the nature of their relationship, after Sullivan's death it became known through his close friends that "Jimmie" and Sullivan were partners. It is hardly surprising that Sullivan was the first professional to use the term "significant other" in describing nonmarital close relationships.

Harry Stack Sullivan was an interesting and influential man who had an enormous influence on the fields of psychiatry and psychology. His lectures, supervision, and training of therapists had, and still has, a significant impact on the theory and practice of psychotherapy.

Erich Fromm

Fromm was born in 1900 in Frankfurt am Main in Germany to Orthodox Jewish parents. He was interested in a variety of academic pursuits and studied law for two semesters at the University of Frankfurt am Main. He also read the Talmud extensively and studied Judaic law and philosophy with a noted rabbi. However, he then took some classes at the University of Heidelberg and began studying sociology and ultimately received his PhD in sociology from Heidelberg. He then started studying and training in psychoanalysis, and after completing his studies in this field, he began his own psychoanalytic practice. Following the Nazi takeover of Germany, Fromm moved to Switzerland and then later to the United States where he taught at Columbia University. With Karen Horney and Harry Stack Sullivan, Fromm began a distinctly different and alternate branch of psychoanalysis that was much more focused on social, relationship, and cultural factors than Freud's theory had been. These three theorists/analysts were working together in the United States to modernize psychoanalysis and to break from traditional Freudian theory and practice to form a new tradition. The three of them formed many organizations and institutes to advance the neo-Freudian approaches to psychoanalysis. Even though Fromm was critical of Freud's theory, he had enormous respect for Freud and considered him to be one of the three most influential thinkers in the 20th century along with Einstein and Marx.

Fromm later moved to Mexico City and spent many of his later years teaching at the university there. In addition to sociology and political theory, he established a section of psychoanalysis in the medical school. He also taught at universities in the United States, including Michigan State University and New York University, while he resided in Mexico. In 1974 he moved back to Switzerland where he lived for the rest of his life, still practicing as his health permitted, and died in 1980.

Because of his breadth of education, interest in law and politics, background in sociology, reading of the Talmud and Jewish philosophy, psychoanalytic training, and interest in Marxist ideology, much of Fromm's writing involved philosophical and political themes as well as neo-psychoanalytic, psychological, and sociological themes. In fact, his book *Escape from Freedom* is considered by many to be one of the seminal founding works in the field of political psychology. Fromm's knowledge of the Talmud and the Old Testament, in general, gave him a basis for examining and analyzing many psychological and cultural areas. Philosophically, he was a humanist, which was certainly something that came from his religious and philosophical studies. A humanist is a person who believes in the basic goodness and value of human beings and who sees people who are free to make choices in their lives and learn from their mistakes and successes. This view of human nature is different from the way Freud saw people, and Fromm shared this perspective with many of the neo-Freudian analysts, including Horney and Sullivan. He saw freedom as a basic element of human nature, and he felt that people could either embrace their freedom and grow to fulfill their potential or be fearful of the freedom and try to escape from it with unhealthy and neurotic coping mechanisms that would inevitably lead to psychological problems and neurosis.

Fromm postulated eight different human needs that are common to all of us although there are differences between people in terms of which needs are most important during various parts of our lives and in different circumstances. These needs are as follows:

1. Relatedness: This deals with our need for meaningful relationships with others, caring about them and being cared for.
2. Transcendence: People have the need to grow beyond their base natures, and rather than killing and destroying people and things, we can create and care about our creations.
3. Rootedness: This deals with our needs to have a sense of roots and belongingness, and to feel at home in the world and with the people in this world.
4. Sense of identity: This need is established by being and feeling a part of important groups and forming a sense of individuality.
5. Frame of orientation: This need refers to our understanding of the world and our place in it.
6. Excitation and stimulation: Being active in striving for a goal rather than just responding to situations.
7. Unity: Having a sense of "oneness" with a person and the world and people in it.
8. Effectiveness: This refers to the need that all people must feel competent and accomplished.

For Fromm, how well people manage and fulfill their needs in healthy and productive ways will determine their adjustment and adaptation to the world and the people in it. Responding to the positive aspects of needs and avoiding or minimizing those negative orientations will be an indication of how well adjusted and happy a person will be. Another element of Fromm's theory that is essential in understanding how he feels that people adapt and approach the needs and conflicts in their lives is found in his "orientations of character." He felt that we relate to the world by (1) acquiring and assimilating things, "assimilation," and (2) reacting to people, "socialization." Unlike Freud who saw our basic instincts as biologically determined, Fromm felt that assimilation and socialization were not instinctive but acquired through experience of circumstances in one's life. He also felt that people were never just one of these basic types, but these two fundamental approaches would be manifest in basic character orientation, of which four were seen to be nonproductive and one as productive. The nonproductive character orientations were receptive, exploitative, hoarding, and marketing, and he called the one positive orientation "productive."

Receptive and exploitive orientations are how an individual relates to others and are socialization attributes of character. The hoarding orientation is an acquiring and assimilating materials/valuables character trait. The marketing ethic is a product of modern times, and this is when the value of a person or thing is determined by its worth in the market. Thus, this is a relativistic ethic whereby value depends on the situation. Despite their struggles, Fromm believed that all people have the capacity for love, reason, and productive work. Very much like Freud, Fromm believed that to be healthy a person must be able to love and to be productive (to work). He also pointed out one of the paradoxes of humankind, and that is to be a healthy and happy person, one must strive for connectedness with others and simultaneously establish a sense of independence and self-reliance. In his theory, Fromm believed that one way people can meet their needs and fulfill their sense of identity is by being productive. His belief was that value in life comes from being meaningfully productive and effective. It seems clear that this idea reflects Fromm's interest in Marxist political philosophy and is another example of how he would integrate psychology, neo-Freudian psychoanalysis, sociology, and political philosophy in his approach.

Fromm was an important and influential theorist and practitioner and along with his other neo-Freudian colleagues had an important influence on American psychology and psychiatry. They founded journals; opened training centers; taught in universities and medical schools; and were important teachers, practitioners, theorists, and role models. Many of Fromm's ideas have been influential in the emergence of modern approaches to psychotherapy, and his ideas can be found in many different forms of treatment. Remembering that many of his ideas are 50–75 years old should remind us that at the time he was writing, his ideas were largely new and even revolutionary. With all the scholarship and research that has gone on in recent decades, most of the newer approaches today have transcended the ideas of Fromm and his contemporaries. This, of course, does not minimize the importance of his contributions but does remind us that good theories are not cast in stone but evolve and move beyond what was known and believed before.

Melanie Klein

Melanie Klein was an innovative, brilliant, and strong voice in the emergence of newer models of psychoanalytic theory and practice. She was born in Vienna to Jewish parents and had a challenging and traumatic life that involved the death of a much-beloved older sister when Klein was four and the sister was eight, and she was also made to feel responsible for the death of her brother. She married, had a family, and later divorced; her son died in a tragic climbing accident that might have been suicide, and she was estranged from her psychoanalyst daughter and they never reconciled before Klein's death.

Klein was well trained as a psychoanalyst but did not have much formal education, never having completed a bachelor's degree or any other higher education. She was quite unique as a woman without higher education in a field dominated by male physicians. However, she was quite influential as a therapist and training analyst. She departed significantly from Freud's fundamental ideas, but she always respected him and claimed to follow his basic tenets. She did, however, differ enough from Freudian tradition to have significant conflict with German and Austrian psychoanalysts, and she and Anna Freud were critical of each other. Klein did find more acceptance of her ideas in Britain, and she moved to London where she spent most of her professional life there and died there at age 78 in 1960.

Klein is important in the neo-Freudian group for several reasons. First, she was one of the first to apply psychoanalysis to children and introduced the use of toys to facilitate analysis of the youngsters, even working with children as young as two years old. She saw play as the fundamental way in which children would communicate and deal with their most significant issues and instincts. There was significant conflict between the followers of Klein and those of the other major proponents of psychoanalysis with children—Anna Freud. Klein was influential in Britain although less so in continental Europe and North America. She still has a strong influence in psychoanalysis in Britain and South America, but only one psychoanalytic training center in the United States is primarily Kleinian in its orientation.

In addition to her contributions to the development of psychotherapeutic methods with children, Klein was recognized as one of the first theorists to develop "objects relations theory," an approach that examined the ways children (and later adults) would develop love relationships with significant others and things and how these relationships would result in the dynamics of important conflicts and issues, including love and aggression. She was a strong and dynamic woman who had a major impact on a field where there were few nonphysicians and fewer women—her contributions are still felt today.

Erik Erikson

Erikson's mother came from a prominent Jewish family in Denmark and was married to a Jewish stockbroker. However, they became estranged, and she was involved with a man of whom little is known other than he was a non-Jewish Dane. When she found that she was pregnant, she moved to Germany to raise her son. She was studying to be a nurse and married Erik's pediatrician Theodore Homburger who adopted Erik and told him that he was his real father; Erik changed his name to Erik Homburger. He was not told the truth about his father until late in his childhood, and he was bitter about this. Erik was tall and blond and was teased by his fellow students in Jewish school, who called him an Aryan, but in public school he was also teased for being a Jew. It is not surprising that he was the first theorist to write extensively about the "identity crisis."

Erik was a good student, but after high school, against the wishes of his father, Erik chose to go to art school rather than medical school, and he studied art for a while but then dropped out of school and wandered around Europe for about year, which was a common practice for young men of prominent families. During this Wanderjahr, Erikson supported himself by drawing pictures for people and later by being a private art tutor for children of wealthy families. He enjoyed this and related well with the children. At age 25 a friend of his invited him to come to Vienna to teach art to students whose parents had come to Vienna to be treated by Freud. Freud's daughter Anna saw how well Erikson worked with the children and encouraged him to begin psychoanalytic training, which he did and later completed his training and received a diploma in psychoanalysis. He was also working with the private school for children in Vienna; he studied the Montessori method of teaching and received a diploma in this discipline as well. When the Nazis came to power, Erikson (then still Homburger) went to Denmark but had difficulty obtaining citizenship because of the residency requirement, so he moved to the United States to teach and practice psychoanalysis; this was also when he changed his name from Homburger to Erikson (a name he gave himself). A man who went to college only briefly and who never completed a university degree of any sort became one of the most influential psychologists in the United States, having academic jobs at the University of California in Berkley, Yale University, University of Pittsburg, and Harvard University. He was influential, and one survey listed him as the 12th most-cited psychologist in the 20th century. In addition, he won many awards for his work, including a Pulitzer Prize and a U.S. National Book Award.

Erikson focused his theory and treatment on social development, and while his approach differed significantly from Freud's, he always claimed that the two theories were not in conflict but were parallel processes, and his approach was not an alternative to Freud's but a different approach *in addition* to Freud's psychosexual development—Erikson was interested in "psychosocial development." Like most of the neo-Freudians, he was more interested in social and interpersonal factors than the unconscious sexual and aggressive instincts. He was also more interested in ego processes (adaptive and more rational aspects of psychological functioning) and was seen by many as one of the originators of "ego psychology."

Erikson was recognized as a gifted teacher and psychotherapist but is best known for his theory of psychosocial development. His theory postulates eight stages of development, and each stage has a conflict associated with it, and resolution of the conflict allows the developing individual to progress to the next stage. Of course, sometimes people are less than successful in resolving their conflicts, and this disruption in their development could lead to psychological difficulties later in their lives. Obviously, this model of pathology is much like Freud's although the nature and quality of development and the specific stages are quite different. For Erikson, the main stages of development are as follows:

1. Hope, basic trust versus basic mistrust: During infancy (approximately 0–18 months) the child faces new and difficult challenges and is largely in the hands of caring adults who help the infant meet their needs. If they grow up in a healthy and supportive environment, they develop a basic sense of hope and trust. If they grow up in a less-supportive environment, then they will see the world as inconsistent and unpredictable and will have a basic sense of mistrust.
2. Will, autonomy versus shame: In early childhood (1–3 years), the child is learning to function more autonomously and to exert their will. They learn to talk, to walk, and start to recognize that they have control over the things and people around them. Successful progress through this stage means that the child will develop a sense of their ability to have an impact on the world and that they can function independently. Difficulties during this stage will result in a child who feels powerless and dependent and has a sense of shame for their lack of willpower and autonomy.
3. Purpose, initiative versus guilt: During preschool years (3–5 years), the child is learning to plan and to initiate actions to accomplish goals. In a healthy environment, they will learn to make decisions, start caring for their own needs more effectively, play with others, make up their own games, and feel more accomplished. Problems during this stage lead the child to feel that they are not capable and that they have not fulfilled the expectancies that others have for them, and they will feel a sense of guilt.
4. Competence, industry versus inferiority: During early school age (6–11 years), the child's peer group becomes more important, and they start learning how to get along with and support (and be supported by) their peers outside of the family. They are also learning to deal more with nonparental adults (teachers, coaches, etc.). This is when they start learning many of the skills that they will take into adulthood, and they also start learning the kinds of things they are good at and some of the things they are not as capable of. It is important at this stage that they are supported and encouraged to pursue the things that they are good at and to enjoy but not feel bad about things that they are not as good at but others might be. Successful completion of this stage yields a child who feels competent and capable and sees value in working hard to be good at things they enjoy; this also means that they learn to accept that they are not good at everything and that is not

bad. Problems at this stage result in a youngster who feels inferior and incapable of producing anything of value and is unwilling or afraid to initiate activities.

5. Fidelity, identity versus role confusion: During adolescence (12–18 years), the youngster is starting to deal with issues of identity: Who am I? How do I fit in? Where am I headed in life? They begin to deal with more significant interpersonal relationships and learn the importance of close friendships and start experiencing early feelings of intimacy in relationships. As they move through this stage, they should learn that people can be trusted and may sometimes disappoint you, but they are important in our lives. They also begin developing a more coherent sense of themselves and their identity. As they progress though this stage, they should emerge with a sense of trust and appreciation for relationships, and a stronger sense of their own idea and who they are as an individual. For those who have problems during this stage, they will show role confusion and not be sure of themselves or what is important to them. They will vacillate between roles and never have a clear sense of who they are and what is important to them.
6. Love, intimacy versus isolation: Early adulthood (18–40 years) is when people begin to develop close and intimate social connections that will result in lasting relationships like marriage or other committed attachments. People will form relationships that make them feel safe, secure, loved, and intimate. Those who are unable to form these important and lasting relationships will feel isolated and alone.
7. Care, generativity versus stagnation: This second stage of adulthood (40–65 years) is the time of life when people generally settle into a lifestyle and have a good sense of what is important to them. They will make progress or develop a sense of completeness in their chosen live work (be it a career, family role, or other), and if they choose to have a family, they will enjoy raising their children and participating in activities that are enjoyable and meaningful. They will have a role and relationship with society and find a meaningful place to make contributions to their community and profession. People who do not find a role and/or sense of purpose during this phase of their life may find themselves regretting choices they have made in the past, resenting those whom they feel contributed to their "failures," and will often feel useless and unproductive and lack a sense of meaning.
8. Wisdom, ego integrity versus despair: This stage is for those 65 years and older, and for people who have gone through the other stages with some degree of success, they will have a sense of fulfillment and accomplishment with their life and will accept the successes and failures of their life without regret or resentment. They will have gained wisdom and understanding of their life and existence and start to face the reality and acceptance of the fact of death. Feeling guilty about mistakes in the past, resentment for having been mistreated by others, or failure to accomplish important goals will often lead them to feel depressed and have a sense of despair.

Although Erikson did not postulate another stage of life, he did start to feel that there was an additional era that might be studied further, and this was the period between adolescence and adulthood. During the mid-20th century, it was common for young people to go to training, college, or the military before starting to fulfill their role as an adult. Other theorists today have referred to this stage as "youth," but Erikson did not get to the point of proposing this as a new stage. However, he and his wife Joan (who had been his frequent collaborator) were discussing the developmental issues of the most elderly people, and in their 80s, they realized that many of their issues were quite different than those they had faced in their 60s and 70s. After Erikson's death, Joan collected their notes and wrote some of their thoughts about this last stage of life, "very old age." During this stage, the person reverts to the issues of the first stage—trust versus mistrust. For example, "Can I trust that my legs will work properly today?" "Can I trust that I will wake up tomorrow?" "Can I trust that my heart will keep beating?" In their thinking, the last phase of life means coming to grips with the aspects of physical and mental changes associated with old age, and with people living longer than ever before, many more people would be facing these issues, and the theories of development needed to accommodate this reality as well.

Erikson was a brilliant and important theorist and practitioner whose influence is widely felt today. His views of human development were based on the thoughts of many of the neo-Freudian analysts who preceded him, but his theory was the most complete and well-developed model of psychosocial development that had been developed. His insightful and useful ideas have impacted how psychologists, other researchers, and people, in general, view human development.

How Is This Utilized Today?

Although there are few psychotherapists who would label themselves as practicing specifically in the mode of any of the neo-psychoanalytic theorists or therapists, they still have significant influence on the teaching and practice of psychotherapy. Horney's impact on the field is being realized today because her introduction of the psychology of women as a legitimate field of study has led to the introduction of scholarly endeavors, including women's studies. It is also true that all the neo-psychoanalytic practitioners were more interested in ego processes than in the unconscious, and this is certainly true today. The subfield of ego psychology grew directly from the work of the neo-psychoanalytic theorists.

Although the psychodynamic approaches are not utilized to the same degree today as they have been in the past, there has been a resurgence in recent years, and the newer approaches are much more focused on social and interpersonal processes and stress the importance of ego processes. One other difference in the psychodynamic approaches today is that they are much more involved with and based on research than in the past. It is also true that Erikson's theory of psychosocial development is still taught and has influenced thinking and research in psychological development. His name and theory are virtually always found in introductory psychology and developmental psychology texts even today.

Clearly, there are contemporary psychotherapists who would identify their approach with the neo-psychoanalytic therapists, but probably their main influence is found in how they have impacted the practice of psychotherapy, in general. Almost every approach to psychotherapy that is used today will utilize some techniques or concepts that can be traced back to the neo-psychoanalytic psychotherapists, and this influence will continue to be felt for a long time. These newer approaches are also much more time efficient and are effective with shorter-term approaches than traditional psychoanalysis.

Concerns and Critiques

Although the neo-psychoanalytic approaches were much more comfortable being based on research and modern theory and methods, they are still more conceptual than empirical in their approaches, and many of their ideas are not easily studied experimentally. Thus, while they are more "scientifically based" than their Freudian forefathers and mothers, they are still not as empirically based as other approaches. For some this is not a major issue, but the theories and psychotherapeutic approaches that are scientifically sound and validated are the ones that are most likely to last into the future.

Another interesting criticism of the neo-psychoanalysts comes from the more traditional Freudian analysts. From their standpoint, the neo-analysts have "sold out" to the more scientific models and are neglecting the more important unconscious psychodynamics that are directly determinative of human psychology. They also feel that by aligning with the "shorter-term" psychotherapies, the neo-analytic practitioners are neglecting the more core issues and are practicing on a superficial basis.

While these newer approaches have had significant influence on psychotherapy and on theory, they will not be taken seriously by some because they are not as "scientific" as other new approaches. However, what is likely to happen is that the neo-analytic approaches will be merged with or incorporated into other methods, and their influence may be more indirect but will still be felt.

CHAPTER SIX

Humanistic and Existential Therapies

Although in the early part of the 20th century Freudian psychoanalysis was the most important and influential form of psychotherapy, there were many others in addition to the neo-psychoanalysts who were critical of traditional psychoanalysis and were looking for other models and approaches to deal with psychological difficulties. Philosophically, many people did not accept psychoanalysis because of its strongly deterministic view and felt that if all behavior, thoughts, and feelings were determined by unconscious instincts and developmental factors, then this left little room for such ideas as free will and freedom of choice in one's life.

Further, many were concerned that Freud's view of human nature was unreasonably pessimistic and felt that there was much more to human motivation than sexual and aggressive impulses. As philosophers and other scholars struggled with these issues, their concerns started to impact psychology and psychiatry, and some therapists began basing some of their ideas and practices on different philosophical models of human nature. Specifically, the humanists and existentialists provided a philosophical basis for models of psychotherapy that looked at human nature and psychotherapy in different ways than did Freud and his followers.

History and Development

Humanism is a philosophical and ethical approach that emphasizes the inherent value and worth of human beings and their capacity for self-determination. This approach is grounded in critical thinking based on the foundation of rationality and empiricism and was opposed to opinions and thought based on dogma and superstition. While humanism was an intellectual and rational approach to assessing reality, it was also seen as being in opposition to religion and other dogmatic approaches to "truth."

Throughout history in many parts of the world, there is evidence of thinkers rejecting supernatural explanations for more rational, human-centered philosophy, and there is written evidence from India, Greece, and Iran dating back to 1000–600 BCE, proving that people discussed these issues. In fact, many medieval Muslim thinkers pursued humanistic, rational, and scientific discourses throughout the Middle Ages. Similar thoughts were found in Renaissance Europe in the later period of the Middle Ages and the early modern period.

Different types of humanism were based on the sources of the ideas. Renaissance humanists were looking for cultural and educational reforms to move beyond the traditional Aristotelian scholastic approaches that had dominated the academic and religious world for centuries. These thinkers wanted an educated and literate populace (including women) that could think and discuss issues based on knowledge, logic, and rationality dispensing with the dogmatic and pervasive influence of the Church.

Also Nontheistic humanists were referred to as secular humanists who embraced a worldview characterized by human reason, metaphysical naturalism, altruistic morality, and distributive justice. They rejected supernatural claims, theistic faith and religiosity, pseudoscience, and superstition. This approach was seen by many as a proposed "replacement" of traditional religion and was felt by many to be heresy and the "work of the Devil."

However, there later developed a group, referred to as "religious humanists," who maintained that there could be a blend of religion and humanism that allowed for differing belief systems regarding "higher powers" but would still be based on the notions of human worth and value, freedom of choice and will, and accepting reason, empiricism, and science as part of the human experience and reality. These groups have taken on the role of traditional "churches" but have done so as an alternative to organized religion but attempting to serve some of the same purposes.

Humanistic psychology arose in the United States as an alternative to the strictly deterministic psychoanalytic and behavioristic models that asserted that all behavior is determined and the idea of free will is an illusion. Many people, including some psychologists, were uncomfortable with the idea that people had little control over what they did, thought, and felt because these things were determined by our instincts, history, and environment. Following World War II, theorists and psychotherapists started to emerge, who offered alternative and more humanistic approaches to psychological theory and practice, and these new alternatives found wide acceptance in the popular culture and in the academic and professional realms as well.

The basic principles of humanistic psychology include the following:

1. The most significant aspect of any person is their present functioning.
2. To be mentally healthy and fulfilled, people must take full responsibility for their actions, regardless of whether their actions are positive or negative.
3. Everyone is inherently worthy, simply by being—while an action a person takes might be negative, this does not cancel out their value as a human being.
4. The goal of living is to attain personal growth and understanding. Only through constant self-improvement and self-understanding can a person ever be truly happy.

These principles underlie the theories and psychotherapies of all the psychotherapists who align themselves with this basic approach to people and to therapy.

Existentialism is a much more recent approach than humanism and is largely associated with early- to mid-20th-century European philosophers. Although their ideas differed considerably from one another and from the humanists, there were some key similarities that made them viable alternatives to the more deterministic models that were popular at the time. However, the fundamental ideas of existentialism date back to philosophers in the 19th century; it was identified by that term until the 20th century when Jean-Paul Sartre accepted that label to describe his work and approach to philosophy and life. Søren Kierkegaard is generally considered to be the first existential philosopher who proposed that everyone—not society or religion—is completely responsible for establishing meaning to their life and living it passionately and sincerely as best they can—namely, "authentically." Existentialism became popular in the years following World War II and influenced many disciplines in addition to philosophy, including theology, drama, art, literature, and psychology.

Key Individuals and Their Contributions

Humanistic Therapies

Carl Rogers

Rogers was an American psychologist who is largely credited with founding the humanistic psychology approach, although he was influenced by and shared ideas with his contemporary Abraham Maslow. Rogers (and Maslow) felt that the strong reliance on deterministic approaches like behaviorism and psychoanalysis had lost sight of the fact that we are dealing with unique and important human beings who have life and freedom to make choices to help develop into the beings they could become. In addition to being a founder of this new approach, Rogers was important as one of the first to undertake scientifically sound research in psychotherapy and was given the Award for Distinguished Scientific Contributions by the American Psychological Association. His person-centered approach to life, psychotherapy, and education led to such innovations as "client-centered psychotherapy" and "student-centered learning," which are approaches that are still guiding our thoughts and practices in these areas. He was also given the Award for Distinguished Professional Contributions to Psychology by the American Psychological Association and served as president of this organization. He was highly valued as a teacher, researcher, psychotherapist, and theorist, and in one study he was found to be the sixth most eminent psychologist in the 20th century and only one of two clinicians (the other being Freud).

Rogers, like Maslow, was a humanist psychologist who believed that for a person to become healthy they need an environment that provides them with genuineness, acceptance, and empathy. If these qualities are not present, a healthy personality cannot develop, and the person will not become the best person of which they are capable. Rogers believed that every person can achieve their goals, wishes, and desires in life, and when this happens, the person is said to have "self-actualized." He believed that human beings have only one basic and dominant motive—to self-actualize. Rather than being guided by history and instincts (Freud) or by situations and stimuli (behaviorism), Rogers believed that we act, feel, and think in ways in which we do because of our unique perception of every situation, and since we are the only person who ever truly knows how we perceive things, we are the only true "experts" on our own reality. Clearly, this approach was different from the other dominant psychological models of the time but was compelling and influenced many people.

Rogerian theory is based on several propositions, but he starts with the assumption that all people exist in a dynamic, ever-changing world of experience of which they perceive themselves to be the center. Further, reality for each person is the perception they have of the world around them and the events and people in it—for all people, reality is as reality is perceived by the experiencing person. The only fact any of us ever truly knows is what we are perceiving from our ongoing experience. To understand how people react to their perceived world, it is also important to recognize that their perceptions and reactions are made as a fully complete and whole individual, and we are a unified, experiencing, and reacting entity; we cannot be understood by reducing our complex experience to instincts, traits, learned behaviors, and so on. As we are experiencing the world around us, and as we develop as an infant, at some point a part of the perceived world becomes differentiated and experienced as the "self." Thus, we become aware of the fact that we exist as part of but distinct from the other parts of our total world of perception and experience. The main goal for each person throughout their life is to self-actualize—that is, to facilitate the self to develop into the most complete and healthy self of which each person can become.

To fully understand a person, we can understand them only from their own perspective, and thus to really know another person, we must understand them from their unique perceptions and interpretations of reality. Rogers would never believe, as some people do, that you can know someone better than they know themselves. Our behavior is best understood as goal-directed efforts that are trying to facilitate self-actualization. Similarly, emotion is also related to goal-directed efforts toward self-actualization, and the quality of the emotion depends on the congruence of the behaviors with the goal of self-actualization; when we are doing things that are helping us to actualize, then we will feel good—how good depends on how important the behavior is to our goal attainment. Conversely, negative emotions emerge when our behavior is not taking us in the direction of self-actualization.

As we experience life and develop psychologically, psychological adjustment exists when our behavior and experiences are consistent with the values and needs of the self, and when our behavior and experiences differ from what is important to the self, then psychological maladjustment will result. Experiences different from what is important for the self will be experienced as a threat, and the more of these threats that are experienced, the greater the likelihood that the self will become rigid and unchanging, and self-actualization will be impossible to achieve, and Rogers would say that this is when "neurosis" would emerge. If the person's experiences are so traumatic and intense that they cannot be incorporated into the self, then the self may disintegrate, and this is when "psychosis" would result.

Rogers also focused considerably on what it meant to be a psychologically healthy person. According to Rogers, a fully functioning person would have a growing openness to experience, meaning they become increasingly less defensive, are open to the reality around them, and accept it for what it is and what it means to them. They would also develop and continue the existential lifestyle, meaning they would live each moment fully, accepting each for what it is and learning to grow and appreciate what life brings them. To be able to live life fully and without reservation, it is also necessary for people to learn to trust themselves and their own judgment; no one knows themselves better than they do, and they need to learn to trust that fully. The healthy person also is free to make choices and decisions about their lives without constraint or outside influence. While they must understand and consider different perspectives and issues, they must be free to trust themselves and to make choices based on what they feel is right for them.

Further, the healthy person needs to be creative and to express their creativity. This does not mean that everyone must be an artist or poet, but rather, each must be able and willing to try new things, express themselves uniquely, and explore new and different ways of experiencing life and fulfilling their own needs. An essential element of being psychologically healthy is to be reliable and constructive, meaning one will be consistent and can be trusted to do the right thing and to provide important contributions to meaningful activities and situations. Finally, the healthy person will live a rich and full life, experiencing many different things and making sure that they have a balanced and meaningful life filled with experiences and relationships that help them become the self-actualized person that they can become.

Since many people experience events in their lives that interfere with their healthy development, Rogers felt that psychotherapy could provide an opportunity for people to correct some of the challenges in their development and get back on track with a healthy and productive life. Of course, he believed strongly that all of us have the capacity to be healthy and fulfill our potential and that rather than directing or instructing people how to change, psychotherapy should provide an environment that would allow a person to trust themselves and start to express and experience the healthy drives that are already inside themselves. This is also why he objected to calling the people he was helping "patients," which implied that they were sick and disturbed; he called them "clients," and his approach to psychotherapy is often called "client-centered therapy" or "nondirective therapy."

For psychotherapy to be beneficial, Rogers felt that three core conditions would make psychotherapy effective and helpful. First, the therapist must display "congruence," meaning being open and honest and not hiding behind a personal or professional facade. Second, the therapist must display "unconditional positive regard," meaning accepting the client for who they are, without judgment or conditions of worth. There should never be conditions placed on a person's value as a human being—for example, "I will like you if you will do this for me." Finally, the therapist must display "empathy"; they must communicate the desire and willingness to appreciate and understand their client's perspective and personal values and reality. Rogers felt that if a client experienced these conditions in psychotherapy, then they could utilize their inner strength and resources to grow and develop into the person they can become and can overcome the problems and difficulties that have impeded their growth in the past.

Although subsequent experience and research has revealed some difficulties with Rogers's approach, his impact has been monumental. He has certainly been one of the most influential people in the training of mental health professionals and in the utilization of psychotherapeutic practices in the history of psychotherapy. We discuss the strengths and weakness of his approach later in this chapter, but suffice it to say that Carl Rogers is one of the most important people in the history and development of psychotherapy.

Abraham Maslow

Maslow is probably best known for his theory involving the hierarchy of human needs. He felt that people must be motivated by more than the sexual and aggressive instincts that Freud proposed, but he also thought that human beings were also much more than a history of stimulus–response connections. He even felt that the neo-Freudian theorists were too limited in their emphasis on social needs. Maslow proposed that people had a hierarchy of needs ranging from the physiological and fundamental survival drives through safety and security needs, love and social connectedness needs, esteem needs, and, finally, self-actualization. Like Rogers, Maslow believed that all people had a fundamental need to become the best individual of which they were capable. Although this theory has been found to be inadequate in many ways by today's standards, at the time this was proposed in the mid-20th century, it was quite a revolutionary idea.

Another point that Maslow focused on that set him apart from most psychologists (except the other humanists) was the idea that most of the theories of personality were developed by clinicians who did most of their work and research on people suffering from psychological problems. Maslow insisted that being psychologically healthy is more than simply not being crazy, and he felt that rather than studying pathology and then inferring what healthy might mean, we should study healthy people and find out what makes them different from those who were suffering from mental health problems. He even went beyond this notion and did studies on people whom he felt were "self-actualizers": those who had done the most with what they had to contribute. His emphasis on psychological health was an important difference between his approach and that of most psychologists and psychiatrists of his era. He attracted a large and enthusiastic following, and like Rogers, he was also elected as president of the American Psychological Association. One study done in 2002 ranked him as the 10th most frequently cited psychologist in the 20th century.

Maslow's approach to psychotherapy is based on his views regarding human nature and the innate capacity for people to self-actualize. To establish ideas about what people could become, he studied many self-actualized individuals to determine what made them different than others, and he found that all of them shared some important personality traits. All were "reality centered" and were able to differentiate between what was real and what was fraudulent. In addition, they were "problem centered," meaning when confronted with difficult situations, they would seek to find solutions rather than avoid or ignore them; thus, they were not overwhelmed by life's challenges but looked at these as problems to be solved rather than obstacles or failures. He also noted that self-actualized people had healthy interpersonal relationships although they were perfectly comfortable being alone. Further, they tended to have a few close relationships rather than many superficial ones. Self-actualized people are spontaneous and creative and are not unduly bound by strict convention. However, they were not unnecessarily oppositional or revolutionary but would approach situations logically and meaningfully based on their own values and the nature of the situation and the people involved. They understand and accept reality, and they also understand and accept themselves for their strengths and their limitations. Independence and self-reliance are qualities shared by self-actualizers, and they are aware of the need to foster and develop their own potentialities and inner resources.

In studying people, their needs, drives, and motives, Maslow also studied some of the aspects that made life special and meaningful. In addition to meeting their needs and drives, he felt that people have moments of extraordinary experiences that are profound moments of love, understanding happiness, or rapture, during which a person feels more whole, alive, and self-sufficient and yet a part of the world and more aware of truth, justice, harmony, goodness, and so on. He referred to these as "peak experiences," and while everyone can have these, many people are not in touch with their true selves to be able to have these experiences. Another concept he introduced was the idea of "metamotivation," which is used to describe self-actualized individuals who are driven by forces beyond their basic needs that allow them to transcend simple existence and explore their full human potential.

Maslow approached psychotherapy as a way of providing an environment where people could explore themselves and their needs in such a way as to get back on track toward self-actualization. Thus, like Rogers, Maslow was nondirective and client centered. He noted that other schools of psychotherapy tended to approach psychotherapy in a way that was more determined by the type of therapy practiced rather than by the needs of the client. One of his most famous observations was, "If all you have is a hammer, everything looks like a nail" (Maslow, 1966). Therefore, in psychotherapy he was more focused on the client's needs than on the "took kit" he had. Rather than a collection of techniques used to change the client, Maslow saw the therapeutic relationship as a way of validating a client as a unique and valuable individual who was worth developing and helping to grow. He did not create changes for the person but rather provided a healthy, supportive, and accepting environment that allowed the individual to blossom and become that person that had always been there but had never been fully revealed and expressed.

Fritz Perls

A German-born man of Jewish descent, Perls was expected to study law but went into medicine instead. After having served in the army during World War I, he finished his medical training and specialized in neuropsychiatry and worked with brain-injured soldiers after the war. He eventually gravitated toward psychoanalysis, and after the Nazis came to power, he and his wife Laura moved to the Netherlands; one year later he moved to South Africa. During his time in South Africa, he served as a psychiatrist in the army and attained the rank of captain. After World War II he and his wife moved to the United States and lived and worked in New York City. They started a new approach to psychotherapy, called Gestalt therapy, and practiced out of their apartment in Manhattan and even started the Gestalt Training Institute.

The German word "Gestalt" refers to "whole," and this came about in part because of earlier experimental psychologists who studied perception and sensation by looking at whole and integrative processes and not just reducing sensation and perception to neurochemical events. Perls liked this idea and borrowed some notions from other psychologists and philosophers and worked with people from the standpoint of focusing on the whole person and dealing with current perceptions and thoughts and avoided dredging through a person's history and development. "What is going on with you now, what does it mean to you now, and how does it make you feel now" would be a limited example of how the Gestalt therapist would approach psychotherapy.

Perls eventually moved to Los Angeles (having left his wife in Manhattan) and started practicing and teaching Gestalt therapy. Eventually, he moved to Big Sur, California, and worked and lived at the Esalen Institute there. Finally, he moved to Vancouver, Canada, in 1969 where he also established a training institute and a psychotherapy practice. In 1970 he went to Chicago for treatment of his heart condition and died of heart failure shortly after having had surgery.

Gestalt psychotherapy is much like some of the other humanistic types of therapy because it is client centered and focuses on the patient's experience as it is perceived in real time. It may examine the patient's history but only from the standpoint of what it means to the patient now and how it makes them feel now. The Gestalt therapist also believes that the only way to fully understand another person is from their own unique and individual perspective. It will also utilize many other techniques like art, drama, literature, and dance as a way of helping the person become whole and self-fulfilled. While Gestalt therapy is not the only approach that uses techniques from other disciplines, it is the one that depends heavily on the integration of many different elements of what is important in any given individual's present life. There are not many practicing Gestalt therapists who utilize only or primarily the traditional approaches and techniques; however, many different types of therapeutic approaches and many different types of psychotherapists will use specific techniques from the Gestalt tradition, and that is where its impact is largely felt today.

Existential Therapies

Existentialism is a philosophical approach that is typically linked to 19th- and 20th-century philosophers. Søren Kierkegaard is usually credited as the first of the existentialist philosophers, although he did not use that term to describe himself or his approach. Although the various philosophers who are existentialists vary considerably in their theories and perspectives, they seem to agree about a few things. First, people are defined not just by their thinking, as some philosophers asserted, but also by their capacities and qualities as acting, feeling, and living individuals who are unique entities with free will and independence. For existentialists, the primary virtue of humankind is "authenticity," or living one's life in accordance with one's values, needs, goals, and aspirations. While Kierkegaard is thought to be the first existentialist, Jean-Paul Sartre in the 20th century was the first to accept that label as defining his approach although he had initially rejected it.

One of the basic concepts in existentialism is the notion that "existence precedes essence." Sartre made the case that it is not the labels, relationships, roles, stereotypes, or other preconceptions that define a person; rather, it is their existence—independently acting and responsible, conscious beings. This means that their being or existence is what defines them as a person and not the categories or labels that others use to describe them.

Existentialists are also concerned with the theme of authentic existence and feel that this is core to this approach to understanding the human condition. Authenticity means that in acting as a person, one should act as oneself, not as one's history, one's genes, one's family, one's race, or any other essential element of their lives would dictate. The authentic act is one that is in accordance with one's freedom and not influenced by any outside forces, people, and so on.

Existential psychotherapy is based on the principles of psychodynamic psychotherapy, humanistic psychology, and existential philosophy. In addition to

Kierkegaard and Sartre, other influential philosophers like Martin Heidegger, Edmund Husserl, Fiodor Dostoevsky, Franz Kafka, Albert Camus, and Friedrich Nietzsche had an impact of the field. Although sometimes misunderstood as being morbid, arcane, pessimistic, impractical, and overly cerebral and esoteric, existential psychotherapy is practical, concrete, positive, and flexible. At its best, this approach deals with many of the ultimate realities of life—freedom, responsibility, death, loneliness, loss, suffering, evil, meaninglessness, to name a few. This approach does not avoid dealing with the negative elements of existence like pain, anxiety, apathy, alienation, nihilism, shame, addiction, depression, guilt, anger, and rage. However, since modern psychotherapy is managed by insurance companies that are most interested in getting quick resolution using medication or brief psychotherapy, many consumers are finding that the complex and difficult-to-diagnose issues that they face do not fit well into the prepackaged brief approaches that are usually available. Many are finding that approaches like existential psychotherapy that deal with some of the core issues in life are much to their liking, and there has been a resurgence in interest in this type of approach to psychological difficulties.

Rollo May

May is without doubt the most well known of the existential psychologists and psychotherapists. He was born in 1909 in Ada, Ohio, and had a difficult childhood. His parents had an unpleasant relationship, and his home was filled with conflict; his parents finally divorced. Further, his sister had severe psychological difficulties and ultimately had a psychotic break and was diagnosed with schizophrenia. He went to college and studied divinity and graduated with a degree in divinity. He also studied with Alfred Adler and studied psychoanalysis at the White Institute where he met people like Harry Stack Sullivan and Erich Fromm. He went into graduate school and received the first PhD in clinical psychology that was awarded by Columbia University. From there he taught in several top universities and published numerous books dealing with existentialism and existential psychology and psychotherapy.

May postulated some psychological stages of development that are not the same types of stages as those formulated by Freud or Erikson. May's stages were more descriptions of various issues that people must deal with at various times of their life. The first stage, "innocence," is the pre-egoic stage of the infant. Infants are innocent, in that they do only what they need to do, and they will learn to exercise their will to accomplish the goals they want or need to fulfill. Another stage that May describes is "rebellion"; the rebellious person wants freedom but does not understand or appreciate the responsibility that comes with freedom, and therefore, this may be a time of tumult and conflict. During the "ordinary" stage of development, the adult learns responsibility, but when it becomes overwhelming, they will seek refuge in conformity and traditional values. The authentic adult will reach the "creative" stage, which is the existential stage where they are self-actualizing and transcend simple egocentrism.

May also had perspectives on a variety of psychological issues and realities and discussed them at length in many of his books. "Anxiety" is a major focus of May's work, and his view of anxiety is not dramatically different from Freud or many of the other psychodynamic and humanistic theorists. He saw anxiety as the apprehension triggered by some threat to a value that the person holds as essential to his or her existence as a self or independent being. He felt that feelings of threat and powerlessness give people the opportunity and the motivation to be free, make choices, and fulfill their goals and needs. If not dealt with properly, anxiety can become fear, which can become paralyzing if not managed properly. Anxiety is inevitable but can lead to growth and self-actualization when seen as a challenge rather than a curse.

"Love" is a topic about which May wrote extensively. For him, love is not a simple thing, and he conceived of many different types of love and explored various types of relationships between people some of which involved physical intimacy and sex, while others were more like what we consider to be friendship and acquaintanceship. He did point out that the relationship between sex and love is complex and frequently misunderstood, but he also felt that both were important and that they could involve the type of complete and fulfilling intimacy that makes life richer and more meaningful.

For May, one of the other problems of life is "guilt," which occurs when people deny their potentialities, fail to perceive the needs of others, or are not aware of how much they depend on the world for their own needs to be met. We can feel guilty because we do not realize our existence in the world, which is happening more today when technological advances lead people to be less involved with nature and become removed from that nature that is part of the reality of their lives. We can also feel guilty because we do not fully understand the needs of others and then feel inadequate in our inability to meet their needs. Finally, we can also feel guilty about our denial of our own potentialities or our failure to fulfill them.

May has been enormously important in integrating psychology and existentialism and exploring ideas that have been neglected by many in psychology today. Perhaps his greatest strength has been as a teacher—both at the university level and with the lay public. His books are well written and understandable and have sold well with the public. His contributions are still felt today, and many of his books and other works are relevant in today's world; many find them topical and important even decades after they were written.

Viktor Frankl

Frankl, a fascinating man, was an Austrian neurologist and psychiatrist, who, as a Jew in World War II, was treated terribly and finally was incarcerated in a concentration camp. Following the war, he was able to use his knowledge, background, and experiences to help describe the torment and trauma experienced by those who were victims of the Holocaust and the inhuman treatment that many experienced at the hands of the Nazis. His mother, brother, and wife were all murdered in concentration camps by the Nazis; the only other member of his family to survive was his sister, who later moved to Australia.

Frankl was the son of a Jewish family of civil servants, and his interest in psychology surfaced early. After graduating from the Gymnasium (like our high school), he studied medicine at the University of Vienna and later specialized in neurology and psychiatry. His early development was influenced by Freud and Adler, but he later diverged from their approaches. His approach to psychology and psychotherapy was called "logotherapy," which is a form of existential analysis. For Frankl, people are primarily motivated by a "search for meaning" in their lives, and his experience in concentration camps convinced him that survival depends on one's finding meaning in one's life (even in the most extreme circumstances) and that without a sense of meaning life is empty and without value. His approach to psychotherapy is much like other existential forms of treatment focusing on freedom, responsibility, authenticity, and so on. Therapy, therefore, helps people discover and exercise the freedom that they have in their life but also to recognize and accept the responsibility that comes with freedom. He famously suggested that with the Statue of Liberty on the East Coast of the United States, there should also be a Statue of Responsibility on the West Coast. Of course, like most existential therapists, Frankl wanted to help people fulfill their goals and needs and "evolve into" the authentic individuals they can become.

How Is This Utilized Today?

Not many therapists today would describe themselves as "existential psychotherapists," but that is not because this approach lacks value or validity. There is no doubt that the existential approach has influenced how therapists practice, and perhaps more important, it has educated the public about psychotherapy, what it is about, and what it can do to help people. May and Frankl both were prolific writers who usually focused their books and articles on the "lay public," that is, nonprofessional men and women who want to learn more about psychology and psychotherapy.

The humanistic psychotherapists have probably had a more obvious impact on the field of psychology and the practice of psychotherapy, and that is due, in part, to the dynamic and influential champions of this approach like Rogers and Maslow. Similarly, not many therapists today call themselves "humanist therapists," and that is partly because psychotherapists today are so much more broadly trained that they will usually use a wide variety of techniques for the needs of the clients whom they serve. However, the humanists and existentialists as psychotherapists have changed many ways in which therapy is practiced.

For example, these approaches focus on the unique individual who seeks psychotherapy and does not stigmatize them as "patients" who have something wrong with them but rather as potentially healthy individuals who are trying to improve their quality of life. Today, most therapists are not as sensitive about this distinction and will use the terms "client" and "patient" interchangeably, but at the time that these humanistic and existential therapists were having a major impact on the field, their emphasis on the importance of recognizing the uniqueness and value of each client was a significant change in the field and a change that is still felt today.

Another thing that these professionals did that was helpful was to challenge the need for our theories and therapies to be so rigidly deterministic in their conceptions of the human experience. Primarily from the psychoanalytic and behaviorist perspectives, all thoughts, feelings, and behaviors are determined by knowable causes. The humanists and existentialists took exception to this approach and pointed out that people have free will and the ability to be active in their environments and to change situations by making active and deliberate choices. Even for those psychologists who are scientifically and deterministically oriented, it is important to recognize that even if it is an illusion, the sense of freedom and free will that people experience as their personal reality will have an impact on them psychologically, and this must be part of what we consider when dealing with them. It is important to recognize that the humanists and existentialists (even if you disagree with them) reminded us that ultimately we are dealing with people—human beings who are unique, thinking, feeling, and active individuals who sometimes need help sorting out the challenges and trauma of their lives, and that is where psychotherapy might have something to offer that might even be helpful.

Concerns and Critiques

As important and influential as the humanistic and existential approaches to psychotherapy have been, there are limitations on their value and the impact that they have had. Probably the main concern is that because of their antideterministic and antiscientific persuasion, it is very difficult to study and understand these approaches because many of the aspects that are important to them are not observable (directly or even indirectly), not measurable, and not amenable to systematic study and research. Certainly, Rogers was an exception because he did and stimulated considerable research on his approach to psychotherapy, but unfortunately much of the research that was done was not particularly supportive of Rogers's ideas. However, his contributions to the scientific study of psychotherapy were enormous and important, even if it did not always support his theory and approaches.

Another problem with these approaches is that in their efforts to destigmatize psychological difficulties and psychotherapy, they also minimized the reality that some people do suffer from severe psychopathology that is much more than just a "problem in living." Some forms of psychopathology are based, at least in part, on biological, neurophysiological, and genetic factors, and in this sense, some of these types of problems are much like "illnesses" in the conventional sense.

Finally, one of the limitations that the humanistic and existential forms of treatment have is similar to the problem with most of the psychodynamic approaches—they are appropriate only for a subtype of people who need psychotherapy. All these approaches work best with intelligent, well-educated, and verbally facile individuals. Of course, this does not describe most people who require psychological or psychiatric assistance.

Because of these limitations, it is likely that the humanistic and existential approaches to psychotherapy will not be in the mainstream of modern treatment methods, but that is not to say that their influence will not continue to be felt. The contributions of these important therapists and theorists have left their mark, and the field of psychotherapy is better for it.

CHAPTER SEVEN

Cognitive Approaches

Cognitive psychology is the study of mental processes such as attention, memory, perception, problem-solving, creativity, and thinking. While this is a relatively new area in psychology, there are many examples throughout history of philosophers, theologians, and educators being interested in studying how and why people think and what goes on inside the mind when people are alert and even when they are not. For many philosophers, the importance of thinking could not be understated, and they saw this as the foundation of human existence. For example, the French philosopher René Descartes famously stated, "Cogito ergo sum"; "I think, therefore I am" (1911). Thus, he saw thinking as the fundamental proof of his existence. He was also one of the philosophers who discussed the dualistic nature of the human condition, that is, the separation of mind and body as two entirely different and separate entities.

History and Development

Philosophers and scholars have discussed and speculated about thinking for centuries, but psychologists have only been systematically studying thinking and cognition for a little more than 100 years. Some of the early psychologists like Freud and other psychodynamic theorists and therapists considered the most important aspects of people's mental life to be the subconscious instincts and drives that determine the thoughts, feelings, and behaviors of people, and the cognitive elements of human psychology are simply the tip of the iceberg and are just outward manifestations of what is going on inside the mind. The behaviorists did not emphasize instincts but were more interested in a person's learning history and looked at their psychological state as a product of their history and environment. Again, cognitive factors were felt to be unknowable and nonobservable and therefore nothing that could be directly studied and were therefore not available for experimental research and validation. However, some psychologists felt that cognitive factors should play a part in human learning, and one of the first to try to make inroads into this area was the American learning theorist Edward Tolman, who made strides in introducing cognitive variables into the study of learning and did much of his work in the first half of the 20th century.

Another psychologist who was interested in cognition was the Swiss developmental psychologist Jean Piaget. He studied cognitive development in children and had a detailed and thorough analysis of how children learn to think and to reason. Most of his research was observational, and he did not personally do much empirical research although this theory has stimulated many decades of research in the areas of childhood cognitive and moral development. Starting in the late 1920s, Piaget continued to do research and write well into the 1970s and 1980s.

Following World War II, psychologists and other researchers and theorists started getting more interested in cognitive factors, and this was largely stimulated by the growth of the information age and the introduction of computers and other forms of information technology. People were interested in how human beings processed information and how understanding this would also help us understand people and how they think and function. During this era, primarily in the United States, the behaviorists were becoming much more influential, and the psychodynamic approaches were starting to lose ground as the primary approaches to understanding people and helping them change through psychotherapy.

However, there were many critics who felt that the behaviorists were misguided in their approach to understanding people, and by largely ignoring mental activity and focusing only on overt behavior, they were missing a large part of what was the essence of human nature. Certainly, the humanists and existential psychotherapists were vocal critiques of the strictly deterministic and reductionist models of psychology that they felt were dehumanizing and simply wrong. However, many more scientifically oriented psychologists were not as comfortable with these less scientific models but also felt that there needed to be more than just instincts and learned patterns of behavior to fully understand human beings.

Some theorists and researchers from different backgrounds started to come together to examine the role of cognition in human psychology more closely, and in 1967, Ulric Neisser put the term "cognitive psychology" into common use, and this provided a background on which others could build. Similarly, some behavioral psychologists began looking for ways to introduce cognitive factors into more scientific behavioral models, and Albert Bandura started doing research in the area of social learning theory and was able to experimentally demonstrate how much human learning and behavior change could occur without the person actually doing the behavior in question—that is, they could learn things cognitively that could later affect their behavior. For example, people could learn by observing the behavior of others without engaging in the behavior themselves.

During the 1950s another theorist/therapist, psychologist Albert Ellis, started working on an approach he called rational therapy, later changed the name to rational emotive therapy, and finally named it rational emotive behavior therapy. This approach was also oriented toward working with people's erroneous beliefs and methods for helping people change how they think, act, and feel. These two approaches (Bandura and Ellis) were the two of the most impactful cognitive approaches that were beginning to emerge, and they would significantly influence the development of modern psychotherapy.

Contemporaneously, another psychologist, George Kelly, was starting to develop a theory of personality based on the ways in which people anticipate and deal with their environment. Although he resisted labeling his approach "cognitive," this theory was much involved with perception, thinking, planning, and memory, all processes usually thought of as being in the cognitive realm. The reason Kelly felt that "cognitive" was the wrong label for his approach was that he also talked about behavior and emotions; however, the basis of his approach is usually described as cognitive. He did speculate and work on approaches to psychotherapy based on his theory of personality, and he did work directly with patients and students.

While Ellis and Kelly had discussed their approaches to therapy somewhat earlier, cognitive therapy as a specific approach to psychotherapy was first discussed by psychiatrist Aaron Beck in the 1960s; although trained traditionally as a psychiatrist using medical forms of treatment, he was also trained in psychoanalytic psychotherapy. In working with his patients, he found that people could deal with their difficulties and help reach their goals by overcoming or changing problematic or inaccurate thinking, dysfunctional behavior, and distressing emotions. Beck found that with collaboration between the patient and the therapist, the patient could build new skills for testing and changing beliefs, identifying distorted thinking, modifying behaviors, and relating to others in better and healthier ways. He was convinced that the key to making these changes was cognition—how people interpret and use information.

Key Individuals and Their Contributions

Traditional Approaches

George Kelly

Kelly is considered by many to be the father of cognitive clinical psychology, although that is not how he described his approach. Kelly's theory of personality was called Personal Construct Psychology, and his approach to therapy was based on this theory. While he did not like his approach to be compared with or linked to other approaches, his model was often compared to humanistic and cognitive theories, and clearly, elements of his approach are similar to both. Personal construct psychology views personality from an interesting perspective. Kelly felt that people approach the world like naive scientists who see things through a perspective that is based on their unique systems of construction developed over their lifetimes, and these help them understand and anticipate events. Why this is like "naive" scientists is that they use their constructs like theories to help understand and organize their experiences of life, and sometimes these constructs are distorted by idiosyncratic experiences that they have encountered; thus their interpretations and expectations might be less than accurate or adequate. How people learn to deal with stressful events is based on their history and their constructs.

Interestingly, some of the more modern approaches to psychotherapy, like cognitive behavioral therapy (CBT), depend on Kelly's approach that treats everyone as a unique experiencing entity who interprets their world in ways consistent with their past, the experiences that they have had, and the systematic way that they interpret social information. He felt, as most psychologists today, that people are not primarily motivated by instincts like sexual and aggressive drives but are more likely to strive to characterize and predict events in their social world. Kelly is less deterministic in his theory than the psychodynamic and behavioral approaches because he feels that people can change the way they view the world, and by doing this they can also change the way in which they interact with this world and feel about it and even change how others react to them. In this way, there are elements of the existential approach as well as the humanistic. However, Kelly would resist the notion that his model could be grouped with any of the other basic types of theories and that his approach was completely different and was not like any other.

George Kelly was an original and important thinker who changed the way psychologists think about personality and psychotherapy. Not many people today conceive of personality in exactly the way Kelly did, but few modern theories of personality do not bear the marks of his ideas. Similarly, there may not be many who conduct psychotherapy as Kelly would have, but all the major approaches to psychotherapy today have been impacted by Kelly's ideas either directly or indirectly; while he may not be as well known as some of the other theorists and therapists we have studied, his contributions have been legendary. In addition to his theory and approaches to psychotherapy, his role as an educator and advocate for psychology was enormously important, and he had much to do with the way the field of clinical psychology developed and matured to what it has become today.

Albert Ellis

Originally trained in psychoanalysis, Ellis had great respect for Freud and his approach. He was also trained in Jungian analysis and felt that analytic types of psychotherapy offered the best in-depth type of treatment. However, as he gained more experience as a professor and clinician, his faith in psychoanalysis started to decrease, and he started reading the works of Horney, Adler, Fromm, and Sullivan and became convinced that approaching therapy from more of a social perspective was important. He also became interested in applying rational thinking as an approach to psychotherapy, and he pointed out that his approach was not entirely new since others who had preceded him had also championed the ideal of rational persuasion as a good basis for psychotherapy and behavior change; he started calling himself a "rational therapist," and he began using a more active and directive type of psychotherapy. This approach was not well thought of by the psychodynamic community that looked at rational/cognitive therapy as superficial and shallow. Further, by being active and directive, the humanistic and existential therapists felt that Ellis's approach was too directive and did not allow the "client" to express their own ideas and to explore their own unique needs and goals. However, as Ellis expanded his approach to include emotions (rational emotive therapy) and then behavior (Rational Emotive Behavior Therapy [REBT]), his approach began to attract more followers and was certainly one of the main influences in the emergence of cognitive behavior therapy as it is widely practiced today. In fact, in a study conducted with U.S. and Canadian psychologists, Ellis was the second most influential psychotherapist in history (with Carl Rogers being first and Sigmund Freud being third).

In the later part of Ellis's career, he branched out into other areas and started studying behavioral integrity, focusing on reliability, honesty, and loyalty as psychosocial behavior. He also got heavily involved in research and practice as a sexologist treating and helping people with sexual difficulties. In addition, he conducted research on sex and love as important parts of the human experience and continued to write about these topics for the remainder of his life and developed some theoretical ideas that contributed to our understanding of human sexuality. Although Ellis had never presented himself as a religious person and was generally critical of religious institutions, in his later years he talked and wrote about religion, and like many of his ideas, his thoughts about religion moderated during his life. Raised in a Jewish home, Ellis considered himself to be an atheist and felt that religion was largely harmful to people by shaping their thinking in ways that were not healthy or realistic. He was also careful to point out that REBT was independent of his atheism and noted that there were many religious people who were REBT therapists, including some ordained clergy. As he aged, his views on religion, and other topics as well, "softened" a bit, and he was more accepting of differing perspectives. Further, he was a lifelong advocate for peace, and he opposed militarism, which brought him in contact with similar perspectives in people from religious backgrounds.

Ellis was well known to be vocal about his feelings and judgments, and many found him rude and insulting. However, he was certainly genuine and direct in his viewpoints and left little ambiguity in his opinions. His ideas and approaches to psychotherapy have had a profound effect on how therapy is practiced today; still people in his institute practice REBT much in the way Ellis taught them, and many people seek out the institute as an opportunity for training and experience in psychotherapy.

More Recent Approaches

Aaron Beck

Aaron Beck is a psychiatrist who spent most of his professional life at the University of Pennsylvania and is considered by many to be the father of cognitive therapy. Although there were some psychotherapists who were cognitive therapists whose work preceded Beck, he was one of the most influential and visible practitioners at the time. In addition to his work on cognitive therapy, he did significant research on depression, anxiety, and psychotherapy. He wrote extensively on the cognitive basis for depression and designed treatment programs to deal with these issues directly and effectively. He was also a champion of improving our systems of identifying patients with depression and treating them earlier, and he developed the Beck Depression Screening Inventory that is used frequently in primary care medical offices and in other sites where depression screening might be helpful. He also later developed the Beck Anxiety Screening Inventory, which is widely used as well.

Beck's commitment to theory and research, detection and diagnosis, education and training, and the development and implementation of reasonable and effective methods of treatment was the reason why his impact and stature in the field are so important. He also founded the Beck Institute for Cognitive Behavior Therapy with his psychologist daughter Judith S. Beck. He has had a huge influence on psychiatry and psychology, and he was judged to be one the five most influential psychotherapists of all time by the *American Psychologist* in 1989.

Beck was born in Providence, Rhode Island, and was the youngest of four children in a family of Russian Jewish immigrants. In 1950 he married Phillis W. Beck, who was the first woman judge on the Appellate Court of the Commonwealth of Pennsylvania, and they had four children. After graduating from Brown University, he went to Yale Medical School and originally began studying neurology, which he found fascinating. Due to a shortage of psychiatry residents, he had to do a six-month rotation in that field and he became absorbed in psychoanalysis even though he had originally been wary of that approach. As he began exploring new approaches and ideas, he started investigating different cognitive approaches to personality and was interested in and explored Kelly's personal construct theory and Piaget's cognitive schemas. He first started writing about cognitive theory of depression in 1963 and 1964 but was maintaining the context of ego psychology; however, he became more interested in the realistic and scientific approaches to cognition and started applying these ideas in ways to meet psychotherapeutic needs.

Albert Ellis was probably the psychologist who influenced Beck the most, and Beck was interested in the pragmatic and realistic approach to therapy. As interested as he was in Ellis's approach, he felt that Ellis was too directive, and Beck preferred to help patients learn for themselves empirically and through their own experiences. As Beck continued to work with depressed patients, he found that they experience streams of negative thoughts that seemed to pop up spontaneously, and he called these "automatic thoughts." He found that these automatic thoughts fell into three categories: negative ideas about themselves, the world, and the future. Beck's approach to therapy was based on the idea that patients could learn to identify and evaluate these thoughts, and by doing so the patients could start thinking more realistically, which led them to feel more positive emotionally and to behave more functionally. This approach to psychotherapy was probably the first example of CBT, and this approach grew to become the most widely accepted and used form of psychotherapy today.

As widely used as CBT is today, it has also been thoroughly and systematically evaluated, and it is an empirically validated therapy often found to be the most effective type of psychotherapy for many disorders. However, as important and widely used as CBT is, it is not without its critics. Some feel that it is too mechanistic and does not get into some of the deeper and more fundamental problems that a person might experience. It is certainly true that the CBT approach is not the most effective psychotherapy for all patients, and some seem to do better with different approaches. For one reason, some patients find that the approaches in CBT are too difficult or unpleasant for them, and they just do not want to do them. There is no doubt that CBT is a generally effective and widely accepted form of therapy, but to conclude that it is the best approach for all patients is neither realistic nor accurate. In fact, no single approach to treatment is the best for everyone. However, CBT is an approach that has proven its value in treatment settings and in the research and clinical literature.

Martin Seligman

"Marty" Seligman is an influential psychologist who did some important research that impacted how we look at, conceptualize, and treat depression.

His work on "learned helplessness" was well done and theoretically important but also paved the way for new ideas about depression. Working with dogs he found that when normal dogs were placed in a cage and then shocked, they would immediately escape the aversive part of the cage to go to another part where they were not shocked. They learned quickly to get out of the section of the cage to avoid the shock. However, another group of normal dogs were put in the cage, but when shocked, they were prevented from escaping the shock and had to stay in the cage and just endure it. Later, when the same dogs were put in the cage and shocked, the partition that prevented them from escaping was removed, but they stayed in the same part of the cage and continued to endure the shock because they had learned that they could not avoid it "so why try." This finding was called "learned helplessness," and Seligman pointed out that this was similar to what we find in depressed patients who are in difficult and stressful situations but will often remain in those situations even when they could escape or leave them because they have learned that it does not make any difference what they do because it will be bad anyway—so they just stay in the aversive situation: learned helplessness.

Although trained as an experimental psychologist, Seligman, who got his PhD from the University of Pennsylvania, decided to start working with Aaron Beck to learn more about the clinical side of depression, and the two of them together began to reformulate their approach to the treatment of depression, which led to the development of what is now called cognitive behavioral therapy. With the background provided by Ellis and Kelly and the early work by Beck, this approach soon became the treatment of choice for depression and many other conditions.

Seligman continued his work on depression and anxiety and was influential as a researcher, teacher, supervisor, and therapist. He also was elected president of the American Psychological Association as some of his predecessors had been as well. However, he also became more interested in a new trend in psychology, and this involved some of the "softer" elements of the field drawing much from the background of historical cultures across the millennia involving virtues that have been highly valued from ancient China and India, through Greece and Rome, to prevailing cultures today. Working with Christopher Peterson, they developed six character strengths: wisdom/knowledge, courage, humanity, justice, temperance, and transcendence. They did not feel that there was a ranking of these virtues but that all of them were important as virtues representing the best in what humankind was capable of and what we should all aspire to. This is a big part of the movement in psychology that is known as "Positive Psychology," and Seligman is a major reason why this approach has become so popular.

One thing that Seligman has done that is enormously important is that he has written several books addressing some of the issues of positive psychology, and although he is a well-trained experimental psychologist, he has approached this field in an easy-to-read, commonsense way that has made his ideas accessible to the public. In his book *Flourish* Seligman talks about how he measures "well-being" using an approach he calls "Well-being Theory." He concludes that there are five elements to well-being, and he describes them with the mnemonic PERMA:

- Positive emotion
- Engagement
- Relationships
- Meaning
- Achievement

From his perspective, Seligman feels that these are the five things that will determine to what extent people experience well-being. In addition to his theoretic work in this area, he and many others have done quite a bit of research on well-being and on positive psychology, in general. Drawing from its background in cognitive psychology and CBT, positive psychology has become one of the most important new developments in psychotherapy in recent years.

How Is This Utilized Today?

The cognitive approach to psychotherapy is widely used and influential in many different areas of the field. One of the appealing facts about the cognitive approach is that it fits in with the commonsense reality of most people's experience of life. We are thinking, active beings, and when we have problems, it seems logical that we should try to fix them by thinking differently and then doing something consistent with our new way of thinking. Of course, if it were really that simple, we probably would not need psychotherapy at all, and people could figure it all out by themselves. However, reality is far more complex, and it is a rare problem that can be quickly fixed with a couple of new thoughts. There is no doubt that by using thinking as a predominant tool in psychotherapy, it is much more understandable and acceptable to many people who are the consumers of psychotherapy.

Today, CBT is the most widely utilized psychotherapeutic approach, and while it is partly behavioral, its history and basis is clearly from the cognitive heritage. One of the reasons why this approach has been so influential is that it has been proven time and again to be a superior form of treatment that usually demonstrates its effectiveness over other forms of therapy, including medication. Because it is easier to study experimentally than other types of therapy, it has also led to more research that has supported its reputation and effectiveness.

However, it is a mistake to assume that CBT is the only type of cognitive therapy that is available, because there are many other approaches that rely heavily on cognitive methods as well. For example, even some of the newer psychodynamic approaches like interpersonal psychotherapy primarily use cognitive methods to deal with therapeutic issues. Similarly, still practitioners use REBT as developed by Ellis. Finally, for those who use humanistic and existential approaches to therapy, their therapeutic practice largely relies on cognitive techniques and theories as well. Clearly, many therapeutic techniques from different backgrounds have been consistently and thoroughly influenced by the cognitive approach to therapy.

Originally, the psychodynamic approach dominated the psychotherapeutic landscape; then the behavioral, humanistic, and existential approaches started making some inroads. As important as these new approaches were, it is equally clear that the "cognitive revolution" in psychotherapy has been the most influential paradigm shift in the field of psychotherapy in recent years, and its impact will be felt for many years.

The newer cognitive and cognitive-behavioral approaches have proven to be effective for several reasons. First, they teach people to assume a sense of self-empowerment that is essential for any behavior change technique to have a lasting effect. Second, they emphasize the importance of self-efficacy, meaning people need to learn to think and believe that they are capable and have the skills to make positive changes. Finally, these approaches emphasize the importance of dealing with the "here and now." We cannot change history and the future is unknown, so learning to focus on things that are happening now is the best way to help people start making changes that will make a difference in their lives. These newer cognitive approaches are typically brief interventions that make them time- and cost efficient; it is more likely that people can and will use the approaches since they will not be committing themselves to years of therapy, which was typical of psychoanalysis, and it is more likely that people's insurance companies will pay for at least some of the expenses of therapy.

These modern cognitive approaches are "learning oriented." They emphasize the importance of understanding how their thoughts and behaviors have created problems for them in the past. Teaching them not only why these dysfunction approaches have caused problems but learning new ways to think and behave will hopefully make the person's life less fraught with problems of their own making. The cognitive and CBT approaches focus on what the person has control over (e.g., their own behavior and thoughts) and how to learn more effective and positive ways to think and act. It is pragmatic, outcome oriented, and usually consistent with common sense and reasoning.

Concerns and Critiques

As important and influential as the cognitive approach to psychotherapy has been, it is not without its critics, and realistically, it cannot be the only set of techniques that will meet the needs of all clients, all ages, all different ethnic and cultural groups, and so on—it can never be the only approach that will work in all situations. Probably the most common problem with these approaches is that they require that people learn new ways of thinking and doing things, and sometimes this is difficult, and some people get discouraged and frustrated and drop out of therapy. Others simply may not have the discipline and organizational skills needed to accomplish some of the "homework" assignments that are part of therapy. Another problem may be that the client may not have the "motivation" to do the things necessary to change. This is a problem when the client or patient has come to treatment because someone else (e.g., spouse, parent, the court) has insisted that the person come into treatment. A therapist can often help a person change who is motivated to change, but a therapist can rarely make a person "want to change" if they really are not interested.

Another problem with cognitive types of therapy is that they depend on the client's ability to understand, process, and act on sometimes rather complex ideas. Also, it is not uncommon for these types of treatments to use homework assignments that may require reading, and therefore, literacy may be an issue for some clients. A good therapist will gear the therapy to the specific needs and limitations of each client, but sometimes this is very difficult to do, and some clients just may not be able to do what is needed.

Finally, these approaches to therapy depend on people's willingness and ability to make changes in their behavior and thinking, but this is rarely easy, or most people would not even need therapy. It is almost always the case that the behaviors and thoughts that create difficulties for people are based on patterns that they have been "practicing" for years and thus are a deeply ingrained and important part of their psychological profile. This does, of course, make change difficult and often painful—some of the patterns that may need to be changed might just be those that the person really does not want to change (e.g., eating habits in an obese person who comes to therapy to help deal with their food issues). Patients soon recognize that they are trying to change the ways that they have been doing for a long time, and for obvious reasons, this makes change sometimes difficult.

Some of the concerns regarding cognitive types of therapy are based on scientific and methodological issues. With some of the early approaches like those of Kelly, many of the behavioral theorists and scholars felt that the concepts were too "mentalistic" and did not lend themselves to rigorous empirical validation and were therefore not of a scientific standard that many felt were acceptable. However, with the growth of cognitive neuroscience, this criticism is moot; now substantial and high-quality empirical research is bridging the gap between the neurophysiological and cognitive psychological factors, and thus, this complaint is no longer relevant.

Others have complained that Ellis's approach was not adequately validated empirically and did not measure up to other approaches that were more rigorously studied. Further, some felt that Ellis's approach was based more on his subjective ideas about what was good for people rather than any objective empirical evidence. Ellis, however, was neither concerned nor bothered by these issues and felt that if his approach seemed to work, that was all the evidence that he needed. This does, incidentally, sound much like Freud's defense of psychoanalysis; he asserted that the process of psychoanalysis was a way of collecting data, and his analysis of the data was the only scientific validation that his approach needed. Further, he felt that psychoanalysis could not be evaluated by anyone who was not an analyst since they would not fully understand the information. Ellis having been initially trained as an analyst seems to use the same line of thinking regarding his defense of his own REBT approach.

Finally, some researchers have complained that even some of the more widely studied cognitive approaches like CBT are not validated by double-blind studies. Experiments that evaluate the effectiveness of certain drugs usually have an experimental group that gets to try the new medication and a control group that gets a completely neutral drug that does not really do anything (e.g., a sugar pill). In the experiment, the researchers know who gets which drug, but neither the doctor who administers the drug nor the patient who takes it knows whether they have the actual medication or an inactive substance that looks just like the drug. Then the patient and the doctor evaluate the patient's response to the drug they took, and neither knows which one they took until the study is over. Thus, since neither the doctor nor the patient knows which drug was taken, it is a "double-blind" study.

Although this is a good method for studying drugs, it is probably not a reasonable criticism of studies evaluating psychotherapies. How could you expect that the therapist would not know what kind of therapy they were providing or that a patient would not know the difference between real therapy and a neutral, nontherapeutic interaction that is not designed to help in any way? The way in which this issue is usually handled is that in addition to the ratings by the patients and the therapists regarding therapeutic outcomes, the patients are usually evaluated by using measurement devices like psychological tests, and/or therapists who did not provide the treatment will evaluate therapeutic outcomes without knowledge of the type of treatment that the person received.

In summary, the cognitive approaches have been well received and have demonstrated their value in treatment. Further, they have influenced most of the different approaches that are being used today. However, they are not the *only* way to treat people, they do not work optimally for every patient, and there are some patients who do not desire or do well with these types of approaches. As we learn more about psychotherapy, we can use techniques more effectively and choose the approach that is most likely to be helpful for everyone.

CHAPTER EIGHT

Behavioral Approaches

Although there are many different types of behavioral therapies, there are some common elements that all share. First, all of them are based on learning theory approaches to understanding behavior. Second, they are all based on and validated by empirical research. Third, they are all deterministic models—this means that they believe that all behavior is caused by identifiable and knowable causes. Finally, they tend to be briefer and directive types of therapy with specific and measurable goals and outcomes.

However, the behavioral approaches to psychotherapy differ from other types of therapy in several ways. First, purely behavioral approaches focus *only* on overt behavior and avoid dealing with nonobservable events like thoughts and emotions. Of course, they do not deny that thoughts and emotions exist but point out that all we have to work with when dealing with these inferred states is the self-report of people and observations of their overt behavior. We cannot directly observe or measure mental events, and the strict behaviorist would avoid trying to deal with these types of variables. These theorists and therapists emphasize the importance of the person's environment (the context of their behavior) and their reported and observed history to understand them. When conducting therapy, they try to focus on the current environments, relationships, and situations; and since history cannot be changed, they look only at historical factors for understanding the learning patterns that have developed over time and try to establish a context to help understand the person's behavior now. The behavioral approaches assume that all behavior is learned, and changing behavior is primarily about helping people "unlearn" maladaptive patterns and learn some new and more adaptive and functional ways to act and behave—learning is the key.

The behavioral approach is also deterministic—all behaviors have an identifiable and knowable cause. While the behaviorists are primarily concerned with learned patterns of behavior, they would not deny genetics, reflexes, neurophysiological factors, and so on, but they would quickly point out that these are the domain of biologists and physiologists and are not a concern for psychologists. Other psychological approaches like psychoanalysis are also quite deterministic, but many other psychotherapeutic approaches (e.g., humanistic, existential, some cognitive approaches) are not deterministic and find the strict determinism of psychoanalysis and behaviorism to be dehumanizing.

History and Development

When we look at the origins of behavioral approaches, we need to consider the entirety of human history. Since people have existed, there have likely been attempts to change behavior using rewards and punishments—these tools have been used by parents, teachers, courts, the government, and others to modify people's behavior. However, the difference is that the present use of behavioral techniques is based on systematic research and theory and is organized as a collection of techniques and methods that address different ways to alter (improve) people's behavior to help eliminate or reduce the frequency of dysfunctional behavior and to introduce and increase the presence of more functional and adaptive behavior.

In recent years, behavioral approaches have melded with other types of approaches resulting in more eclectic methods that draw from other models as well; the most obvious example is CBT, which is a blend of behavioral and cognitive techniques. Even some of the newer psychodynamic approaches like interpersonal psychotherapy also use some behavioral methods. Many of the behavioral therapists have started introducing new ideas into their practices, including "mindfulness" and "positive psychology," which are quite different than the techniques used by the strictly behavioral therapists. However, still some behavioral therapists rely almost completely on purely behavioral methods and continue to do so.

The behavioral approach to therapy is based on learning theory, which is a branch of psychological research and theory that dates back to the late 19th and early 20th centuries. However, the roots of behaviorism go back much further and may be found in ancient philosophical approaches like Stoicism. Philosophers in the past few centuries have attempted to understand human nature and the human mind, and some of them (e.g., the British empiricists) were instrumental in providing a philosophical base for this approach. The early learning theorists like Edward Thorndike, John Watson, and Edward Tolman were instrumental in doing research and developing theories that led to better understanding of how people learned and how different behavior patterns were acquired and modified. In fact, Thorndike seems to have been the first person to describe "modifying behavior" in 1911.

Interestingly, the first actual model of learning was developed by a Russian physiologist, Ivan Pavlov, and he was not even interested in studying learning. Pavlov was studying digestive processes in dogs and was interested in the role of salivation in digestion, so he had tubes in the salivary glands of his dog subjects, and then he would put meat paste on their tongues and measure the amount of saliva that was produced. After having done this a few times, he found that when he walked into the lab, and even before he put the meat paste on the dogs' tongues, they started to salivate. This, of course, is hardly surprising to anyone who walks into their home thinking about a wonderful dinner their mother or father must be getting ready to prepare and starting to salivate. However, from Pavlov's physiological perspective, there was not a good explanation as to why this would happen. As evidence of his brilliance as a researcher, Pavlov decided to try to find out why this unexpected salivation occurred, and he designed some experiments to try to understand this.

Although he resisted having his work considered to be "psychology," Pavlov developed what was the first empirically validated model of learning. His most well-known experiment involved dogs that were restrained and had equipment to monitor their salivation. All the dogs would salivate when meat paste was placed on their tongues (this was an unconditioned stimulus [US]—meat paste, which led to an unconditioned response [UR]—salivation). If a bell were rung when there was no meat paste in the dogs' mouths, this was a conditioned stimulus (CS) that yielded no response. However, if meat paste (US) was placed on the dogs' tongues and a bell (CS) was rung at the same time, salivation would occur (UR). After a few such pairings (sometimes only one was needed), the bell (CS) would result in salivation, which was a new conditioned response (CR) that occurred only after the pairing had occurred. Thus, the dog "learned" to salivate in response to the bell.

This model of learning has been known by several different labels, and all of them are correct and interchangeable: classical/Pavlovian/respondent conditioning; this approach started to generate considerable interest and research. Interestingly, although he designed and executed the original research, Pavlov was not interested in pursuing that line of study; several of his students (especially Vladimir Bekhterev) did quite a bit of work on this model, and their work gained interest primarily in the United States where behaviorism was starting to take hold as a major influence, but some psychologists in the United Kingdom were interested in this approach as well.

Key Individuals and Their Contributions

Early Models

John Watson

John Watson, an American psychologist, was professor at Johns Hopkins University and a "radical behaviorist." He felt strongly that all behavior was determined, and all was learned though experience. He was not interested in mental events or nonobservable variables like thoughts or feelings and made claims that if he were given an infant and total control of its environment, he could shape it to be anything he chose—doctor, lawyer, laborer, artist, and so on. One study that he did on a youngster was enormously influential and highly controversial. He recruited an 18-month-old boy, Albert, who was developmentally normal (it was later discovered that he was the son of a single mother who worked as a cleaner in Watson's laboratory building). Watson let Albert play in the lab and he introduced a white rat in the room which avoided Albert, but the little boy could see and watch the rat but showed no interest or reaction to the animal. Later, Watson put the rat closer to Albert, and behind the little boy he struck an iron bar with a hammer and produced a loud and startling noise and Albert started crying. When he stopped the noise and removed the rat, Albert settled down. Later, when Albert was playing in the room, he brought the white rat back into the room, and as soon as Albert saw the rat, he started crying loudly and continued crying until the rat was removed. Watson also found that Albert was afraid of things like white stuffed animals and even a white towel that was crumpled up in the corner.

This demonstration was important for several reasons. First, it demonstrated that by using Pavlovian conditioning techniques, a child could learn to fear a previously neutral stimulus (the rat). Second, it demonstrated that abnormal behavior (a fear reaction or phobia) could be learned. Third, it showed that a learned fear reaction could spread to other previously neutral stimuli (generalized fear response like a phobia). This demonstration of learned abnormal behavior also suggested the possibility that learned abnormal behavior might be modified by learning new, more functional behaviors.

As important as this research was, Watson attracted considerable negative attention for the work. People were outraged that he would do research and teach a fear response to a youngster (in fact, there is no way that this study would be approved today because of the ethical implications). Not only was his work negatively viewed by the field of psychology and the academic community in general, but also he was front-page news in the Baltimore newspapers. Further, Watson had an affair with one of his graduate students, and he divorced his wife of 17 years and married his student. This was also front-page news, and the board of trustees at Hopkins finally decided that Watson was too much of a liability to the school and he was fired. It should also be noted that Watson went on to work in business and started to apply psychological ideas to advertising and marketing and retired as a successful multimillionaire. Although he had been dismissed by the American Psychological Association (APA) for his unethical research methods, in his later life the importance of his contributions was also recognized, and he was given a lifetime achievement award by the APA. He was thrilled by this award, but at his advanced age, he was unable to attend the annual meeting to receive his award.

To help restore his reputation, after Watson was fired from Hopkins, some of his students decided to do another study where they could demonstrate that if it were possible to condition abnormal behavior (phobia), they could also condition healthier behavior. After the original study with little Albert, with all the publicity, his mother took him and moved to another town without telling anyone where they were going. Therefore, when they wanted to do another study, they had to find a different subject, and they were able to locate a boy who was the age that Albert would have been had they located him (about two-and-a-half years old). This boy already had a fear of white furry objects, including white rats, and he became the focus of the new study. By using conditioning methods, they were able to help the little boy find more adaptive and healthier responses to white furry objects, and he no longer had the same fear that he had before. This study was important because the researchers were able to demonstrate that conditioning methods could be used to successfully treat abnormal behavior and return the subjects/patients to a healthier and more "normal" condition.

B. F. Skinner

As important as the classical conditioning model had become, many felt it was too limited a model to explain all the different types of learning, and new and different models needed to be explored. One of the most important psychologists in the 20th century emerged to begin studying a completely different model of learning and conditioning, and B. F. Skinner started work on a model that became known as operant conditioning (sometimes called Skinnerian conditioning). While the Pavlovian model depended on an existing relationship between US and UR, Skinner felt that it was unnecessary to identify the original cause of a behavior, because he felt that behavior was largely shaped by its consequences. This was an approach that was similar to what Thorndike had presented in the early decades of the 20th century when he postulated the Law of Effect. According to this law, "Behaviors followed by pleasant outcomes tend to be 'stamped in' (repeated) and behaviors followed by unpleasant outcomes tend to be 'stamped out' (eliminated)" (Thorndike, 1905). Skinner found that the simple law of effect did not capture the complexity and richness of this new approach, and he based his model on the concept of "reinforcement," which refers to the idea that anything that increases the likelihood of a given behavior being repeated is a reinforcer. Positive reinforcement refers to a situation when the addition of a positive outcome increases the likelihood of a given response recurring, and negative reinforcement is when the removal of an aversive outcome would also increase the likelihood of a response recurring. On the other hand, punishment involves the addition of an aversive outcome or the removal of a positive outcome with the intention of decreasing the likelihood of a response recurring. Skinner felt strongly that the use of aversive outcomes (e.g., negative reinforcement or punishment) would yield less predictable results and would also create unwanted collateral outcomes (e.g., the subject learning to fear and avoid the punishing agent). To eliminate unwanted behavior, Skinner preferred to identify the unwanted behavior, analyze the situation, and determine what the reinforcers were, and by removing the reinforcers, eventually the behavior would be eliminated (this is called "extinction"); this outcome is more stable and predictable than the use of aversive outcomes.

Traditionally, the two models of learning were considered to represent two different types of learning, and they remained somewhat separate although not really in conflict or competition. It was clear through clinical practice and research that both approaches were valid and important. When behavioral forms of treatment started to be used, some tended to use the label "behavior therapy" to describe approaches that relied primarily on the classical conditioning approach and "behavior modification" for approaches primarily based on operant conditioning. Today it clear that these two approaches do not really represent different kinds of learning but rather just different kinds of techniques to accomplish the desired results. In fact, today the two terms ("behavior therapy" and "behavior modification") are often used interchangeably to describe types of behavior therapy that rely primarily on behavioral learning approaches. Those that relied heavily on the operant techniques were able to demonstrate a broad range of symptoms and behavior problems that could be treated effectively using operant methods, and these approaches did not even depend on language facility to be effective. Thus, these approaches could be used with children, developmentally disabled people, severely mentally ill psychotic patients, and others who could not understand or speak the language used by the therapist. These techniques were even applied in organizations to deal with problems such as social loafing at work, poor performance, theft, and conflict. Applied in this way, the approach is called "organizational behavior modification," and it has proven to be effective to deal with work-related behavior problems.

Historically, others have used the classical conditioning approach to deal with a wide variety of clinical problems as well. After World War II, Joseph Wolpe developed an approach called "systematic desensitization" to treat phobias, and this approach is widely used even today. Hans Eysenck from the United Kingdom also demonstrated how classical conditioning approaches could be used to treat a wide variety of mental health problems, and he and his followers contributed significantly to the use of conditioning-based approaches for the treatment of psychological disorders.

Recent Approaches

Peter Lewinsohn, Derek Hopko, and Others

Although most of the newer forms of psychotherapy depend, at least in part, on cognitive techniques and strategies, this is certainly the case with many of the behavioral techniques like CBT; some behavioral therapists and researchers feel strongly that the cognitive aspects of treatment are not necessary and that purely behavioral approaches can be optimally effective by themselves. Some have pointed out that current thinking suggests that the cognitive elements of psychotherapy are the main reason why cognitive-behavioral approaches are so successful; however, they also point out that this conclusion may be premature and ill advised. For one thing, they assert that even with approaches like CBT, most of the significant therapeutic changes occur during the first parts of therapy where the predominant techniques are behavioral and not cognitive. The behavioral therapists have a long and impressive history of dealing with significant psychological issues like anxiety and depression and have proven themselves to be effective for many decades. Even Skinner as early as 1953 suggested that depression involved problems where the reinforcement patterns for normal healthy behavior were interrupted, and less functional (depressive) forms of behavior began to predominate the person's behavior. Further, C. B. Ferster suggested that over time the reinforcers for healthy behavior were disrupted or even punished, and some form of reinforcement for maladaptive behavior emerged to keep the unhealthy behavior persisting over time.

More recently, Lewinsohn and his coworkers are among those who continue to work on a behavioral model of abnormal behavior that is sound and empirically and clinically validated. He suggested that behavioral treatments for depression (and for other forms of maladaptive behavior) were aimed at increasing access to pleasant events and positive reinforcers as well as decreasing the intensity and frequency of aversive events and consequences. He went on to assert that the fundamental elements of behavioral treatment for depression are based on the following:

1. Reintroduce clients to pleasurable events and activities.
2. Appropriately reinforce the correct behaviors—extinguish others.
3. Help improve social skills.

Other researchers and clinicians have followed Lewinsohn's approach and have been working on other techniques and methods for applying purely behavioral methods to the treatment of psychological difficulties, and because depression and anxiety are such common problems, many of the studies deal with either or both types of problems. For example, Hopko and his colleagues have developed behavioral activation (BA) therapy. This approach is based on the idea that if people with psychological problems are going to get better, they cannot simply sit around and wait for it to pass—they must become more active and get themselves involved with situations where they will be able to experience more pleasurable events and people and hopefully start feeling better and acting more normal for themselves. The three fundamental aspects of BA are as follows:

1. Extinction (removing the reinforcers) for dysfunctional behavior
2. Fading (gradual removal of the therapeutic structure so that the new, more adaptive behaviors become a permanent part of the person's behavior repertoire)
3. Shaping (gradual approximation of the desired final behavior patterns)

Some have questioned whether purely behavioral changes would also result in cognitive and emotional changes that will help the client feel and act better and not just appear to be better. Interestingly, some compelling studies have demonstrated that using purely behavioral approaches resulted in cognitive and emotional changes equally as effectively as cognitive types of techniques, suggesting that at least for some (probably many) clients, the cognitive techniques are not necessary to evoke cognitive changes, and perhaps the behavioral approaches can be adequate in and of themselves.

Other Recent Approaches

Another recent approach called brief behavioral activation therapy for depression (BATD) has been introduced and evaluated. This approach is structured and time limited and usually lasts for 8–15 sessions, and early in the treatment, the intention is to weaken access to positive reinforcement for dysfunctional behaviors (e.g., sympathy) and to avoid or minimize negative reinforcement (e.g., avoiding responsibilities). This approach may seem mechanistic and impersonal to some, but the first stages of treatment involve building a rapport between the client and therapist and educating the client about the approach and techniques and answering any concerns or questions that they might have. It is true that both BA and BATD are similar although BATD is more structured and conducted within a brief time frame. Both approaches involve the following:

1. Learning relaxation skills
2. Increasing pleasant events

3. Social and other problem-solving skills
4. Skills training
5. Contingency management
6. Incorporating verbal-cognitive methods such as
    a. cognitive restructuring
    b. self-instruction training

In addition, both BA and BATD use additional approaches such as the following:

1. Rating mastery and the pleasure of activities
2. Mental rehearsal of assigned activities
3. Therapist modeling
4. Periodic distraction from problems or unpleasant events
5. Mindfulness training or relaxation
6. Self-reinforcement
7. Additional skills training
    a. Sleep hygiene
    b. Assertiveness
    c. Communication
    d. Problem-solving

It is clear from these lists of therapeutic approaches that the newer behavioral therapies are "technique oriented" and are fundamentally grounded in behavioristic theories and empirical research. The researchers and clinicians who have developed and are using these new types of therapy have done an excellent job of developing new approaches, applying them to a wide variety of different problems areas, and validating them with empirical research. While it is not realistic to assume that one type of therapy will be the optimal approach for every client or problem, it is also true that the work that has come out of the behavioral approach has been impactful and impressive, and even for therapists who prefer to use a wider variety of techniques, much is to be gained by applying some of the behavioral techniques to the approaches that they use as well.

How Is This Utilized Today?

We are finding an increased interest in the behavioral techniques today for a variety of reasons. First, and most important, they work. One cannot dispute the fact that the behavioral approaches continue to demonstrate empirically and clinically that they are powerful tools that have broad and important applicability in helping people with psychological difficulties improve their quality of life and decrease some of the difficulties that they are experiencing. Further, the behavioral techniques, as mentioned earlier, can be used with many different types of clients, including those who are typically not usually good candidates for traditional forms of psychotherapy. For example, there is considerable evidence for the effectiveness of behavioral techniques in working with young children who may be preverbal or who will not be able to sit in a chair for an hour and discuss how they feel about their parents. We have also seen the effectiveness of behavioral techniques working with severely mentally ill patients like schizophrenics who would not be able to participate in traditional psychotherapy. There is also an extensive literature regarding the use of behavioral techniques with developmentally disabled children and adults. While behavioral techniques would certainly not "cure" schizophrenia or a chronic developmental disability, these techniques have been effective in helping severely disturbed individuals become more independent and functional and live a more productive and enjoyable life.

One other factor that makes the behavioral techniques important has less to do with choice of therapeutic techniques for the patient's benefit but rather how the treatment is paid for. Whether we like it or not, many of the decisions about mental health treatment are made by insurance or managed care companies that will determine how, by whom, and how long mental health treatment can be used (if at all). Therefore, the briefer forms of treatment are more likely to be approved and supported by the people who make the decisions about paying for treatment. While this might seem like an unfair and even ridiculous consideration, it is the reality that we are dealing with in the mental health care environment as well, which is also one of the reasons why fewer people are choosing to go into fields like clinical psychology and psychiatry today.

Another factor that makes the behavioral techniques so important today is that they can be applied in many different situations and even at the group and organizational levels. There are many examples of the use of behavioral techniques to impact the behavior of students in school settings (e.g., finding ways to reinforce positive behaviors and discourage negative behaviors). Further, using techniques like organizational behavior modification, there have been many examples of how behavioral techniques can be applied in the organizational setting to improve the quality of work, productiveness of employees, workplace safety, and job satisfaction. In fact, research in this area is so compelling and important that it is hard to understand why more organizations are not using these techniques, but the resistance is usually based on ill-informed misconceptions of how psychological interventions can be positively applied to organizational settings. Most organizations tend to resist any kinds of changes unless they immediately impact the financial position. For example, there is ample evidence that spending money on improving the quality of work life will pay off in the long run, and in fact one group of many studies showed that every dollar spent on programs to help provide a better work environment and better treatment for employees will result in a $5 gain for the organization within five years.

Concerns and Critiques

Although the behavioral techniques have proven to be effective in clinical, educational, and organizational settings, they still do not have the impact that they probably should have. One reason for this is that these approaches are seen by many as outdated and "old school." Since they may not be the most widely accepted and used approaches, there may be some reluctance to go against the current cognitive-behavioral trends, and thus, there may not be as much incentive to do research in these areas as in the more mainstream methods. In a similar vein, academics and scholars may not be as enthusiastic about these approaches because they feel that they need to be using, researching, and teaching the methods that are most widely accepted by the professional community. Consequently, the problem in the underutilization of behavioral techniques may be, in part, a marketing issue; those who are most familiar with the behavioral techniques and who use them most frequently might do a better job of writing, researching, teaching, and talking about these approaches. This criticism might be unfair, but it does seem that students, many young psychologists, and the public are probably not as aware of the potency of these behavioral techniques; in some way, word of these approaches does seem to need a louder voice.

One important concern about the behavioral techniques is that practitioners may get caught up in the techniques and lose sight of the fact that each client is unique and different and will not react the same way to a therapeutic program as others might and even if the program is presented in precisely the same manner. This has been a consistent criticism of the behavioral techniques and with some validity. Although we know that these behavioral techniques are applicable to a wide range of problems and to varied and different groups of clients, some practitioners tend to focus more on the symptoms and less on the people they are dealing with, and yet the best behavioral therapists will tell you how important it is to remember that each patient is different and you cannot practice this type of therapy by using exactly the same approach with each person. Although it is true that some of the behavioral techniques are "manualized," the individual differences between patients and clients must be respected and kept in mind. In manualized treatment, the therapist uses a specific set of techniques precisely as they are laid out in the manual, and each person gets the same program. However, even in manualized treatment programs, the initial part of the intervention deals with factors like goals, expectations, symptoms, and concerns, and the treatment proceeds with these concerns in mind. Thus, while this is a legitimate criticism and concern, patient uniqueness and individuality can and should be part of every treatment approach, including the behavioral ones.

One major problem with the use of behavioral approaches is that because they tend to be technique oriented, some feel that all they have to do is to learn the specific techniques and then they can use the behavioral therapy as an "expert." Therefore, people who are not adequately and fully trained may be trying to use these techniques. To be a behavioral therapist, one must have extensive training in a wide range of related areas, and one must fully and completely understand patients or clients and have a thorough understanding of the problems they are facing. In a related example, if one read through the book as to how to repair a hernia and watched the surgery a few times and passed a test on surgical hernia repair, would you really want that person to do the surgery on you? Hopefully, you would want a surgeon who was fully medically trained, was experienced in conducting the surgery, and could manage complications that might arise. The APA and all the state and provincial (in Canada) psychological associations have strict ethical standards governing the practice of psychology, and people are forbidden to practice in areas or with techniques on which they are not fully trained and capable. However, practitioners who are not psychologists might try to use these techniques but feel that they could provide this kind of treatment because they went to a workshop that taught them how to do it—this type of practice is complex and requires a high level of training and experience before trying the techniques on clients. It is important when receiving treatment to make sure that the person has the appropriate credentials to provide the care that they offer.

One of the other frequent complaints about behavioral techniques is that they treat only the superficial symptoms and do not get to the root cause of the problems. Particularly, the psychodynamic therapists have voiced concern that by treating only symptoms and ignoring the underlying problem the treatment will not and cannot be effective. They frequently use a medical analogy, saying that if a physician treats only the symptom (e.g., a headache) and ignores the underlying disease (e.g., a brain tumor), then the treatment will certainly not be effective and could even be fatal. As logical as this analogy sounds, it really is an inappropriate comparison in most cases.

If behavioral treatment of the symptoms was really dealing only with the superficial manifestations of a problem and ignoring the core issues, then one would expect that by treating the symptoms only, one of two things would occur. First, one might suppress the symptoms temporarily, but then they would emerge again; second, by suppressing one type of symptom, another symptom would arise in its place (this is called symptom substitution). However, numerous and good studies have been done to determine if these concerns were valid, and the results of these studies have been compelling and unequivocal. By suppressing symptoms with behavioral treatment, there is no evidence of either symptom return or symptom substitution. Consequently, the fear that behavioral treatments covered up only the real problems seems not to be a valid concern at all.

Perhaps a more interesting question is, "Why does symptom return or symptom substitution not occur following behavioral treatment?" Since behavioral symptoms are usually not like medical symptoms, there is no reason to expect that they will behave the same way. In fact, what seems to happen is that regardless of what originally causes abnormal or dysfunctional behavior to occur, the behavior patterns become deeply ingrained in the persons' behavior repertoire, and they develop reinforcers that keep the behavior active, and the original cause is now irrelevant because the dysfunctional behavior has developed a "life of its own." This is called "functional autonomy," and it refers to the fact that a behavior that has emerged in the history of an individual will continue only if there are processes that sustain it over time; when this happens, the original cause of the behavior is no longer relevant to the behavior in question. The evidence seems clear: using behavioral treatment to deal with abnormal behavior does not simply cover up or ignore underlying problems that will resurface or cause other problems later. In fact, what seems to happen is that when people begin to learn more functional ways of dealing with their problems, they also begin to think and feel differently, which makes them much happier and self-fulfilled. They also learn that regardless of the situations in their past that created some of their difficulties, they can still be healthy and happy and are not trapped by events in their past—they can rise above the problems that they faced earlier in their lives. Another way to think about this is, "We are products of our history, but we do not have to be victims of it."

CHAPTER NINE

Group and Other Forms of Therapy

Throughout the history of humankind, one of the factors that enabled us as a species to succeed and to evolve was our need (probably genetic) to band together with others for protection, care, provision of sustenance, breeding, support, and so on. Human history that is known to us has made it clear that people lived and worked in groups, and therefore, issues of group dynamics, conflict, communication, and control must have always been a part of the human condition. We know that people have always looked to groups as a way of dealing with issues and solving problems, so even if they did not have formal group therapy, it is likely that living, working, and dealing with one another in groups also gave people a reference group for support and guidance when that might be helpful.

Group Therapy

Formal group therapy is a much more recent advent into the treatment arsenal for dealing with various mental conditions. For example, in the early 1900s it was found that it was helpful for tuberculosis patients (who were largely removed and segregated from "normal" or healthy society) to get together in groups and talk about their problems. It was also noted that in World War II, soldiers who were suffering from "battle fatigue" seemed to benefit by talking with groups of others who were having similar problems. Several psychotherapists in the East Coast of the United States worked with therapy groups in the first half of the 20th century, and one who had considerable influence was Jacob Moreno, who made some inventive and important innovations in group therapy, including the development of a structured form of group therapy called "psychodrama." In the 1950s some therapists at the Tavistock Institute in London started experimenting with conducting psychotherapy in groups rather than individually, and this was probably the first actual use of group therapy psychotherapeutically outside of the United States.

Also, in the 1950s, a brilliant and far-thinking social psychologist named Kurt Lewin was studying groups in a training center in Bethel, ME, and after one of their group sessions where they were dealing with specific assigned problems, Lewin noticed that the members sat around discussing the group and its processes and dynamics. Lewin quickly realized that this was important and could form a basis for an entirely new way to study and to conduct groups. He called this new form of group "T-Groups" for "Training Groups," and he used this as a way of helping groups of workers deal with one another more productively and helping groups be more effective and rewarding. Even though these did not start off as therapy groups, the applicability to the treatment environment was obvious, and many began experimenting with this approach. One point that Lewin emphasized (and this is still important today) is looking at groups—any type of group—in terms of its content (what the group is dealing with) and its "process," *how* the group functions. Most effective groups will deal with these two issues equally, and this goes for therapy groups as well.

The interest in and use of group therapy started to increase during the 1960s and 1970s, and the idea of working in groups to gain support and to help deal with issues also fit well into the emerging culture of those decades and was consistent with some of the approaches that were being developed during this era. T-Groups started to be used in different contexts; some were called D-Groups (Development Groups), and another specific type of group was called the Encounter Group where people would get together and discuss their feelings about one another (sometimes in a brutally honest fashion) and then explore ways to give and receive feedback that would help each person grow, develop, and become much more self-aware and honest. Although many of these techniques could be powerful and therapeutic in the hands of a skilled and experienced therapist, considerable harm was done by practitioners who were not adequately trained and were not able to effectively lead group process in these types of challenging groups.

Although still used today, group therapy is not as widespread and frequently used as it was in the past. Some of the reasons for this decrease in use may be surprising, but all are relevant. Most important, research evaluating the effectiveness of group therapy was not as supportive as had been hoped. Clearly, group approaches to psychotherapy can be used effectively in many settings in the hands of competent and well-trained therapists, but they are not as widely applicable as had once been hoped. Further, while group approaches were consistent with the American culture in the 1960s and 1970s, in later decades people were not as group oriented, and many (probably most) patients preferred to be treated individually. Another real issue was how group therapy was paid for; if a therapist had a group of six to eight persons and these people all had insurance or paid out of their own pocket, that meant that for one therapy session the therapist would have to individually bill each person and/or file claims with each insurance or managed care company that was involved. Because of all the extra office work involved with many claims, many therapists either stopped doing groups completely, or they just charged a flat fee for each participant that they had to pay for themselves; many people did not want to pay for group treatment when they could get individual treatment paid for by their insurance or managed care company.

For these and other reasons, group therapy is not as widely used today as it was in the past, but the main use of therapy these days is for specific types of topics, for example, grief and bereavement groups, anxiety groups, depression groups, PTSD (post-traumatic stress disorder) groups, cancer patient groups, and heart disease groups. These specific topic groups have been found to be helpful for many people, and if possible, to find ways to make it cost effective for providers and for clients, these groups have an important role to fill in the treatment arsenal.

Family Therapy

Although professionals have worked with families in different contexts throughout history, the family therapy approach to mental health treatment probably had its origin in the 19th-century social work movements in the United States and the United Kingdom. This approach, coupled with the emergence in the early 20th century of the child guidance movement and marriage therapy, led to a wider use of family types of treatment. Because some of the early practitioners in family therapy came from the psychoanalytic heritage, most of the early family therapists utilized primarily psychodynamic types of therapies. Later, some people from the social psychiatry field started influencing the practice of family therapy, and later, psychologists from the learning theory and behavioral backgrounds started working with families using methods that derived largely from these theoretical approaches.

One of the major influences in family therapy came in the 1950s from anthropologists and others who were interested in studying family systems. Communication theorists also became interested, and the approach of family systems theory, which emphasized the importance and dynamics of communication, began to emerge. At about the same time, scientists and theorists from many disciplines began working in the area of general systems theory, and many of the ideas and approaches from this new area started to be helpful in conceptualizing and working with families.

Interestingly, some theorists and therapists began studying the role of family systems and communication on the development of schizophrenia, and this proved to be helpful in broadening the treatment of schizophrenia. Although it quickly became obvious that schizophrenia as a complex and serious disorder must be caused by a set of factors that included physical, medical, genetic, learning, and trauma, the finding that most people who developed schizophrenia were from families that had dysfunctional communication systems gave theorists and therapists a whole new range of treatments that could be helpful in guiding patients with schizophrenia toward a more complete and healthy life.

In the 1970s all the different approaches to family therapy began recognizing and accepting some of the other techniques and models, and it became common for many family therapists to be more *eclectic* and to use techniques from several different approaches. This has continued into more modern times, and although some therapists remain wed to a specific school of thought and set of methods, most family therapists are more broadly trained and will use a wider variety of techniques depending on the needs and preferences of the families with whom they work.

One of the main changes that have occurred in the recent past is the use of multimodal therapeutic approaches that integrate care from several perspectives with different providers. For example, if a family has experienced a significant loss, they might work with a family grief counselor but then might also work with a psychologist who will help them deal with behavioral and cognitive strategies for managing conflicts and other issues. Or, they could work with a psychologist, family therapist, or social worker on other types of family issues, problems, communication difficulties, and so on. One change that has become more prevalent in family therapy in recent years is to have family therapists who might be eclectic in their approaches but who specialize in dealing with one problem. Today a family looking for help and guidance is likely to find a broad array of options that might be helpful. While this could be a little overwhelming to try to decide what might be best for each family, this is when referral sources like family doctors, clergy, and professional associations become even more valuable.

Other and Adjunctive Forms of Therapy

Some forms of mental health treatment might be used instead of traditional forms of psychotherapy (or medication), and others (adjunctive) might be helpful when used in concert with psychotherapy. Some of these have proven to be helpful for specific types of problems, and some (e.g., teletherapy) might be used when traditional therapy is not available because of distance or other factors.

Teletherapy

With the advances in computer-facilitated communication, it has become possible to provide mental health and even medical treatment remotely when patients are not able to get to a provider in time or perhaps they are not able to get to treatment at all. One of the first forms of this remote type of treatment was suicide hotlines or crisis hotlines, where someone in crisis or thinking seriously about committing suicide can call a hotline and speak to a trained counselor who can offer suggestions and possibly get the person to a place where appropriate treatment can be provided. In this case, the person on the phone (or online) is not usually a trained and licensed mental health professional, but they are trained in crisis intervention and can be helpful in these types of situations.

One of the first true forms of teletherapy for mental health treatment was in the military, where people who needed treatment were in remote places where professional treatment was simply not available. The military developed some good programs that have been in place for many years and has proven to be extremely helpful in providing care for people who needed treatment but who were not near a treatment facility or outpatient office. This technology has also been proven helpful in treating other types of people in remote areas where conventional treatment is not available: many rural areas, Native American communities, or other people who work in areas far from available treatment. As helpful as some of these programs have been, there have also been some problems. Regulating this type of treatment is difficult because anyone with a phone and/or a computer can set themselves up as a therapist and start providing "care" without appropriate training or licensing, which can be dangerous. Some people feel that simply wanting to help, being a good listener, letting people get things "off their chests," and so on are what therapy is all about. Obviously, being an effective therapist involves considerable education, training, and experience, and the risks of seeing inadequately trained therapists are significant. Most licensed and experienced therapists have had people come to them for treatment who are "causalities" from so-called therapy conducted by untrained providers.

There are, however, some important advantages to teletherapy, and this has become a legitimate and important treatment option. As stated earlier, the main advantage is being able to provide appropriate treatment to people who would not be able to get treatment in any other way. This predominately refers to people who are geographically remote from treatment sites, but it can also refer to people who may be homebound because of disability or their psychological condition, and they may not have any access to treatment at home. Another advantage for teletherapy is that it is more flexible in terms of scheduling and transportation. When people do not have access to private transportation (e.g., a car) and may have to rely on public transportation, this may seriously limit their ability to make and keep appointments. Further, teletherapy saves time and money for transportation to and from therapy appointments. Similarly, for people with young children, it may be difficult, expensive, or impossible for them to take the time of appointments where they must find care for the children.

Depending on the therapist, sometimes teletherapy is less expensive than traditional psychotherapy, and this might make a difference for some clients as well. Unfortunately, for many people there is still a stigma associated with psychotherapy, and they are reluctant to go to an office for treatment for fear of seeing someone they know. Finally, some are more comfortable interacting remotely than face-to-face, and while this might seem to be a good reason for using teletherapy, that is valid only in the early stages of treatment; because the person has the symptom of being uncomfortable dealing with people directly, this must become a goal of treatment, and ultimately this individual would need to "graduate" to in-office appointments.

In terms of disadvantages of teletherapy, there are some significant ones to consider as well. For example, some providers claim that the therapeutic relationship is just as strong as in the traditional face-to-face, in-office type of relationship; however, research evidence and clinical experience would disagree with this. The richest form of communication is that which has the most interpersonal cues available, and that is always face-to-face, real-time communication. You will always pick up on more cues in this setting than in any other type of interaction—it is simply not the same on a phone or through a computer, and it never will be. For example, suppose one of a person's treatment goals is to stop smoking, and you are treating them remotely, and while (for fear of disappointing the therapist) they strongly assert that they have not smoked at all, but if they were present you would smell the tobacco on them. This is only one example, but no experienced therapist would say that they can get the same information through teletherapy as they can get in direct contact. However, teletherapy is important for people who cannot be treated in any other manner, but it is not a legitimate alternative to traditional psychotherapy.

Regulation of providers is another problem with teletherapy. State and national professional associations have been struggling with how to regulate teletherapy to ensure that public health and welfare are protected. Not only should you always seek treatment from an appropriate state-licensed professional, but you must also make sure that they are licensed in a way that covers the teletherapy; for example, in some states the teletherapist must be licensed in the state in which they practice but also in the state where the patient is living and receiving the teletherapy. Another problem may be with insurance or managed care coverage, which may not cover treatment provided remotely or from another state, and if this is the case, then the patient may be facing more out-of-pocket expenses for teletherapy. It is also important to know whether the therapist in question has been appropriately trained to provide teletherapy because it is not the same as traditional therapy, and there are different enough to necessitate additional training. Similarly, quite a few "quacks" and "shysters," who may have impressive credentials, advertise and provide online and other forms of teletherapy, but if you look closely, you will find that they do not have a legitimate state license to practice professionally; these "phonies" should be avoided for teletherapy or any other form of treatment. Finally, with respect to regulatory issues, any professional who treats patients or clients must comply with the Health Insurance Portability and Accountability Act (HIPAA), which protects patient privacy and health records. HIPAA issues become more problematic in teletherapy where patient privacy might be more easily compromised. This can be dealt with, but a person receiving treatment must be assured that their privacy and records are protected in a way that is consistent with HIPAA regulations.

Art Therapy

This approach has been used with children and adults alike and has been an adjunctive type of therapy for many decades. Art therapy is rarely the only or primary form of treatment, but it has been used along with many other different types of therapy and is often helpful. This approach can utilize the creative art-making process itself as a therapeutic endeavor, or the creative expression can be used as a medium for interpretation and/or interaction between the patient/artist and the therapist. The basic tenets of art therapy involve humanism, creativity, reconciling emotional conflicts, fostering self-awareness, and personal growth. As a mental health profession, art therapy uses the creative process of art making to improve and enhance the physical, mental, and emotional well-being of individuals of all ages. A fundamental assumption of art therapy is the belief that the creative process involved in artistic self-expression helps people to resolve conflicts and problems, develop interpersonal skills, manage behavior, reduce stress, increase self-esteem and self-awareness, and achieve insight.

Similarly, art therapists are often like marriage and family therapists and mental health counselors, and in the United States, art therapists may be licensed under several different titles depending on their background and training and on the specific type of license available in each state. Some art therapists are licensed as other types of mental health providers (e.g., psychologists, social workers, nurse practitioners) and then acquire additional post-master's or postdoctoral training in art therapy. Art therapy has been used with all age groups and for many different types of psychological disorders ranging from anxiety and depressive disorders, PTSD, personality disorders, and even psychotic disorders like schizophrenia. The artistic activities may have actual therapeutic value themselves, but they are also often a means of the therapist gaining more understanding and appreciation of the dynamics of the difficulties that the specific patient may be dealing with. When dealing with children, it is often difficult to conduct traditional psychotherapy because of their limitations cognitively, affectively, and linguistically. Particularly when dealing with issues of trauma and abuse with children, art therapy has proven to be helpful.

Another area where art therapy has been found to be beneficial is in working with patients with significant medical conditions like heart disease and cancer. Both as a distraction from worrying about an illness and as a means of expression and problem-solving, art therapy can be helpful for many patients. Some of the other areas where art therapy has made a positive contribution include disaster relief, bereavement (especially with children), homeless youth, incarceration, dyslexia, dementia, autism, and schizophrenia.

Historically, art therapy is relatively new, but there are records of artistic activities used for some patients in the 18th century as part of the revolution in the care of mentally ill patients that later became known as "moral treatment." As a profession, art therapy began in the mid-20th century arising independently in the English-speaking and European countries. The British artist Adrian Hill was the first to use the term "art therapy" in 1942 when he was recovering from tuberculosis in a sanitorium and found significant therapeutic benefit from painting and drawing while he was recovering. Shortly after Hill's reports of his use of art in his own treatment, others in Britain, the United States, and other parts of Europe started exploring and practicing with techniques that would later become the field of art therapy.

Dance Therapy

For thousands of years that we know about, and probably much before that, dance has been used for many purposes, including entertainment, spiritual and religious activities, social and cultural activities, celebration, or recognizing some of life's issues (e.g., birth, death, marriage, fertility, sickness). Using dance as a mechanism for helping people with physical or mental difficulties has certainly been a part of the history of dance. During 1840–1930 a new philosophy of dance emerged in Europe and in America and was based on the idea that dance and/or movement could have effects on various aspects of our lives—both physical and mental, and was not just an expressive art form but could be used for other purposes as well. The formal use of dance therapy began in the United States in about 1940, and Marian Chace, a former dancer, choreographer, and performer, had a dance studio and observed the positive psychological effect that dance had on her students, and this attracted the attention of local physicians who began sending their patients to Chace's classes.

Following this first wave, the second major impact of therapeutic dance came about in the 1970s and 1980s where people started thinking about and using dance as a form of psychotherapy, and this was the point at which dance therapy as a mechanism of therapy emerged. Dance and movement therapy (DMT) assumes that the mind and the body interact, and in both the conscious and subconscious mind, these two systems interact and affect one another. Through the unity of body, mind, and spirit, DMT provides a unifying sense of wholeness to the person. Dance is also physical exercise and a means of social interaction and performance that can be beneficial to many people.

Dance therapy is used in many settings and for many different types of people, patients, and psychological issues. Not only is it directly helpful to the patients who participate or even watch the dance, but it is also a basis to explore and understand some of the psychodynamic elements of a person's functioning and to provide some insight into some of the issues and concerns that they might present. The four stages of dance therapy are as follows:

- Preparation: This is the warm-up stage where a person establishes a safe space to function without obstacles or distractions, a supportive relationship with another person is established, and comfort for the participant is established.
- Incubation: The leader verbally prompts the participant to go into subconscious and open-ended imagery to create an internal environment in which the person feels comfortable in expressing themselves through movement.
- Illumination: The participant through DMT and interaction with the therapist uncovers and resolves unconscious motives, improves and increases self-awareness, and explores the positive and negative effects of this insight and illumination.
- Evaluation: Discuss the insights and results as well as the significance of the process and all that emerged from the experience; at some point, there is preparation for the end of the therapy.

To practice dance therapy, the therapist is expected to have a master's degree in DMT and to be certified by the American Dance Therapy Association (or a similar organization in other countries). If a person has a master's or doctoral degree in a related mental health field, they can become certified as a dance therapist if they take additional coursework and a supervised internship that is approved and certified by the National Association. While not usually a state-licensed specialty, dance therapy is practiced primarily by nationally certified practitioners, some of whom hold state licenses in other professions. Like any other mental health or health-related specialty, if one participates in dance therapy, it is important to ensure that the person has the appropriate training and certification.

Drama Therapy

Drama therapy relies on the use of theater techniques to facilitate personal growth and promote mental health. This mode of treatment is found in many settings, including hospitals, schools, mental health treatment centers, prisons, and businesses, and can be used with individuals, various types of groups, couples, and families; it may be used with adults of all ages, children, and adolescents.

Modern drama therapy (DT) began with the work of Moreno who developed psychodrama, which is an action-based form of psychoanalytic treatment. From this beginning, modern DT evolved, but it is a distinct modality within the creative arts therapies and is not just an evolved form of psychodrama. As a field, DT has grown to include many different forms of theatrical interventions, including role-play, theater games, group-dynamic games, puppetry, and other forms of improvisational techniques. DT has been beneficial to clients by helping them

- solve problems;
- achieve cathartic release;
- gain insight and improved self-awareness;
- understand the meaning and value of personally relevant images;
- explore and transcend dysfunctional personal behavior patterns and improve interpersonal interaction.

To become a registered drama therapist, a person must have a master's degree in DT or a master's degree in a relevant field and then take additional coursework and receive supervision to practice DT. This field has grown in use, and more people around the world are finding this to be a valuable adjunctive form of mental health treatment and a mechanism for people to grow and develop psychologically and emotionally.

Programs to Replace Psychotherapy

Over the years numerous programs have made claims that their program is superior to and more effective in changing psychological problems and "healing" people than traditional psychological and psychiatric therapies.

Typically, these programs have been pseudoscientific and/or pseudoreligious groups that place little value in traditional psychology or psychiatry or any of the legitimate mental health treatment programs. Of course, there is absolutely no reliable or valid information that would support their claims, but for anyone wishing to sign their lives over to these programs and pay increasingly larger sums of money to be "cured," these programs will make outrageous claims as to how they will improve your life and make you a happier and healthier person. Most of them are "pyramid schemes," which means you have to pay money to get involved and each progressive step in the organization costs more money, but you can make money out of it as well by recruiting new people for the organization and getting financial benefit from the money that these new people will pay. Most of these "programs" have been classified as cults, and many of them have had legal and financial difficulties because of their illegal, unethical, unprofessional, and frequently immoral and degrading practices.

The Church of Euthanasia is an example of a "church" that was founded in 1992 and is based on the idea that humans have overtaken the world to the disadvantage of all other species—not a totally unreasonable view. However, they recruit people with the idea of reducing the world's population through voluntary means; the founders claim that this is the only antihuman religion in the world. Their main saying is, "Save the Planet, Kill Yourself." The four main pillars of the "religion" are suicide, abortion, cannibalism (of the already dead), and sodomy (any sexual act not intended for procreation). As bizarre as this organization may sound, it has had many members over the years and is still functioning. From its standpoint, rather than suffer from psychological problems, if you are unhappy, then you should just commit suicide. Probably the only true advantage to this group is that it should not last longer than one or two generations.

Another so-called self-help group that has been in the news of late is Nxivm (neks'ium), which is based in Albany, New York, and offers personal and professional development seminars through its "executive success programs," which a report for the Ross Institute described as "expensive brainwashing." This has also been described as a "pyramid scheme," which has made considerable money for those at the top. Nxivm has also been accused of being a recruiting platform for a cult operating within it in which women were forced into sexual slavery and branded. Early in 2018 founder Keith Raniere and associate Allison Mack were arrested and indicted on federal charges including sex trafficking, and the organization suspended operations in May 2018 by court order.

Originally called the Unification Church (although it had a much longer official name), founded by Sun Myung Moon, many referred to the group and its members as "moonies." Now called the Family Federation for World Peace and Unification, this movement is spiritually based and includes several different organizations, including business, educational, and political. This organization has been declared a dangerous cult by many and has been criticized for its involvement with politics and business but in the name of religion. This group has been widely criticized by religious leaders and scholars, including many Jewish and Christian theologians and scholars. As is true of many of these types of organizations, membership involves personal, social, and financial commitment that has been accused of being abusive and manipulative.

The Family International is an organization that has gone through many different names, including Teens for Christ, The Children of God, The Family of Love, and The Family. Basically, it spreads the word of salvation, apocalypticism, spiritual "revolution and happiness," and distrust of the outside world. It exerted considerable control over its members personally and financially and encouraged members to show God's mercy by being sexually active and promiscuous. The founder, David Berg, went by several titles but ultimately called himself "king," and when he died, his wife married Berg's assistant whom Berg had picked for her next "consort"; she called herself "queen" and her new husband was the "king."

Probably the best known of these "cults" that try to replace the need for mental health care is Scientology, which has been in the news frequently for the abuse and manipulation it inflicts on its members in the name of the "church." Originally founded by a second-rate science fiction writer, Scientology decided that it was a religion and thus did not have to pay taxes like other businesses. It also publicly states that psychology, psychiatry, psychotropic medications, psychotherapy, and other forms of mental health treatment are simply phony ways for mental health practitioners to make money. It has developed a scientific-sounding but totally bogus way of measuring people's mental functioning, and then in exchange for a lot of money, it shows people how Scientology's bizarre ideas can turn them into high-level, fully functioning people.

This organization has been the subject of movies and TV shows, many featuring former members and leaders who finally realized how ridiculous this church was and how abusive it had been to its members. There have been attempts in the United States to deal with Scientology legally, and there have been some cases where it has been found to be engaged in criminal activities. However, in Germany, Scientology is classified as an "anticonstitutional sect," and in France, it has been determined to be a "dangerous cult." The main goal that Scientology has been successful in fulfilling is finding effective means for separating its gullible members from their money.

The one lie that these dangerous organizations share is that they all preach the notion that if you join them, pay the money, take their "classes," do exactly what they tell you, and so on, then there will not be any need for the "phony mental health treatment" provided by licensed psychologists, psychiatrists, social workers, and counselors. These ideas have kept many people from getting the kinds of help they needed, and none of these organizations has ever been found to actually provide the benefits that they claim—they may find a few "true believers" who will tout their value, but not one systematic and valid piece of research supports any of the claims made by any of these groups. While these represent just a few of the types of organizations that would pretend to replace the need for mental health services, many more do the same but are not as well known. What is also truly unfortunate about these organizations is that there are many church and religious organizations, and other types of consulting and training organizations that provide wonderful and needed services, but the few bad apples make people reluctant to get involved with anything that may appear to be the same type of group. It is also true that the valid and helpful organizations would never claim to be a substitute for traditional medical or mental health services.

How Are These Utilized Today?

Group and family types of treatment are widely used today, although perhaps somewhat less than in the past. Many of the group types of therapy that are popular involve specific-issue groups, for example, living with anxiety, coping with depression, and family of origin issues. Of course, there are also many nonprofessional self-help groups like 12-step programs (e.g., Alcoholics Anonymous, Narcotics Anonymous, Emotions Anonymous). There are many other medically related self-help groups like Reach to Recovery for breast cancer patients, groups of patients with heart disease, and many other groups for different types of diseases. There are also self-help groups like Alanon for family members of a person with alcohol abuse problems and family members for Alzheimer's and dementia patients and even groups like the National Alliance on Mental Illness for family members of mentally ill patients. Self-help groups can be enormously beneficial for people dealing with specific medical and psychological problems and for their family members as well. However, these groups are not actually therapy groups because they are not led by licensed professionals, and even if volunteer professionals help the group, the goal is not treatment but support and information sharing.

Group therapy is still used, but as mentioned earlier, it may not be as widely used as it used to be; there appear to be several reasons for this. First, as widely used as group therapy was in the 1960s and 1970s, the research that was conducted to evaluate the effectiveness of group therapy was not as supportive and encouraging as was anticipated. Since some new individual types of therapeutic approaches were effective and empirically validated, many practitioners began using primarily individual methods of treatment. At the same time, insurance companies started to cover psychological and psychiatric services, and the whole idea of billing for services where each person had to be billed separately and with different companies became difficult for providers to find a way to deliver group therapy in a cost-effective manner. Today, group therapy is not usually the first or main type of treatment used but may be part of a treatment package where the patient may have several different types of treatment that are part of their program. As new and different models for delivering health care begin to emerge and are evaluated, it is likely that we may find an increasing demand for group types of treatment, and we will see it used more frequently. Family and couples therapy is still a widely used form of treatment and can be an effective way of dealing with family and relationship issues.

The alternative forms of treatment have varying degrees of usage, but telehealth and teletherapy are being more frequently and widely used; this has brought appropriate treatment to many who would not otherwise have access to treatment. Some of the adjunctive forms of treatment like DT, art therapy, and DMT have certainly proven their value but are not widely used outside of major urban areas or around universities and medical schools where these types of programs can be integrated into existing programs and treatment centers. One of the main limitations in the use of many of these types of adjunctive treatments is the lack of insurance coverage for the treatments, and this is certainly a concern for many patients who might be appropriate candidates for these forms of treatment.

In terms of the so-called programs that replace psychotherapy, still many are flourishing and managing to cost their "clients" huge sums of money and keeping them from receiving appropriate care. Fortunately, the legal and government agencies around the world are watching and collecting evidence on these terribly harmful programs, and hopefully we will see a decrease in the exploiting and harmful programs; the healthy and honest programs will continue and flourish—although still not a replacement for psychotherapy.

Concerns and Critiques

Carl Rogers once said in the later years of his life that one of his biggest disappointments was that research had not supported the effectiveness of group therapy to the extent that he had hoped. Of course, he did not mean or imply that group therapy was not useful but that it was not as generally effective as had been expected. However, research and clinical evidence do demonstrate that group types of treatment (including couples and family therapy) are beneficial for certain types of problems and still have an important place in the treatment armamentarium. Probably the biggest problems with the group types of therapy, as well as the adjunctive forms of treatment, involve using them for the wrong types of problems and using them with providers who are not appropriately trained. Many providers do not have adequate training or education, who take fees for providing services, including group therapy, to unsuspecting clients who think they are receiving credible care. These providers get away with this by claiming education and training that turns out to be minimal or nonexistent, selecting a name for their profession that sounds legitimate (e.g., Professional Group Dynamics Consultant), and even putting phony diplomas and certificates on their walls. However, if they are not state licensed in a mental health specialty, you should avoid them.

Other providers (even some who might be appropriately licensed) will put people in groups without adequately screening them, and it might turn out that group treatment is not what they need, which might do more harm than good. Thus, two of the main problems in group types of treatments and the adjunctive forms of treatment include treatment being provided by inadequately trained therapists and trying to treat people in groups who might do better with other forms of treatment.

From what has already been discussed, it is probably clear that the "cult-like" programs that pretend to replace the need for psychotherapy are exploitive, harmful, frequently illegal, and unprofessional and should not be allowed to exist. The good and legitimate programs that do coexist with traditional medical and mental health care can and should flourish, but the illegal and unethical ones should not be allowed to provide services.

CHAPTER TEN

Medical and Other Physical Approaches

Although medication, surgery, and other physical forms of treatment are not psychotherapies, understanding psychotherapy means that we need to fully appreciate some of the other types of treatments available to treat psychological problems. Throughout history we find evidence that people have considered mental illness to be caused by physical factors like infections, genetic and/or congenital problems, toxins, and injuries. Further, even if people thought that mental illness was caused by other factors like demons and witchcraft, the usual types of treatments that were used were physical in nature.

While there have probably always been wise men or women, shamans, healers, priests, or other clergy who were available to people to talk with and support them during times of tribulation, and much of what they probably did would have been something like psychotherapy today, it must have been rudimentary and probably not effective. However, most of the historical references to treatment approaches for mentally ill persons describe physical types of treatment. In different parts of the world, archeologists have uncovered skulls that have holes cut into them, and it is assumed that cutting or boring holes in the skull was intended as treatment for some type of problem that appeared to originate in the brain. Although it is likely that many of these patients did not survive the surgery, some skulls have been found that show evidence that the holes cut into the skull actually healed and that the person lived for many years following the "surgery." This procedure is calling "trephination" and has been around since Neolithic times.

Many people have stated that these holes were bored or cut into the skull to treat mental illness, and it is assumed that they thought that the cause of the problem was demons or spirits in the brain that would be let out if a hole was bored. While this is a compelling suggestion, the reality is that we have no actual written or pictorial accounts that would prove that this is why these holes were made. It is likely that trephination was used to treat a variety of problems such as severe headaches, brain diseases, swelling in the brain from injury, and mental problems as well. We know that this early form of brain surgery did occur and that some people survived the procedure, but all the reasons why this was used are still based on speculation.

History and Development

Throughout written history, there is evidence of the use of herbs, potions, and so on to treat a wide variety of medical and mental problems. Much of the field of medicine today is based on research and practice dating back for millennia. Of course, we have more information, better science, centuries of clinical practice, and much better understanding of the world around us than any of our ancestors did. There have been many examples of abuse or misunderstandings regarding the use of herbs and potions to treat the ill; in fact, many people who helped people by providing herbs or potions to treat their ailments were accused of witchcraft or sorcery and were punished or killed for their practices of the "dark arts."

Fortunately, as people began to learn more and the field of medicine began to emerge, the use of various natural substances for the treatment of illness, pain, or disease became much more widely practiced and accepted. We have good examples of the use of medicine to treat or cure people dating back to ancient Egypt, Persia, China, Arabia, Greece, and Rome. Even in more primitive cultures, there might be a shaman, witch doctor, medicine man (or woman), or others in the group who served to help, treat, and hopefully cure many people who were afflicted with various physical and mental problems. However, it is also true that most of the "medicines" and procedures that were used historically were probably worthless or dangerous, but it is also true that some of them might have actually worked; the number of medications used today that are derived from or chemically based on naturally occurring substances gives credence to this old and accepted way of treating medical and mental problems.

Although the use of medications was probably the most frequent reasonable approach to treating mental conditions, there were many other attempts to provide relief and/or cures for mental illness. Earlier, trephination (cutting a hole in the skull) was mentioned as a possible treatment for mental illness, but many centuries later when surgery was becoming more sophisticated, other attempts were made to find surgical solutions to psychological problems, and *lobotomies* were tried and experimented with for several decades in the 20th century. The theory was that if the connections between the parts of the brain that were responsible for rational thought were separated from those parts that involved emotion and basic drives and urges, then the person would act more rational. Several different types of lobotomies were used, but none of them resulted in outcomes that would be considered beneficial enough to warrant the risk of brain surgery. Usually patients would become calmer but still suffered from surgically induced brain damage, and most were never able to function normally again. Finally, this surgical procedure was discontinued and was not permitted at all. Fortunately, today a few surgical techniques have proven to be effective in helping some conditions that have not responded to any other treatments, and while they are experimental and rarely used, they appear to be promising for some patients; these will be discussed in depth later in this chapter.

Other, so-called medical treatments from the past were also tried on patients with mental health conditions, and they proved to be as ineffective with mental illness as with physical illness. Bloodletting is a good example of such a treatment; surgically opening a vein and putting leaches on patients were techniques intended to remove either "excess blood" or toxins in the blood that were causing problems. These approaches usually resulted in anemia (caused by low levels of red blood cells) or infections or both. Needless to say, "bleeding" did not last long as a fundamental treatment for mental illness. This approach probably came from the belief of the early Greek and Roman philosophers and physicians that the world was made up of four basic elements: earth, water, fire, and air. Likewise, the body comprises four basic elements: blood, phlegm, yellow bile, and black bile. They believed that an excess of any of these elements would result in disease, and thus too much blood would cause various conditions for which the treatment would be to remove some of the blood.

Purging was another form of "medical" treatment that was used to treat diseases but also used to treat mental illness. This practice usually involved taking substances that caused vomiting, diarrhea, or both. Once again, the intent was to remove toxins from the body that were causing the problem. Of course, there never has been a mental condition where physical purging was an effective treatment. However, to the credit of the people who were trying to help the patients, they were using treatments for mental illness that were typically used for medical conditions. This was important because it indicated that some people were trying to get the message across that mental illness was a condition that could be treated, and since many thought that mental illness was based on demonic possession or someone being in league with the forces of evil (witches and warlocks), elevating mental illness from being evil to being sick was a true improvement. This approach also had some roots in the Greek/Roman belief of the basic four bodily fluids, and when physical or mental illness occurred, it must be because there was an imbalance in these fluids. Of course, they were wrong, but it was a logical step in the direction of making connections between processes in the body and symptoms that a person might experience either physically or mentally.

At different times in history, people in many cultures looked at mental illness as based on religious, spiritual, or moral issues, and they were treated sometimes cruelly since it seemed to some that the mental illness was either punishment for wrongdoing or a condition based on the intervention of the gods or even possession by a demon. Thus, it seemed logical that if people had done wrong, were being punished by the gods, were in league with the devil, or were possessed by evil spirits, then the "patient" should be vigorously punished as a result of their evil deeds or to make the body such an inhospitable place that the demons or evil spirits would leave. Thus, during the Middle Ages treatment of the mentally ill involved many physical "treatments" that were truly torture and many times even led to death. Thus, when the medical model of mental illness started to make headway, this put mental illness in a totally different light and started to lead to more humane treatments even if most of them were not helpful. Restraint, warm (sometimes hot or cold) baths, wrapping patients in sheets to immobilize them, and other physical treatments that were not effective at all were tried and later abandoned.

In the 19th century, most of the treatment for mental illness was purely custodial, and patients were locked up in hospitals that were little better than prisons. Fortunately, some people began to believe that patients would do better if they were treated more humanely and with consideration and support. A French physician, Phillippe Pinel, and some of his colleagues started using what they called "moral" treatment for patients, which meant that although in a hospital, they were treated kindly, were given healthy food, had opportunities for recreational and educational activities, engaged in social activities, and were treated medically when appropriate. In the United States, Benjamin Rush, a physician who had been surgeon general of the U.S. Army during and after the Revolutionary War, also started to make changes in how the mentally ill were treated.

Two other Americans who were instrumental in changing how mental patients were treated were Dorthea Dix, who went around the country advocating for the need to provide reasonable and therapeutic hospitals for the treatment of patients with mental illness, and Clifford Beers, a former patient who was treated, recovered from his mental condition, and toured the country talking about his treatment and how badly patients were treated in most hospitals and encouraging communities to institute better and more meaningful treatment opportunities for mental patients.

As more and better treatments started emerging from medicine and from psychotherapy, it became increasingly clear that most patients did not need or require in-hospital treatment, and most patients were treated in offices and clinics outside of hospitals, which is consistent with what is done today. Of course, we still have mental hospitals, but most in-hospital stays are short, and most treatment is done on an outpatient basis.

Basic Approaches and Their Contributions

Medical Approaches

Psychopharmacology

Psychopharmacology is the area of science and practice that involves the use of medications to treat mental disorders. Many people in most cultures have specialized in the use of plants, herbs, animal products, and so on to develop potions, elixirs, draughts, and many other names for the substances they developed to help treat disease and injury, and these substances were often used to treat psychological and emotional problems as well. This has been a controversial area throughout history, and many practitioners who used these substances were accused of practicing the dark arts and were thought to be dabbling in areas not meant for man or woman to interfere with. However, people's illness, pain, fear, depression, and so on finally resulted in the acceptance of using substances prescribed by someone who knew what they were doing for the treatment of conditions that were impairing peoples' health and well-being.

Today, medications are the most frequently used form of treatment for psychological and emotional conditions. Interestingly, they are not the most frequently used treatment because they are the most effective but more because medications are easily accessible and can be prescribed by anyone who is properly licensed. It would be nice if most people taking medications were followed by a psychiatrist or prescribing psychologist who were responsible for their care. However, there are frequently shortages of doctoral-level mental health providers who are available to prescribe medications for patients. Thus, well over 80% of psychotropic drugs are prescribed by nonpsychiatrists. Usually, a person's psychiatric medications are prescribed by their primary care physician (PCP), pediatrician, OB/GYN, or even subdoctoral-level providers like nurse practitioners and physician's assistants. It is also important to note that if it were not for these nonpsychiatric physicians and subdoctoral-level providers, many people who truly need psychotropic medication would not get anything at all. However, it does point out that we are woefully underserved by the lack of adequately trained mental health providers at the doctoral level, and this is true of psychiatrists and psychologists as well.

When prescribing psychotropic drugs, several different categories of medications are frequently used. These are antidepressants, antianxiety drugs, stimulants, hypnotics, mood stabilizers, and antipsychotic medications. It is not uncommon for people to be on more than one psychotropic medication depending on the complexity of their case, which is referred to as "polypharmacy." It is also common practice to use certain medications for problems other than those for which the drug was originally intended and may be used even in the absence of approval from the Food and Drug Administration (FDA) for the use of a drug for another purpose. However, this is not illegal or unprofessional and just points out that practice may at times move ahead faster than the science, and people may discover useful applications for a drug before research has demonstrated its effectiveness for this new purpose. The use of drugs for things other than what they were intended for is called an "off-label use." When a prescriber uses or recommends a drug "off-label," one should ask, On what basis is this drug being used? Usually the prescriber will say something like, "I have found that many of my patients who are being treated for X Condition do very well on this drug" or "Some new research just came out demonstrating the effectiveness of this medication, but the FDA just has not had time to study it fully." If the drug is safe and is legal to use for something and the licensed provider knows what he or she is doing, using drugs off-label is not a problem.

Antidepressant Medications

Whether it has been called depression, melancholia, the blues, dysphoria, or any other name, this disorder has been around at least as long as recorded history, including references in the ancient Greeks and Romans, the Bible, and Shakespeare. All people have experienced some form of negative mood, but not all people have had true depression. Although this is the most common of all mental health disorders, not everyone experiences it fully. In a year's time, about 12% of American women and 7% of American men experience depression. Over a full lifetime, 21.3% of women and 12.7% of men experience depression, and currently, about 19 million Americans are suffering from this condition. Further, this disorder is one of the most common causes of lost work time and disability, and therefore, it is also one of the most "expensive" health-related problems to deal with. For these reasons, it is obvious why attempts have been made over the years to find suitable treatment for depression, and although medication alone is not considered to be adequate treatment for depression, some good antidepressant medications can be helpful in treating this challenging condition.

In attempts to treat this disorder, various medication strategies have been tried for many years, but only in recent decades have reasonable and safe drugs been developed for the treatment of depression. Since it is not uncommon for people to have depression and anxiety at the same time, it was common for providers to give tranquilizers to people who were depressed to hopefully help them feel better. However, while these drugs might help with anxiety, they really did not help the depression, and they might even make patients more depressed. Certainly, since many people dealing with depression have difficulty making themselves become more active and involved, a central nervous system depressant like a tranquilizer would not likely make someone more active, and these were not used often as antidepressants. Another type of drug that seemed like it might help was the stimulants (e.g., amphetamines), because it was hoped that they might make depressed people more energetic and become more active. Unfortunately, while these drugs might give people more energy, they did not make them less depressed, and therefore, patients might develop an "agitated depression," which might increase their suicidal risk.

During the 1950s a new class of antidepressants emerged, and these drugs seemed to work well in helping reduce depressive symptoms. They appeared to work by preventing some of the neurotransmitter substances (a drug that sends messages between neurons in the brain) from being reabsorbed too quickly and remaining more active in the brain, and they were called the monoamine oxidase inhibitors (MAOI) and included medications such as the following:

- Nardil (phenelzine)
- Parnate (tranylcypromine)
- Marplan (isocarboxazid)
- Emsam (selegiline)

While these drugs appeared to be helpful with depression, they were difficult to use because they had some serious and sometimes fatal side effects. These drugs interacted badly with some foods and medications, and their use required dietary restrictions that were problematic for many people. Although these drugs are used more frequently in Europe, they are not used much in the United States unless a person has simply not responded to or could not tolerate any other form of antidepressant drug.

Another class of antidepressants, the tricyclics were first identified in the 1950s, and they also proved to be effective in treating depression and did not have as many serious side effects as the MAOIs did. However, they did tend to have some side effects, including constipation, dry mouth, blurry vision, weight gain, and heart arrhythmias that were problematic for some patients, but they were a distinct improvement nonetheless. This class included such drugs as the following:

- Elavil (amitriptyline)
- Norpramin (desipramine)
- Asendin (amoxapine)

- Anafranil (clomipramine)
- Pamelor (nortriptyline)
- Tofranil (imipramine)
- Vivactil (protriptyline)
- Surmontil (trimipramine)
- Sinequan (doxepin)
- Ludiomil (maprotiline)

Like MAOIs the tricyclics worked by keeping some of the brain nerve cells from reabsorbing two of the neurotransmitter substances, serotonin and norepinephrine, and appear to block or partially block acetylcholine and histamine. While they had a better side effect profile than the MAOIs, these drugs were also difficult for some patients to tolerate, and today they are used more frequently to treat insomnia, pain, migraine headaches, and obsessive-compulsive disorder than they are to be used specifically as antidepressants.

Probably the most significant breakthrough in the medical treatment of depression came with the discovery of a class of drugs called selective serotonin reuptake inhibitors (SSRI), and unlike the earlier antidepressants, these drugs work only on the serotonin system in the brain. Serotonin is a neurotransmitter, and when people are depressed, their serotonin levels are too low, and this class of drugs keeps more of the serotonin in the system longer, which helps people feel more "normal" and have fewer depressive symptoms. While these drugs do not "cure" depression, they have been helpful in reducing the symptom burden of depression so that people who are depressed can function more effectively in their lives. Like the other antidepressants, the SSRIs are not addictive, but they have a much better side effect profile than the MAOIs and the tricyclics. Since they are safer and easier to use and are effective, the SSRIs have become one of the most widely prescribed types of drugs in the United States. Drugs in this category include the following:

- Prozac (fluoxetine)
- Paxil (paroxetine)
- Zoloft (sertraline)
- Celexa (citalopram)
- Luvox (fluvoxamine)
- Lexapro (escitalopram)
- Viibryd (vilazodone)
- Trintellix (vortioxetine)

While these drugs are safe and usually effective, they are not free of side effects, and some people have difficulty tolerating them. However, if a person has a problem with one of these drugs, it is likely that they will not have the same problem with one of the others, so it is possible to find one of the drugs in this class that a person can tolerate. Since the SSRIs are safe and helpful, they are prescribed frequently and are widely used by many doctors. Although the SSRIs are antidepressants, they are also effective in treating anxiety and are used frequently with people who have problems with pain, attentional problems, symptoms of menopause and premenstrual syndrome in women, and other issues as well.

Another class of drugs that are like the SSRIs are the selective serotonin and norepinephrine reuptake inhibitors, and they work on both the serotonin and norepinephrine systems and work to keep more of both neurotransmitters in the system. While they work well with depression and anxiety like the SSRIs, they are also good for helping people who are depressed who have problems with fatigue and low energy levels. In general, these drugs also have a good side effect profile and are not addictive; they are, however, sometimes a little more difficult to stop taking and must be tapered down gradually. Usually it is best to taper off most antidepressants when discontinuing them, and this should always be done with the doctor's knowledge and recommendation. These drugs are also used for conditions like fibromyalgia and chronic fatigue syndrome. Drugs in this category include the following:

- Effexor (venlafaxine)
- Pristiq (desvenlafaxine)
- Cymbalta (duloxetine)
- Fetzima (levomilnacipran)

A few other antidepressant drugs are chemically different than any of the other classes and may work on some of the other neurotransmitters in addition to or instead of serotonin and norepinephrine, and they are somewhat different from one another as well, so they are often referred to as "atypical antidepressants." None of them are addictive, and they usually have mild side effects, but again some people have difficulty tolerating them. Drugs in this category include the following:

- Wellbutrin (bupropion)
- Remeron (mirtazapine)
- Desyrel (trazodone)
- Trintellix (vortioxetine)
- Serzone (nefazodone)

These drugs are used primarily for depression although each is a little different and may be used for other things as well. For example, Wellbutrin, which works on the dopamine neurotransmitter system, is also used for smoking control and attention deficit hyperactivity disorder (ADHD) in adolescents and adults and may lead to slight weight loss. Trazodone is an antidepressant, but one of its side effects is that it makes people drowsy, and consequently it is frequently used as a sleep aid. Since it is not addictive and safe to use, it is more widely prescribed than sleeping pills for many people. In general, these drugs are safe, but they do have side effects, and not everyone will respond well to them or can tolerate them.

There is also another newer antidepressant, Edronax (reboxetine), is a norepinephrine reuptake inhibitor and works well with major depression. It is also used off-label to treat panic disorder and ADHD.

Antianxiety Medications

Several different medication strategies can be used to treat anxiety disorders, and each of them works slightly differently, and sometimes they might be used in combination depending on which symptoms are the focus of treatment. One similarity in the medical treatment of anxiety and depressive disorders is that medication alone is rarely adequate treatment for either of these types of disorders. Although psychotherapy alone may be used to treat either of these types of disorders, the combination of medication and psychotherapy is frequently used, primarily because medication will often have a quicker effect on reducing some of the symptoms, but as attractive as this might seem, the trade-off is that when one tries to come off of the medication without psychotherapy, the symptoms usually reappear. The types of anxiety treatment strategies include the following:

Anxiolytic medications: These drugs work directly on anxiety and are intended to reduce anxiety and make the patient feel more comfortable. Often, the azapirones and the benzodiazepines are called "tranquilizers" because they are supposed to calm people down. Some of the classes of anxiolytics are as follows:

- Azapirones: for example, BuSpar (buspirone).
- Benzodiazepines: for example, Ativan (lorazepam), Dalmane (flurazepam), Klonopin (clonazepam), Halcion (triazolam), Librium (chlordiazepoxide), Restoril (temazepam), Serax (oxazepam), Valium (diazepam), Xanax (alprazolam).
- Antihistamines: Although often used for allergies or insomnia, they are sedative and may also be used to treat anxiety, for example, Atarax or Vistaril (hydroxyzine).

Antidepressant medications: Interestingly, even though these drugs do not act directly on anxiety, some do have a positive effect and usually will reduce some of the symptoms of anxiety and make them easier to deal with. For example, these drugs often reduce the frequency and intensity of panic attacks. They often work well in combination with psychotherapy.

Anticonvulsants: These are rarely used to treat anxiety alone but may be used as augmentation therapy, meaning they may improve the effectiveness of another medication by boosting its impact in treating anxiety, for example, Gabitril (tiagabine), Neurontin (gabapentin), Depakote (valproate), Lamictal (lamotrigine), Topamax (topiramate).

Noradrenergic agents: These are usually used to treat high blood pressure but may be helpful in specific types of anxiety symptoms.

- Beta blockers: for example, Inderal (propranolol), Tenormin (atenolol)
- Alpha blockers: for example, Minipress (prazosin)
- Alpha agonist: for example, Catapres (clonidine), Tenex (guanfacine)

Atypical antipsychotics: These drugs are also rarely used to treat anxiety disorders alone but may be used in combination with other antianxiety drugs to improve the therapeutic impact of the medication, for example, Abilify (aripiprazole), Geodon (ziprasidone), Risperdal (risperidone), Seroquel (quetiapine), Zyprexa (olanzapine).

Mood Stabilizers

This class of drugs is frequently used in the treatment of bipolar disorder but may also be used to treat other conditions where the person's mood is variable and may swing from high to low frequently. There are certain personality disorders as well as anxiety and depressive disorders where mood instability is a problematic symptom, but the person does not meet the criteria for the diagnosis of bipolar disorder. Lithium salts were the first mood stabilizer that was identified, and this class of drugs is still used today; lithium carbonate is typically used and is found in several different drugs like Eskalith, Carbolith, and Lithobid.

In addition, anticonvulsant medications like Tegretol (carbamazepine), Trileptal (oxcarbazepine), Depakote or Depakine (valproic acid and salts), Lamictal (lamotrigine), Neurontin (gabapentin), Lyrica (Pregabalin), and Topamax (topiramate) have been effective in the treatment of mood instability. In addition, some of the second-generation antipsychotics like Zyprexa (olanzapine) might also be used as mood stabilizers.

Antipsychotic Medications

This group of medications is used to treat psychotic disorders that are serious mental disorders like schizophrenia. These are powerful drugs, and although not addictive, they have other qualities that can be problematic.

However, these drugs are effectively used to treat psychotic disorders (for which they are usually the main form of treatment) and may also be used for bipolar disorder, insomnia, nausea, severe anxiety, and other conditions where agitation might be an issue. In fact, several of these drugs are used with major depression and seem to be helpful when used to supplement antidepressant medications.

Some of the older antipsychotic medications (often called first-generation antipsychotics) were a breakthrough in the treatment of schizophrenia and led to severely ill patients being able to be treated in less restrictive environments, including outpatient treatment. Prior to these drugs being available, most psychotic individuals were "warehoused" in hospitals where they were kept in primarily custodial care because they could not function outside of the hospital well if at all. These drugs, while frequently effective, also have some significant side effects and must be monitored closely. Some of the first-generation antipsychotics include the following:

- Largactil, Thorazine (chlorpromazine)
- Haldol (haloperidol)
- Orap (pimozide)
- Stelazine (trifluoperazine)
- Dolmatil (sulpiride)

More recently, some newer antipsychotic medications have been introduced, and while they are not without side effects, they tend to be safer and easier to use than the older drugs; this group is often called "second-generation" antipsychotics. Some of the drugs in this category include the following:

- Solian (amisulpride)
- Abilify (aripiprazole)
- Clozaril (clozapine)
- Zyprexa (olanzapine)
- Seroquel (quetiapine)
- Risperdal (risperidone)

Stimulants

This class of drugs was used to treat depression because when a person is depressed, they are often fatigued or sluggish, and it was thought that an energizing drug might help. However, all this seemed to do was create a condition known as "agitated depression" and did not really help at all. However, stimulant drugs are primarily used to treat attention deficit disorder and attention deficit disorder with hyperactivity. They are also used for some people who have medical conditions that make them sluggish or even neurological conditions like narcolepsy when people fall asleep unexpectedly at any time during the day. This category includes methylphenidate (Ritalin, Concerta), dexmethylphenidate (Focalin), mixed amphetamine salts (Adderall), dextroamphetamine (Dexedrine), lisdexamfetamine (Vyvanse), and methamphetamine (Desoxyn).

Hypnotics

This class of drugs is used to treat insomnia, and sleep problems are common in people who suffer from psychological difficulties. Two classes of hypnotics, barbiturates and opiates, are sedating and relaxing and can make people sleepy. However, they are rarely used to treat insomnia in recent years because they are both addictive and dangerous when overdosed. Since many effective sleep aids are much safer to use, these two classes of drugs are rarely used.

One class of drugs, which is also used to treat anxiety, is benzodiazepine medications that are addictive, but are generally easier and safer to use than barbiturates and opiates, but are not used for a long period of time because of their addictive quality. Some of the benzodiazepines that are used for insomnia include Prosom (estazolam), Dalmane (flurazepam), Doral (quazepam), Restoril (temazepam), Halcion (triazolam), and Valium (diazepam).

Some non-benzodiazepine hypnotics that are often used as sleeping pills are zolpidem (Ambien, Ambien CR, Intermezzo), zaleplon (Sonata), ramelteon (Rozerem), chloral hydrate (Noctec), dexmedetomidine hydrochloride, and eszopiclone (Lunesta). Although these drugs can often be effective sleep aids, they can be abused, and some may have some problems with addiction. Therefore, they are usually not used for longer-term sleep needs.

Today, it is more common for prescribers to use various antidepressants for difficulties people might have with sleep. These drugs usually have a better side effect profile and are not habit forming. The most commonly used antidepressant for insomnia is trazodone, which is easily tolerated by most people and might even augment the effectiveness of other antidepressants that the person might be taking. Some of the tricyclics like amitriptyline can also be used as sleep aids and are tolerated well by most people. Mirtazapine is also used for insomnia by some.

Many over-the-counter sleep aids are used by many people, and most of these are antihistamine types of drugs like diphenhydramine (Benadryl) that may be used for allergies but are also sedating and nonaddicting. A naturally occurring hormone in the body is melatonin, and this can be taken safely by people who have sleep difficulties. In addition, other substances are sold in drugstores and natural food types of stores, and although there is not much evidence supporting their effectiveness, some people find them helpful. An important comment, however, is that even though something might be bought over the counter, might not require a prescription, and is "naturally occurring," that does not mean that these substances are without risk. Some can have negative effects on their own, and others can interact badly with other medications that a person might be taking. Never add any type of substance to your medication regime without informing your PCP and other providers you may be working with.

Other Physical and Medical Forms of Treatment

Electroconvulsive Shock Therapy (ECT)

Treatment of several different mental health conditions has relied on the use of electricity or chemicals to induce seizures, and this was done to relieve some of the symptoms of various problems—especially depression. Although there are some "horror stories" about some of the awful things that shock therapy has done in the past, it is much more effectively and safely used today. Today people are anesthetized prior to shock therapy, and they are not aware of the shock or its effects; there are no overtly obvious seizures, no broken bones, and so on. The most common side effect is memory loss following the ECT, which usually involves only short time spans before, during, and following the treatment, and this usually improves in a few days or so. In addition to anesthesia and drugs to relax the patient, the equipment and procedures are far better than they used to be; smaller doses of electricity and more effective and safer methods are also true of this procedure today. ECT has proven to be effective for treating serious depression, and while it is not usually the first-line treatment, it is often used when a patient has not responded to any other form of treatment and may not tolerate the antidepressant medications. This somewhat "scary" type of treatment is said by some to be safer for the elderly and for pregnant mothers than medication.

Psychosurgery

In the past, psychosurgery was used as a treatment for several types of mental illness, including depression bipolar disorder and schizophrenia. The typical technique was a lobotomy where parts of the brain were separated by surgically severing some of the connections between the frontal lobes and some of the other parts of the brain. This approach was always controversial and produced more serious complications than it did cures. These approaches are not used any longer, although a few forms of psychosurgery have been used experimentally for disorders like severe obsessive-compulsive disorder that has not responded to any other types of treatment. However, psychosurgery is still controversial, has potentially serious (even deadly) complications, and has not proven to be effective enough to warrant using them frequently. However, with the technical advances in surgery and better and safer forms of anesthesia, the hopes for new and effective forms of psychosurgery are still there and may yet be realized.

Light Therapy

As mentioned earlier, people who live further away from the equator (either north or south) are more prone to seasonal affective disorder (SAD), and many people find that even if they do not have SAD, winters (in the north and summers in the Southern Hemisphere) are difficult times for many people. Light boxes have been used to help people with seasonal components to their mood disorders, and although the results are mixed at best, there is some evidence that light therapy can be helpful for mild to moderate depression. Light boxes can be purchased and usually cost several hundred dollars. However, keeping your home or office bright during the day (or evening) and going outside for a walk or just to sit in the sun for a while are even more effective than light boxes. It is not uncommon for people in the extreme latitudes to have low levels of vitamin D, and if this is the case, their PCP could give them vitamin D supplements, and this is sometimes effective in improving mood.

Exercise

There is a substantial amount of research and clinical evidence that for people with mood disorders, anxiety disorders, and other mental health problems, exercise is therapeutic. Most professionals recommend three to four times per week for at least 30 minutes (and more is better). Aerobic exercise is the most important, but using resistance training like weights is fine and can also be helpful for bone and muscle health, but aerobic activities are best for moods and emotions. For those who are infirm or have joint problems, exercises like swimming and biking might be best, but elliptical trainers are also good. Walking is one of the best exercises, and running, jogging, and treadmill are good if you can tolerate them. Several considerations are important when deciding to start exercising:

1. First, check with your doctor and make sure you follow their directions.
2. Start very simply and for short periods of time and build up gradually.
3. Find activities that you enjoy—if you do not like the exercise you are doing, it is not likely that you will continue.
4. If you are inexperienced, go to a gym where professional trainers give you instructions.
5. Find a friend to exercise with—this usually improves compliance.

New and Experimental Medical Treatments

Deep brain stimulation is a sophisticated procedure that involves the implantation of an electrode deeply in the brain to stimulate activity that can hopefully alleviate severe depressive symptoms. This new technique has been approved for use for Parkinson's disease and other movement-related disorders. It is also used for unrelenting pain problems and for certain types of epilepsy.

Another new and promising practice is rapid transcranial magnetic stimulation (rTMS). Unlike deep brain stimulation, this approach uses magnetic currents. The electrodes delivering this stimulation are placed on the scalp, and pulses are sent through the brain. This does not induce seizures and appears to be safe. It has been used to treat depression experimentally, and while some of the results are promising, it is too early to determine if this will be an effective and acceptable new form of treatment.

An approach that also uses magnetic waves is magnetic seizure therapy, and this approach uses a combination of rTMS and ECT. While it does induce seizures, it appears to be safe and has fewer side effects than ECT alone. This is a preliminary type of treatment, and although promising, it has not yet been established as an effective and safe treatment method. Some good research is being conducted on this approach, and new findings will guide future use.

Vagus nerve stimulation is another of the newer experimental approaches that are being evaluated. The vagus nerve is one of the cranial nerves that seem to have some role in depression although it is not yet clear what that role might be. In this approach, an electrode is implanted near the vagus nerve, and a device like a cardiac pacemaker will stimulate the vagus nerve on a regular basis; some of the early findings suggest that this might be another potentially helpful treatment for depression and perhaps other psychiatric difficulties as well.

Some Alternative Treatments

Hypnotherapy

Hypnosis has been used as a mental health treatment method for at least two centuries. Prior to the development of psychoanalysis, hypnosis did have some promising results treating patients with "hysteria," but the therapeutic effects were rarely sustained, and when other psychotherapeutic tools because available, hypnosis was largely ignored by professionals, and it fell into the realm of entertainment and pseudoscience. However, more research and training started finding some therapeutic value for the use of hypnosis in certain situations.

When people expect that hypnosis will quickly and easily treat problems like smoking, overeating, gambling, and alcohol and drug abuse, they are bound to be disappointed; hypnosis does not fix complex problems with simple procedures. In the hands of a well-trained, licensed professional, hypnosis might have a role as an adjunctive therapy that is used in combination with other techniques. It is not used often, although one can find "professional" hypnotists who will claim to treat almost anything—caveat emptor (let the buyer beware). If a person wants to try to see if hypnosis will help them, they should go to a licensed mental health professional who uses hypnosis as one of their therapeutic techniques; this means that the person should be a licensed psychologist, psychiatrist, or social worker. Some counselors may be trained to use hypnosis, but they should be state licensed as well and not just certified by some impressive-sounding bogus organization.

Eye Movement Desensitization and Reprogramming (EMDR)

This approach has been around since the 1990s and has an enthusiastic following. It is a technique that has been used with post-traumatic stress disorder and other types of mental health problems. Substantial research has been done on this approach, but the results have not been impressive. Most of the "successes" are anecdotal and not borne out by systematic research. EMDR proponents will point to some of the "research" that supports this approach, but on evaluation, these studies were largely found to be biased, poorly executed, and the result of experimenter bias. Some of the better studies that have been done do not support this technique for the problems it claims to treat. For every problem that EMDR claims to treat successfully, there are better, more conventional forms of treatment that are more effective and supported by good-quality research and clinical evidence.

Neurolinguistic Programming

This approach was first introduced in the 1970s, and with impressive-sounding concepts and dramatic claims of success, it gained notoriety quickly and attracted considerable attention. Looking for connections between underlying neurophysiological processes, cognition and language, and overt behavior, this approach sounded like it made considerable sense. However, on examination, this was found to be based on poor understanding of neurophysiology, poor understanding of cognition and language, and poor understanding of behavioral dynamics. Any serious scientific investigation of this approach arrived at the same conclusion: this is pseudoscience and ineffective therapy and should be avoided as a treatment method.

How Are These Utilized Today?

Although there have been many advances in psychotherapy, it is still the case that the most common type of treatment for mental health issues is medication. While the quality of medication has improved greatly and there are many good and effective drugs to treat mental health conditions, medication alone is rarely adequate treatment. Of course, with conditions like schizophrenia, bipolar disorder, and obsessive-compulsive disorder, medication is often the first-line treatment, and psychotherapeutic treatments may be secondary but are still very important and particularly with conditions like bipolar disorder and obsessive-compulsive disorder. It is also true that most of the personality disorders (with a couple of exceptions) do not typically respond well to medication as a form of treatment. What is particularly important for most patients is that for conditions like depression and anxiety disorders, medication alone is never adequate treatment, and for these conditions, while medication can be helpful, psychotherapy is the most important aspect of treatment. However, in the area of mental health treatment, medication is still the most common type of treatment used.

Other medical and physical types of treatments are not used nearly as frequently. ECT is used far less frequently than medication but certainly is used more than any of the other medical/physical treatments. This treatment has vastly improved in recent years and is a safe and effective form of treatment, especially for major depression that does not respond to other treatments or for patients who do not tolerate medication well.

Psychosurgery for mental health conditions is rarely used today although there are a couple of specific types of treatments that are occasionally used for seriously ill patients who have not responded to any other forms of treatment. Some of the other experimental types of treatments like rTMS, deep brain stimulation, vagus nerve stimulation, and magnetic seizure therapy have had some encouraging results but are not widely used now.

Light therapy is used more today than in the past, and while this seems to be helpful for some patients, there is no reason to conclude that this form of treatment is as good as more conventional forms of treatment. While it could be helpful, simply having patients be more physically and social active, getting outdoors even for a short time frequently, and making sure that vitamin D levels are appropriate are probably more effective and less expensive than sitting in front of a light box for several hours a day.

One form of physical "treatment" that has proven to be effective for most patients with many different conditions is physical exercise—particularly aerobic exercise. Certainly, for mood disorders and anxiety disorders, exercise is important, and this finding has been demonstrated and replicated in the experimental and clinical literature in many studies. However, when beginning an exercise program, it is important to do so with the knowledge and support of your physician. It is also important to have a realistic and structured program. Start slowly, increase gradually, and use professional guidance from a trainer, physical therapist, or other knowledgeable professional.

For the alternative treatments, caution is usually a reasonable approach. Hypnotherapy certainly has a place in the treatment regime for many practitioners, but it is never a quick or simple "fix" and is more frequently used as an adjunctive treatment to support other forms of therapy. It is important that if a patient wants to investigate hypnotherapy, they approach this preference by working with a licensed mental health professional; if the professional they are working with does not use hypnotherapy, they might be able to suggest a colleague who might be able to help. With EMDR, the picture is not as clear. There are professionals who feel that this approach has been beneficial for some of their patients. However, professional literature is not supportive of these claims, and fewer people are using this approach today than a few years ago. Most practitioners find that other techniques usually work better and faster than EMDR, and there are still many questions about its effectiveness; no good theoretical explanations exist as to how and why it should work at all. Finally, with respect to neurolinguistic programming, there is no evidence to support its therapeutic efficacy, and there is no good reason to seek out practitioners in this approach—it does not appear to work, and the underlying theory has been described by many academics and researchers as "pseudoscience."

Concerns and Critiques

One of the major concerns about the use of medical types of treatments for psychological problems is that the medical model is sometimes not appropriate for mental health issues. In medicine the model is usually diagnosis, treatment, and cure. The implication here is that the diagnosis will reveal a specific medical condition for which there is an appropriate and accepted treatment that will hopefully result in a cure. While there are some types of mental health problems that might fit this approach better than others, most psychological difficulties do not easily fit this model. For example, diagnoses are usually general, and it is not always easy to get exact and specific diagnoses that several experts would consistently agree with. Further, while we often have a good idea as to what type of therapy would work best with specific diagnostic categories, there may be good and honest disagreement as to which type of treatment would be best. Also, since treatment is often protracted, and many conditions are recurrent, the idea of "cure" is sometimes difficult to establish. In fact, one psychiatrist in the 1960s (Thomas Szasz) was totally opposed to the medical model of treatment in psychology and psychiatry (he was a physician) and even said that using the term "mental illness" did not make sense because we are usually not dealing with true diseases, but more accurately we are treating "problems in living."

One other problem with the use of medical approaches for dealing with mental health issues is that medication is often overused and misused because it is an easy type of treatment to implement; it is often prescribed by people who do not have adequate information about psychological problems, and frequently the best information many physicians (nonpsychiatrists) have about psychotropic medications comes from representatives of drug companies selling the drugs. It is also true that insurance and managed care companies often encourage the use of medications because they may think that it works faster, does not take as long as psychotherapy, and can be prescribed with short and infrequent visits. Unfortunately, for many problems, medication alone is not adequate treatment, and the drugs are helpful only while the person is on them, and when they stop taking the medication, their problems come back. Psychotherapy, on the other hand, produces results that are less likely to result in relapse when therapy is concluded.

Other medical forms of treatment may have a role, especially ECT that has proven to be a helpful adjunctive form of treatment for patients who have not responded well to medication and/or psychotherapy. Most of the other medical forms of treatment are still experimental, and their use has not been approved for general use.

Some alternative treatments have a role in the treatment arsenal but are not used as often as the more accepted forms of treatment. Hypnotherapy may be helpful in some situations but is rarely used as a primary treatment and is usually used as an adjunctive treatment. However, it should only be used to treat mental health issues when the person using is an appropriate state-licensed mental health professional. Likewise, light therapy has been found in some studies to be somewhat helpful for mild to moderate depression although there are also more effective and less expensive ways to treat depression. Finally, although both approaches have their proponents, research and clinical literature is not supportive of the use of EMDR or neurolinguistic programming as appropriate and effective means of treating mental health conditions.

PART 3

Case Studies

In this section we present a few brief cases all of which reflect common problems confronted in psychotherapy. None of the cases are taken from a single individual, and all are compilations of issues faced by different patients at different times. Therefore, not one case refers to a single individual, and thus all patient confidentiality is assured. Each case is explained, and the primary referral problem is discussed. Following each case description, a section shows how different psychotherapeutic approaches would deal with the specific problems in the cases. The therapeutic approaches are drawn from the four basic types of psychotherapies, and each case has two examples of how different therapeutic models would try to understand and treat the stated problems. The four basic models are psychodynamic, behavioral, cognitive and cognitive-behavioral, and humanistic/existential. You will see that depending on the case, sometimes the approaches are similar and sometimes they are different. The psychodynamic therapies typically rely on deep case history, examining "underlying causes" of behavior and gaining insight and psychological changes. The behavioral therapies look at the history of the referring problem, the types of reinforcers/punishers that have been used, development of a therapeutic strategy, and the resulting behavior change. The cognitive therapies look at the symptom history, the cognitive processes related to the problem, a therapeutic strategy to help the person think differently about their problems, and then the resulting behavioral change. The cognitive-behavioral approach usually starts with behavioral tactics before moving into the cognitive aspects of the therapy. Finally, the humanistic/existential therapies also look at the history of the difficulties and explore how the person feels about them, the choices they have made, the expectations they have, and then the help they gain more of a sense of control over their lives and the ability to make better and healthier choices.

There are many similarities between the therapies. For example, all start by identifying the referral issues and then determine and agree on the therapeutic goals. Then they explore the person's history and develop a context for understanding the individual's problems. The next step is to undertake the therapy itself, and as therapy progresses, they work toward closure and termination of treatment when the treatment goals are reached.

Case 1: Generalized Anxiety Disorder

Mrs. Smith (a 28-year-old married female) made an appointment explaining that she was having problems with anxiety and that it was getting worse. Her primary care physician (PCP) had evaluated her and started her on an anxiolytic medication (a tranquilizer) and a selective serotonin reuptake inhibitor antidepressant (which is also helpful for anxiety). However, even though the medications were helping, she was still having some anxiety and seemed to worry about almost anything. She was having difficulty sleeping, was not exercising because it made her heart beat faster and that scared her, and she was not socially active because she was afraid that if she went out someplace, she would get anxious. She had always been a nervous person and had been described as "high strung" by many. Her father also had problems with anxiety, and others in her family tended to be a little nervous, but she felt her anxiety was worse than that of the others. She said that her anxiety began getting worse in college and got a little better when she met her husband and got married, but after having her daughter, the anxiety started getting more problematic, and after having her son, the anxiety continued to be an issue. She describes herself as a "worrier" and reports that she will worry about almost anything. She does not smoke or use recreational drugs and only occasionally drinks alcohol and never to excess. She would like to get the anxiety under better control, would like a fuller and more well-rounded life, wants to be a better role model for her children, and would like to worry less about things. She also feels guilty because she feels that her anxiety is keeping her from being the mother, spouse, daughter, and friend that she wants to be. Her children are both in school; her daughter is eight years old and her son is six. She works part-time in medical records for a local hospital and usually works three days per week.

Psychodynamic

The psychodynamic therapist, like all the other schools of thought, would begin by getting to know the patient and establishing rapport to begin developing a productive therapeutic relationship. The therapist (Dr. Schmidt) began looking into the early family dynamics and found that Mrs. Smith's father suffered from anxiety and was not able to be active with family activities, and he was not a warm and comforting person. Mrs. Smith never felt her father cared much for her, although he frequently told her that he loved her. As a child, she rarely brought friends home because they thought her father was weird, and this embarrassed her. Her mother was pretty "normal" but had a busy job and was not as available as the mothers of many of her friends. She had one younger brother, and he was usually off playing with his friends. When she was younger, Mrs. Smith had several close girlfriends and was a good student but was very quiet and did not have many friends, but the ones that she had were close and supportive.

Mrs. Smith noticed that she worried more than most children and she tended to get nervous frequently. She progressed quietly but uneventfully through middle school and high school and did not have many problems with anxiety although she still tended to be a worrier. The anxiety started to emerge more in college where she was more on her own, did not have many social connections, had a few friends, and dated occasionally. She met her husband at a party when they were both juniors in college, and they got along well but did not date for a couple of months. They started getting more serious in their senior year and started talking about marriage. They got engaged three years after they got out of college and got married one year later. Mrs. Smith's anxiety continued to get worse, and she became more of a worrier each year.

Mrs. Smith's therapist noted that as a child, she did not have close relationships with anyone in her family although she felt closer to her mother than her father. Interestingly, Dr. Schmidt felt that she described her husband in terms that were more like her mother than her father and felt that other than her husband, she did not relate comfortably with most men. After some in-depth analysis, the therapist could find no evidence of physical or sexual abuse in her history. He also concluded that her childhood left her questioning relationships and was fearful of getting too close to people because "you never knew if they would respond, lash out, or ignore you." Her early life was also filled with uncertainty about events and relationships, and her worrying seemed to be a function of her lack of trust in events around her. The therapist felt that her therapy should involve her understanding the basis of her fears and anxiety and to learn to develop and trust a relationship other than her husband whom she was likely overdependent on. Therefore, Dr. Schmidt wanted to let Mrs. Smith learn that he was someone who was predictable, understanding, and trustworthy and that as she came to accept that fact, he would help her learn how to broaden her social network and take the risk of getting closer to other people.

Dr. Schmidt would also help her understand that her fear of uncertainty was what was keeping her anxiety active, because no one can predict the future perfectly, and uncertainty was always with us—but that did not have to be anxiety provoking since it was merely a part of life. By learning to accept the uncertainty and not fear the future, she would learn how to be more comfortable and confident with her own life. As she became more comfortable and less anxious, they would begin tapering down their visits to the point of terminating treatment.

Cognitive Behavioral Therapy

After completing her history and establishing the therapeutic rapport, the CBT therapist (Dr. Johann) would want a detailed description of the history of her anxiety—when it started, who else in her family had anxiety issues, what situations were most difficult for her, what things made her less anxious, how had the anxiety progressed over the years—and review her goals and expectations of therapy. He would also discuss the medications Mrs. Smith was taking, how they were working, any side effects, and how she felt about taking them.

The first phase of treatment would be to educate Mrs. Smith about the nature of anxiety and how it related to stress. Then, Dr. Johann would start Mrs. Smith on a program of stress management, which would also help moderate some of the symptoms of anxiety. The therapist would want Mrs. Smith to start an exercise program with her doctor's approval, start gradually with activities that she liked, and then progress to working out in a gym and exercise classes to help her be more comfortable working with others in a social situation. She was also taught to use relaxation techniques and to practice them daily, and this would become integrated with meditation and mindfulness techniques. In addition, the therapist would teach her specific techniques (e.g., structured breathing) that would help reduce her anxiety and manage stress better. The therapist would also examine her sleeping patterns, and the therapist would help her to develop better sleep hygiene and hopefully start sleeping and resting better.

Dr. Johann then introduced more cognitive techniques and would have Mrs. Smith describe situations that made her anxious and some of the situations that she worried about. They would look at these situations and topics and analyze them in such a way as to help her understand how disproportionate her fears and anxieties were relative to the actual risk of the things that she feared and worried about. However, this understanding alone would not "fix" the anxiety and worry, and the therapist would start giving her different ways to think or act when she was in a situation where she felt anxious or when she was worrying.

Finally, the therapist would develop a program where Mrs. Smith would start to confront some of her fears in a systematic and gradual fashion to start becoming more comfortable in situations where she would usually be anxious. For example, Mrs. Smith was terrified about speaking publicly, even in small groups. Therefore, the therapist suggested that she begin a conversation with some of her friends individually, then with two other people, and then in small groups until she was more comfortable speaking to small groups of people she knew. The therapist might then suggest that she join a group that helped people learn how to speak publicly or to take a college or adult education class at a local school or college that taught public speaking. As she became more comfortable with this, the therapist would encourage her to pick another anxiety-arousing situation, and they would develop a similar approach with that fear. As Mrs. Smith became more confident in her ability to address her fears, she would be encouraged to start dealing with some of her other issues on her own and in the same gradual manner. After the anxiety was under better control, they would discuss her medications with her doctor, and when he or she felt that the time was right, they might start gradually weaning Mrs. Smith off the medications as well. While she was tapering off medications or just refining her new coping strategies, they would also start to taper down the frequency of therapy meetings until Mrs. Smith no longer needed them.

Case 2: Panic Disorder

Charlie Grafton is a 32-year-old man who is married with three children (two girls aged 12 and 6 and a 10-year-old boy). He is a computer programmer who works for a large manufacturing company and has a good health insurance plan. Since he was a teen, he has had problems with occasional panic attacks, and they are sometimes so bad that he goes to the hospital emergency room because he feels so badly; he worries that something is seriously wrong, and he is afraid that the panic attacks might cause something medically serious (e.g., a heart attack).

Medically, Charlie is in good condition and takes some medication for high blood pressure but is otherwise in good health. His mother also suffers from panic attacks, and hers had gotten so bad that for years she has been house-bound because of her fear that if she goes out of the house, she will have another panic attack; Charlie is committed to never let that happen to him. When his panic attacks started interfering with his family and work life, he went to his PCP for a checkup and to find what was causing the attacks. His doctor diagnosed the problem as panic disorder without agoraphobia (he is not house-bound—at least not yet). His doctor started him on Xanax (a tranquilizer) to take when he got or started to get a panic attack.

Although Xanax seemed to help by stopping or making the panic attacks less severe (at least some of the time), they were still happening and perhaps even more frequently. In consulting with his doctor, it was suggested that Charlie see a psychologist who specialized in dealing with anxiety disorders, and he gave him several names. When Charlie met the psychologist and they talked for a few times, it was clear that they were dealing with panic disorder without agoraphobia. Charlie's psychologist talked with Charlie's doctor, and they discussed different treatment options. Charlie's doctor decided to also put Charlie on Prozac and keep Xanax for a while but then taper him off that. Prozac is an antidepressant but works well to prevent panic attacks even though it is not a tranquilizer. As well as Xanax was working, it does have some unfortunate side effects (e.g., it is addictive if taken regularly for some time) and is not usually a good long-term treatment. Also, while it reduces the panic attacks, it does not cure them, so when you stop the drug, the panic attacks continue. With treatment coordinated between Charlie's doctor and psychologist, they began Charlie's psychotherapy. The psychologist agreed with the diagnosis and accepted Charlie's goal of reducing or eliminating the panic attacks and finding better ways to manage his fear of having more panic attacks. Like many people with panic disorder, the fear of having another attack was almost as big a problem as having the attack itself.

Humanistic Psychotherapy

After reviewing Charlie's history, his psychologist (Dr. St. Clare) asks Charlie to tell him about his panic attacks, when they occur, and how it makes him feel. He also asks Charlie to tell the therapist about himself, what were his likes and dislikes, what were his important relationships, what he thought about his job, and what he liked to do with his free time. The therapist did not really talk much and seemed to be more interested in hearing what Charlie had to say about himself.

After spending several sessions with Charlie just reflecting about himself and his panic attacks, the therapist started to focus more on the panic attacks, how they made Charlie feel, and, more important, how having panic disorder made Charlie feel about himself. When Charlie was asked to tell Dr. St. Clare about his mother and her panic disorder, it became clear that Charlie had some strong feelings about his mother and her psychological issues. He loved his mother and felt badly about her disorder, but he was also angry at her because she could not be the mother he felt that he deserved, and he also felt that it was her fault that he also had the panic disorder. He was embarrassed about his mother's condition and rarely talked about her to others; he was also embarrassed to admit that he rarely visited her; he did not like taking his children to visit her and often found weak excuses to keep from having to see her. Dr. St. Clare encouraged Charlie to talk about these feelings and made sure that Charlie understood that his feelings were not bad—they were just feelings—and these negative feelings did not mean that he hated his mother or that he was a bad person.

Charlie's therapist then began to explore his feelings about himself and how his panic disorder and his mother's condition affected him and his feelings about himself. It started to become clear that Charlie blamed himself and his mother for his condition, felt weak and helpless, was embarrassed about his condition, and felt "crazy." Dr. St. Clare then focused on some of Charlie's strengths and some of the things in his life that he felt good about. They also explored his history and identified positive aspects of his life and his accomplishments. The therapist also pointed out to Charlie that she (the therapist) liked and respected Charlie and found him to be a decent, hard-working man who was a loving husband and father, a good friend to many people, and someone others looked up to.

The therapist then started working with Charlie to help him internalize and integrate some of these new ways of thinking and feeling about himself and others and encouraged him to start looking for opportunities to act in ways consistent with his new ways of thinking and feeling. As he became more confident and self-accepting, she helped him look more realistically at himself, accept his strengths and weaknesses, continue to strive to be healthier and more self-aware and self-accepting, and learn to accept his mistakes and flaws as simply a part of who he is and use these as goals for self-improvement.

Behavioral Psychotherapy

Charlie met with a behavioral psychotherapist (Dr. Benoit), and they began by getting to know one another and exploring Charlie's history. They also discussed his panic attacks—when they started, how they affected him, when they occurred, and under what circumstances they happened. They then started to work on stress management activities and learning new ways of approaching stress-producing situations. They also learned relaxation techniques and practiced those frequently.

The next stage of treatment involved the use of an approach called "systematic desensitization" that was originally developed by Joseph Wolpe. They began by Charlie listing different situations that were likely to produce a panic attack, and he ranked them from the easiest one to deal with and tolerate to the most challenging situation he might face. The next session, Dr. Benoit got Charlie to relax, and then he started describing the *least* anxiety-arousing situation to Charlie; he would just listen, and if he felt even a little anxious, he would signal the therapist by lifting his finger, and the therapist would stop talking about that situation and talk about something neutral. They would work on this (it might take several times) until Charlie could listen to and think about the anxiety-arousing situation and stay relaxed. They would proceed through the list until they got to the point where Charlie could listen to and think about everything on the list without feeling anxious at all.

The next phase would be for Charlie to continue working on his relaxation skills daily, but then start to gradually approach situations that used to be difficult for him, and to keep doing it frequently enough that the situation no longer produced any feelings of anxiety; this is called in vivo (in real life) desensitization. This phase would continue until Charlie could approach difficult situations without feeling anxious—even if he did not like the situation, he would not feel anxious about it. They also would work on Charlie starting to develop new and healthier ways to approach difficult situations and to find ways to reinforce these new behaviors so that they would continue. At the same time, they would work on removing any reinforcers for less adaptive behaviors like avoiding difficult situations. For example, when anxiety is reduced by avoiding a feared situation, the avoidance is reinforced (by the anxiety reduction), and therefore, it is more likely to occur again. By finding other things to do besides avoiding the situation, they were trying to reduce the reinforcing effect produced by the anxiety reduction, and therefore, the avoidance tendency would be "extinguished" in the absence of adequate reinforcers.

After having worked on these types of techniques, Dr. Benoit helped Charlie learn how to generalize the feelings of relaxation and to confront (not avoid) situations that might have produced anxiety in the past. When they got to the point that Charlie was facing most of his difficulties without difficulty, the therapy would be gradually tapered off and then terminated.

Case 3: Adjustment Disorder with Anxiety

Kevin is an 18-year-old college student, who has recently begun having some problems with anxiety, and it seems to have gotten worse lately. Presently he is living on campus in the dorm and is in a suite with three other men students whom he likes and gets along with. Although his parents are divorced, he sees both frequently, and they get along reasonably well for being divorced. Kevin has two sisters, one older than him and one younger, and they get along well although he does not usually "hang around" with them when he is home.

Kevin finds that whenever he is dealing with someone in authority, he starts feeling nervous, his mouth and throat get dry, he gets sweaty palms, and his hands even tremble a little. He really dislikes these feelings, and he finds them embarrassing. He has spoken only to a few people about this (including his mother), and everyone has been supportive but basically tell him that there is nothing to worry about and just put those feelings out of his mind. Although he knows that they are trying to help, nothing that they have suggested has made any difference at all. One of his friends suggested that he might need medication, and as much as Kevin hated the idea of taking pills for something like this, he did make an appointment with his family doctor who listened to his concerns and then did an examination. He agreed that Kevin was experiencing anxiety, but he told him that since this problem had existed only for the past couple of years or so, it was not likely to be a chronic anxiety issue, and he agreed that medication might help, but he also told Kevin that the medication would not "cure" the anxiety and would just cover it up. He said that before they tried medication he would like Kevin to make an appointment with a psychologist who would possibly be able to help him learn how to deal with the anxiety-producing situations more effectively.

All of this was new to Kevin because he had never had any mental or emotional problems before. He had enjoyed high school, had played in the band, had a "garage band" with several of his friends, and was socially active. He was a decent student and usually made Bs with a few As and some Cs but was college bound like most of his friends. He would occasionally have a few beers with friends in high school, but he never got drunk or did anything stupid like drinking and driving. He tried marijuana a couple of times, but he did not like how it made him feel, and he was afraid of being caught and getting into trouble. In college he would drink with his friends at parties on weekends and had gotten drunk a couple of times, but he did not like that feeling either and rarely drank to excess; he did not use any recreational drugs. He finally decided that he would take his doctor's advice and make an appointment to see a psychologist.

Cognitive Psychotherapy

The cognitive therapist (Dr. Sanger) met Kevin, spent some time getting to know him, and took a careful history, including Kevin's description of his anxiety issues. After some discussion, the therapist found that Kevin had started having difficulties with anxiety in high school, and it appeared that Kevin was afraid of getting into trouble with teachers or school officials because his parents had been insistent on the idea that if he got into any problems in school, that would make it very difficult for him to get into a good college.

Whenever Kevin was called on in class or when he had to go to the school office to take care of some business, he would become nervous and really did not like to do things like that. He became good at avoiding any contact with authority figures and kept as low a profile as possible. Dr. Sanger started to explore these situations with Kevin and asked him to speculate as to what kinds of things could happen if he dealt with authority figures directly. It turned out that Kevin was harboring some frightening and unrealistic beliefs about authority figures, what they could do to him and how much power they had. He also pursued Kevin's belief about himself and how he saw himself relative to authority figures.

When they discussed his beliefs and took them to the extremes that seemed to underlie Kevin's fears, Kevin could see how unrealistic and even ridiculous those things sounded when you said them out loud. For example, he appeared to have the belief that people in authority had enormous power that they could use on a whim and that they were looking for opportunities to harm him personally. While he knew that this was not true, it did feel like this was the kind of thing that made his fears feel real. There also seemed to be a belief that if he ever did anything wrong or even if he was accused of doing something wrong, his life would be ruined, and he would be a failure forever. Kevin also seemed to feel that if he got into trouble people would see him as a total "loser" and would not want to be friends with him; further, he felt like if he really got into trouble, he really would be a loser and would not deserve to be liked and respected by others. It also became clear that his fears and anxiety got even worse when he was in college because it seemed that the professors, deans, and officials had even more power and control over his future and his reputation.

The therapist explored each of these beliefs, and they would discuss them and discover how unrealistic and exaggerated these beliefs were. It appeared that Kevin needed to find new and better ways to think about authority figures, their power over him, and his feelings about himself. It also became clear that simply understanding how unreasonable his beliefs were did not change his feelings or the anxiety, and in fact, these insights even seemed to make him feel worse because they pointed out that he could not even think correctly about important things in his life.

At this point, the therapist started taking each of the dysfunctional beliefs that Kevin had and discussed and explored what would be more realistic beliefs to have about each of the issues they had discovered. They discussed them to the point that Kevin could see what reasonable beliefs would be, but he also got to the point where he understood and believed the new points of view. The next step involved the therapist helping Kevin start to experiment with acting in ways consistent with his new beliefs, and this also meant being more assertive about his own needs, approaching others (including authority figures) when he needed to, standing up for himself, and not avoiding things just because he was anxious. As Kevin got better at doing these things, feeling less anxious, and not avoiding situations, they began decreasing the frequency of his visits and ultimately were able to terminate treatment.

Psychodynamic Psychotherapy

Kevin was referred to a psychodynamic psychotherapist (Dr. Abraham), who, he was told, had a lot of experience dealing with anxiety disorders. When Kevin met the therapist, she was pleasant and spent a lot of time getting to know Kevin and exploring his history. She wanted to know about his family, his parents, his siblings, and his extended family as well as his friends, professors, and any other people in his life who were important to him.

Dr. Abraham was interested in his relationship with his parents and other family members, and they spent a lot of time discussing them. It became clear that Kevin loved and respected both of his parents, but he felt closer to his mother than his father. He was nine years old when his parents divorced, and he lived most of his time with his mother although he saw his father frequently and stayed with him every other weekend and on most vacations. He and his father liked to go fishing and play golf together, and they usually had a good time. Although Kevin's father was not mean or punitive, he was never one to praise his children much, and he had high expectations for them and wanted them to do well and to be successful in whatever they chose to do. His father came only to see him play in the school band once or twice and never seemed to show much interest in Kevin's musical ability. In fact, Kevin had the feeling that he never quite measured up to what his father thought he should be doing, and it did not seem to matter how hard he worked; it never felt good enough. He also felt that his father was disappointed that Kevin was not involved in sports.

Kevin's mother was more accepting and more positive about Kevin's abilities and accomplishments, but that did not seem to have much of an impact on him because "that is what mothers do." Although Kevin got along with his sisters, he did not spend much time with them because they had their own activities and friends; one of his sisters was a talented soccer player, and he did notice that his father rarely missed one of her games. It was also true that Kevin was the only one in the family who had problems with anxiety, meaning he rarely talked about it to anyone in the family because he felt he was kind of a "wimp" as the only one in the family with anxiety.

The therapist started exploring the people and situations where he felt anxious, and gradually it became clear to Kevin that, at least in part, he was acting toward authority figures as if they were like his father and that they would never approve of him, and if he made a mistake, they would be upset with him. Although Kevin felt much more accepted by his mother, he found that women authority figures were not easier to deal with because as authority figures, they were more like his father than his mother.

The next phase of Kevin's therapy involved his starting to learn how to be more comfortable with authority figures, and his therapist suggested having a few meetings with his academic advisor (whom Kevin liked) and discussing the fact that he had trouble relating to authority figures; then with his advisor's advice, he would start meeting some of the officials in the school and discussing his major, his goals, and his questions with them. The therapist was hoping that by dealing with these people directly, Kevin could separate in his mind these officials from his father and see that they were not the same.

After starting to deal more with these people, the therapist suggested that they invite Kevin's father to join them for a session or two and discuss Kevin's fears and concerns. She expected that Kevin's father would want to be helpful, and she wanted the two of them to be more open in their communication with one another. As Kevin became more comfortable dealing with authority figures, had a better understanding as to where his anxiety was coming from, and started talking more and being more direct in dealing with his father, they would start tapering off the treatment and would ultimately terminate their sessions.

Case 4: Major Depression

Mary is a 57-year-old woman who has been divorced for 10 years and has little contact with her former husband. She has one daughter who is 32 years old and lives locally. Her daughter has two daughters aged 8 and 10, is married, and works in the local community library; her husband is a mechanic and works at a car dealership. Mary's parents are both deceased, having died about five years ago and died within two years of each other. Although Mary did not see her parents often, she still misses them very much. She has one older brother, who lives in a different part of the country; she loves and respects him, but he is so busy with his career that they rarely see one another and usually just get in contact during the holidays and other special times.

Mary works as a secretary in the local city office and likes her job and the people with whom she works. Her health is generally good, although she takes medication for high blood pressure and high cholesterol. She is a little overweight but otherwise is in generally good health. She lives alone with her cat Cheshire and rarely goes out socially. Although she is religious, she usually does not go to church, and she feels bad about that. Her health habits are good, and she does not smoke and rarely drinks alcohol.

Mary has struggled most of her adult life with depression, and she has been hospitalized several times for this condition; she even had electroshock therapy on one occasion about 10 years ago. Presently, she sees a psychiatrist who has prescribed antidepressant medications, but she is not seeing a psychotherapist. Recently, the depression has been coming back, and although she is getting to work and taking care of her major responsibilities, she can see that the depression is taking more out of her, she is becoming more isolated, and she is sleeping most of the day on weekends. Others have noticed that she is not feeling particularly good and have asked if she is sick. While she thinks it is nice that people are concerned about her, she wishes they would just mind their own business. She talked with her psychiatrist, who suggested that she start seeing a psychotherapist again and gave her a couple of names of therapists he felt would be appropriate for her.

Existential Psychotherapy

Mary made an appointment with a therapist, Dr. Rollomay, who was suggested for her, and she met with him in his office. He was nice and easy to talk to. After getting to know one another and gathering information from Mary's history, Dr. Rollomay asked her about why she had come to therapy and what she expected from therapy. Mary explained that she had been treated for depression for many years, and it seemed like every few years or so, she would have another episode of depression, and she felt like this was coming on once again.

Dr. Rollomay started asking questions about Mary's history and family and was interested in when the depression had started and when and how it recurred. Although sometimes there were events that seemed to set off the depression, for example, her divorce, many times it just came on without anything seeming to have caused it. It seemed like she was more likely to get depressed in the winter, but there were some winters that she did not get depressed at all, and there were other times when she got depressed during the spring or summer, so clearly it was not just a seasonal type of depression.

In the process of therapy, they began to look at Mary's life, the people who were important to her at different points in her life. They also examined her roles and relationships and focused on her self-image at different stages of her life. She had been close to her parents when she was a child, but after she graduated from high school and went to college, she did not see them often. She met her husband in college, and he was two years older than she was; after he graduated, they decided to get married, so she dropped out of college and got a job working in the office of an insurance company. After the birth of her daughter, she stayed home to care for her and to be a full-time homemaker. Over the years, she and her husband were drifting apart, and one day, when their daughter was five years old, he told Mary that he no longer loved her and that he was leaving and wanted a divorce. He was willing to let Mary have custody of their daughter, but he did want regular and frequent visitation. He also paid her child support and paid Mary maintenance payments for three years after they separated. Mary felt badly about the divorce, and particularly because of her daughter, but she also had to admit that she really had not felt close to her husband for many years and did not even feel that she loved him anymore—he was more of a habit and a source of security than anything else.

Mary was surprised when her therapist said that one of her problems was that she had no idea who she was. He pointed out to her that she seemed to identify herself primarily in terms of her relationships. For example, he asked her, if they took her personality and removed the parts of her that were a mother, wife, daughter, friend, coworker, and so on, what would be left? This brought tears to her eyes, and she replied that it felt like if they took all her relationships away there would not be anything left. Very warmly, her therapist pointed out that what was left was truly who Mary really was, and what therapy would be about would involve Mary uncovering and knowing just who she really was and what was important to her as a person.

Mary and her therapist spent many hours looking at Mary's life, her values, her choices and decisions, her relationships, and how these things had drifted along without Mary understanding much about herself or her life. As they delved into these issues, Mary started to realize that there were things in her life that were important to her and choices that she could make to improve her life and how she felt about herself and those around her. As she became more comfortable with herself and could see what she was becoming as a person, she was able to look forward to a future that was hopeful and full of prospects for a meaningful and rewarding life. She could look forward to being herself and becoming the best "Mary" she could be.

Mary also understood that depression might also be a part of her future, but rather than feeling victimized about that, she realized that this was a condition that she might not have full control over, but she did have control over what she did about it, how she felt about it, and how she could actively seek the treatment that would keep the depression from controlling her and her life.

Cognitive-Behavioral Psychotherapy

After getting to know Mary and going through her history, her CBT therapist (Dr. Etkin) took an inventory of her health habits and let her know that he expected her to be following the nutrition advice given her by her nutritionist; he wanted her working on her sleep hygiene, getting more exercise, and trying to get more socially involved with things around her. Having started her off on the basics, he also recognized some of the dysfunctional thought patterns she had about herself and about other people.

Rather than start working on her thoughts, he wanted her to get started changing her behaviors. For example, he wanted to find out what kinds of social activities that she typically enjoyed. He even asked her, "If you were not feeling depressed, what kinds of things would you probably be doing?" Recognizing that physically and socially she would not be able to just start off doing things the way she used to, he suggested that in terms of physical activities, she should either join a class that met three times per week or find a friend that she could go to the gym with three times per week. He wanted her to start gradually and build up slowly to get to exercising 30–45 minutes three or four days per week. He also wanted her working out with other people, which would make it more likely that she would follow through, but also would have her doing something social. To work on other social activities, he wanted her to start by going to some social type of situation (e.g., church or clubs) where she would be around other people and to also have one social activity involving one or more friends or family where they would do something together (e.g., a meal, shopping, a movie) and do that once per week.

The therapist also had Mary keep track on a sheet he prepared to track her mood, daily activities, sleep patterns, and any other significant events. In each of their meetings, they would begin by reviewing the chart and see how it compared to previous weeks. They were also tracking how she was progressing with her physical and social activities. At this point, they also started working with her thoughts and beliefs. For example, if she was ruminating about something negative, she needed to immediately change activities and do something else—even if she was at work. Whenever she had a negative thought about herself, she had to come up with two or three positive qualities about herself before she could return to the activity she was engaged with. She also had to keep track of the number of times she had negative or unpleasant thoughts, under what circumstances they occurred, and what she did to change them. As they tracked her progress, the more gains she made, the more they spread out the therapy visits until they were able to terminate treatment.

Case 5: Persistent Depressive Disorder

John is a 45-year-old man who is married and has a 12-year-old son and a 15-year-old daughter. He is a social studies teacher at the local middle school and has been a teacher since he finished college. He likes his job, enjoys the students, and has friends at work. His mother struggled with depression for most of her life, and he remembers that she was "never" happy, complained all the time, and rarely showed much love or positive emotions. John's father was reported to be a good provider, but worked a lot, and was not home with the children very often. John has three older sisters, and while they were pleasant to him, they did not have much to do with him because they were older and had their own friends and activities.

When John was a child, he remembers having friends and enjoying playing with them, but he rarely brought friends over to the house because there was not much to do, and his mother made no secret of the fact that she did not want "the house full of screaming kids." John was a decent student and rarely got into trouble at school. He did not play any sports or get involved with any other after-school activities because his parents neither encouraged him nor supported his interest in the activities his friends participated in.

John's parents had not provided any support for his going to college, but his guidance counselor felt that he was college material and encouraged him to take the college entrance examinations and then to apply to state schools where the tuition would be lower, and he would qualify for student aid. He was accepted at several different schools, and he decided on one that was one of the smaller universities in the state but one that had some of the courses of study that he was interested in. He was not sure what he wanted to do when he finished school but decided that he would try to be a teacher, and that is what he majored in and what he ended up doing. He liked history and thought that would be good for him to teach, so he became a social studies teacher in a middle school. He had friends and dated occasionally and met a young woman who was also a teacher, and they married and had two children (a boy and a girl). They had a strong marriage and were happy together, and their children were successful in school, and both went to college and had professions.

Throughout his life, John felt that he was not as happy as other people seemed to be; he had chronic problems with sleep, he did not socialize much even though he had friends, and he was not physically active. As a young adult, he decided that he would talk to his doctor about the fact that he just never felt that he was as happy as he should be with all the positive things in his life. His doctor put him on an antidepressant, and after a few months, John could see that he was sleeping better and even felt a little better. He started becoming more physically and socially active but still did not feel like he thought he should. Then he started seeing a psychologist, and while he respected her and what she did, he did not feel that they were making any progress, and so he stopped going to see her. A few months later, he decided to try again and saw a male psychologist, thinking that this might be better for him, but the same thing happened again, and although he liked the man, he did not feel that it was making any difference.

John spoke to his doctor again, and this time he recommended that John see a psychiatrist for a medication consultation; he also suggested a clinical psychologist who specialized in treating depression. After John's psychiatrist got him on a medication regime that seemed to be helping, and he was sleeping better, he decided to try psychotherapy again.

Humanistic Psychotherapy

When John had her first appointment with his new psychotherapist, he was not sure if he was going to like her or not, but he decided to stay with it for a while and see how it went. His therapist (Dr. Klein) was nice, but she did not say much, and when she did, it was normally just following up on what he had already said or asking questions to clarify some of his comments. At first, he did not feel like they were really doing anything but just talking about random things, but after a few sessions, his therapist asked a question that he did not expect; she wanted to know if he thought that other people liked him, and if so why, and if not then why as well. John had always had a few friends although he tended to keep his relationships "situation specific." That is, he had his friends at work, but he almost never saw them outside of work; he had neighbors whom he visited with in the yard but almost never did anything with them socially; and he had family members that he would see during the holidays but rarely any other times.

It was hard for John to think about what others might like about him, and he joked with the therapist about his "popularity" and what people thought about him. However, she stuck to her question, and finally he had to start looking at himself closely, and with prompting he came up with a few qualities that he thought that his friends might attribute to him, although he was embarrassed to talk about these things. When asked to come up with qualities about him that people might not like, this was even harder, and the things that he came up with were usually situation specific; for example, someone might have been upset with him because he did not finish a task on time or perhaps did not meet their expectation in other ways. However, when pressed on the question as to whether there were people who did not like him as a person because they thought that he was bad, lazy, thoughtless, or some other negative quality, he could not come up with anyone. His therapist then pointed out that it seemed like people saw a lot of more positive things in him than he did himself. He could not disagree with her, but he found this observation to be a little surprising.

John's therapist then began to focus on his mood, and she asked how often he felt depressed; he said that he rarely felt depressed, but she pointed out that he had been diagnosed with persistent depressive disorder, implying that he is depressed most of the time and had been for a long time. He knew that this was his diagnosis, but he was not sure if that was accurate. She then asked how often he truly felt happy or joyful, and he could think of only specific situations like a wedding or birthday where he was happy about what was going on in a situation, but he could not relate to the idea that he could be happy—even joyful—without that being tied to an event; this was confusing to him. She also pointed out that not feeling badly was not the same as feeling good. The next part of their therapy focused on John's learning how to recognize and experience his emotions without having to tie them to specific situations—just experience the emotion for what it was.

After John got better at recognizing his feelings, he could see that even though he did not often feel sad, it was also somewhat rare when he really felt good. They then worked on his recognizing the variance in his moods during the day and starting to understand, accept, and even enjoy how he felt. They also worked on his being more open about his feelings with others and even risk talking about his emotions with others whom he trusted and enjoyed spending time with.

As John got more competent and comfortable with his own feelings and could experience and talk about them, their therapy was almost completed. The last part of the treatment involved his learning how to integrate his feelings, his self-perceptions, and others' feelings about him into a more coherent, realistic, and positive self-image; to feel good about himself, who he was, and what he did; and to enjoy the people and events around him more than he ever had before.

Behavioral Psychotherapy

John met his therapist (Dr. Watson) for their first visit, and he was a little surprised at how quickly they got right to business; the therapist wanted to know what John thought was the problem and why he came into treatment; he also wanted to know what John expected to get out of treatment. John told him that he had been diagnosed with persistent depressive disorder, and while he did not feel sad or depressed most of the time, he did admit he also did not feel happy often either.

The therapist took a careful history of John's life and was particularly interested in how John dealt with challenges in his life and the kinds of things he enjoyed and some of the things he did not like and tried to avoid. He told John that to begin with they needed to start an exercise program and that he wanted him to be socially active and not to avoid doing social things he was invited to. John felt that this was okay but also thought it was unrealistic to add these things to an already-busy schedule. However, his therapist worked with him to set up specific times to do his exercise and had him make some social goals, such as having a "date night" each week with his wife and making sure to have lunch at school with a friend or group of friends rather than sitting in his office eating lunch and grading papers like he usually did.

They also talked about the things in John's life that he enjoyed and the kinds of things that he really looked forward to. His therapist pointed out that many of the things that John really enjoyed were not that difficult to attain, but John rarely did any of them. John reluctantly agreed with the therapist but did not see what this had to do with how he felt. His therapist pointed out that the kind of depression that John had was more about not having many positive things going on in his life rather than just feeling sad or depressed. He told John that it looked like he was simply going through the motions of life without taking the time to enjoy the quality of the things around him that were positive and pleasant.

They then started using a technique that the therapist called "contingency management." What this amounted to was John making up a list of things that he liked and enjoyed, another list of things that he wanted to change in his life, and somethings that he would like to accomplish. They then designed a system where John would start making gradual changes in the areas he wanted to modify, and he would add outcomes that he enjoyed, therefore, when he finished or accomplished something he wanted to do. Sometimes these would be small, like just taking a few minutes to talk with his wife or kids about their day and what they did. By using this approach, John was starting to make some changes he wanted to and was certainly experiencing more pleasant and positive things in his life. As these changes were occurring, he also noticed that he was feeling better, was happier, and was enjoying his life more than he ever had.

Case 6: Bereavement

Erin is an eight-year-old girl who was raised in an intact family with a mother and a father and an older sister. She thought that their lives were "normal," and not much exciting ever happened to them. Her father sold insurance and had a good job; her mother is an attorney and worked with a firm in the city. They have a nice house in the suburbs, and Erin had many friends in the neighborhood. With both of her parents working, she wished that they had more time together as a family, but she was proud of both of her parents and what they did for jobs. After school, they had a lady come in to take care of them, take them to their lessons, and supervise their homework and chores, and the lady stayed with them until one of her parents got home. Although they were busy, she and her sister both took dancing lessons, and they both played soccer, but since her sister was two years older than Erin, they did not play on the same team. As busy as her parents were, they almost always were able to come to their games and performances, and she was happy that they did.

Last year their father did not seem to be feeling well, and he was going to the doctor's quite a bit. One evening, her parents sat down with Erin and her sister, and they said that her father had gotten sick with cancer of the stomach and that he was going to be taking some time off work so that they could treat the cancer and hopefully make it better. Erin was not quite sure what all of this meant, but since everyone seemed so serious and worried, she thought it must be bad. Her father had surgery, and when that was done, he had to go to take some medicine that made him very sick and they called it "chemo."

After what seemed like a very long time, the chemo was over, and Erin's father started to gain weight, feel better, and seem more like himself; he even started going back to work for a few hours each week. Finally, it seemed like things were back to normal, and she was glad that everything seemed fine. Then one day, they sat down in the evening again, and her parents told them that the cancer was back and that since it had come back so strongly, they did not think that they would try the chemo again because it probably would not work, and it would just make her father sicker. When they said that, her sister asked if her father would ever get better, and their mother said, "No, we are afraid that there is nothing else that can be done." Although that was all that they said, she and her sister talked about it later, and her sister said that this meant that her father was going to die. Erin wanted to know when, but her sister did not know.

Over the next few months Erin's father kept getting weaker and sicker; he lost more weight; and eventually, he just stayed in bed all the time. Finally, they had to take him to the hospital because he was just too sick to keep at home. All of them would go up to the hospital to see her father every day after school and on weekends, and there were nice doctors and nurses who always talked to them about their school and sports. One day before they went to see their father, their mother sat down with them and told them that their father had died. They all cried and felt awful, and family members started coming to town because of the funeral (although Erin did not really know what that meant). After the funeral, people started leaving and going home, and Erin and her sister went back to school; all their teachers were very nice to them; they talked with the social worker a few times; their friends did not really know what to say, so no one said much about their dad. Erin really missed her father, and she cried when she thought about him. It also really upset her to see her mother so unhappy and worried. She tried to talk to her sister about her feelings and concerns, but her sister just did not want to talk about anything having to do with their father. Erin did not feel good much of the time, and she had missed quite a bit of school, and although people understood this, it was becoming somewhat of a problem, so it was suggested that Erin should talk to a psychologist about what was going on with her. She really did not want to talk to a stranger, but her mother convinced her to try it and see what she thought.

Psychodynamic Psychotherapy

Erin really did not want to just talk to anyone about her father, but when she met the lady psychologist, Dr. Cass (her sister called her the "shrink"),

Erin thought she was very nice, and other than saying that she was really sorry to hear about Erin's father, they did not talk about her father at all; in fact, they talked mostly about Erin, her school, her friends, and the things she liked to do.

Eventually, the psychologist did want to know more about Erin's mother as well as her sister, friends, teachers, and others in her life. She wanted to know what these people were like, how Erin felt about them, and the kinds of things that they did together. It became clear that Erin's father was the main male adult influence in Erin's life, and there really was not anyone else who filled even part of that role. Erin had one male teacher on her team, and a male soccer coach, but her uncles lived in another state, and she really did not know them very well anyway.

Erin and her psychologist talked about loss and what it meant when someone important to us dies or leaves us in other ways. Although this made Erin a little sad to talk about it, she was kind of glad that there was someone whom she could talk to about her father who did not get upset when she talked about him. Erin started realizing that a lot of what she had been feeling after her father's death was because she missed him, because she not only lost him but also lost a relationship—her father—and she also lost something else: her family was not the same as it used to be.

Erin and her psychologist spent quite a bit of time talking about how important Erin's father still was in her life and the ways that he still influenced her. They even talked about ways that Erin could remember him that was not just about sadness and loss. Her psychologist asked her what one of the things that Erin missed most about her father, and she said it was his stupid jokes. Therefore, it was suggested that Erin should write a book (just for herself) that had all the bad jokes that she could remember that her father had told her, and every time she remembered a new one, she would write it down. It was even suggested that Erin could go to the cemetery occasionally and take some flowers for her father but also take a joke that she could tell him there too.

Erin and her psychologist also talked about ways that Erin could reach out to other men in her family and her life and start to develop these relationships; this was not to replace her father but to remember him and to have others with whom she could relate and enjoy activities with just like if her father was there. Even though he was not there, this was just one more way that she could remember him and the things that they loved doing together.

As Erin started feeling better and was getting her life back to normal (i.e., a new normal), she did not need to see Dr. Cass often, and eventually they were able to end their visits. However, she told Erin than any time she wanted to come back and talk that, all she had to do was let her mother know, and they could make an appointment.

Behavioral Psychotherapy

When Erin went to her first appointment with her new psychologist, Dr. Thorndike, she did not know what he would be like, but he seemed to be a nice man. He told her he was sorry about her father and then asked her to tell him about herself and what kinds of things she liked to do. He had a cool office because there were lots of toys and books and other things for kids. He even told her that while they were talking, she could play with anything she wanted to in the office. She found a cute little pony, and she picked it up and held it for a while. Then she saw some Legos, and she started playing with them. While she was playing, the psychologist sat with her and even helped her with the Legos when she could not find the right piece. They also talked while they played, and they talked about her friends and family and all the things she liked to do.

For the next couple of visits, they mostly played with toys and talked while they did that. They started talking about how her life was different after her father died, and they also talked about some of the things that she liked to do with her father that she was not doing anymore. He then told her that they were going to make a list of things that she liked to do in the office and things that she liked to do at home or with her friends. They even set some goals about things that she would really like to do, such as go on vacation, go to movies, and visit her grandmother.

Each week at their visit, they would talk about things that Erin wanted or needed to do but had not be able to do them since her father died. They would pick one thing like having one of her friends come over to play and have a sleepover. She loved to do that but just had not done it since her father died. If she was able to accomplish that goal, she would get to pick whatever toy she wanted to play with at the psychologist's office that week. If she did not accomplish her goal, then they would just have some quiet time and read or talk, both of which things she also liked to do.

The psychologist talked with Erin's mother, and they agreed to have several big goals that would be recognition of how well she was doing, and after having five weeks in a row where she accomplished her goals, she would get to have a visit with her grandmother. They had a few of these kinds of things that Erin could work for, and when they had finished her therapy, her mother agreed that she would take both girls to Disney World (which they had planned to do anyway, but now it was going to be in recognition of the hard work that Erin would do).

One week, the psychologist asked Erin if she liked playing games with him, and she was pleased to tell him how much she liked working and playing in his office. He then pointed out that even though he was not related to her at all, she could have fun doing things with a man who was not her father, and that would be another way of remembering her father and not missing him so much. She did not realize that he was helping her learn to have fun with other people, including men, and that she was going to "generalize" this learning to other social situations where she could be more comfortable and have more fun.

Although it seemed mostly like playing games and having fun, Erin would later understand that what her psychologist had done was to "condition" her to learn new ways to deal with social situations that allowed her to enjoy doing things that she used to enjoy with her father but to also be able to remember him and feel good about what she was learning to do. She was also finding new ways to start to live a more normal life and not feel so sad all the time. None of this made her miss her father any less, nor did it make it okay that he was no longer there, but she felt that her father would have wanted her to be happy and to enjoy her life, and this was her way of remembering him.

Case 7: Adjustment Disorder with Depression

Mary is a 35-year-old woman and was a beautician, who worked primarily as a hairdresser and rented a space in a large salon where she was one of seven women who worked there. Most of the women worked part-time, and almost all of them had school-aged children. Although Mary was married, she and her husband had been separated for three years, and it did not look likely that they would reconcile; he had a new girlfriend, and Mary heard that they were very happy together and getting out socially. Since it sounded like her ex-husband and his new girlfriend were often seen at the same places where he and Mary had gone, she really did not want to bump into them socially, so she did not go out much. She had a couple of dates but nothing serious and nothing that she was interested in pursuing.

Since Mary and her husband had never had children (by his choice primarily), she lived alone with two cats. She did not go out very often with friends and usually just went to work and then came home, did chores, and watched TV until it was time to go to bed. She usually worked six days per week, and since she really did not have anything else to do, she felt that she might as well work and make some money. She was not careful about her nutrition, and so she would eat fast food or frozen dinners or just not eat at all. However, between the junk food, sodas, potato chips, and lack of exercise, she had gained some weight and was now finding it difficult to fit into her clothes. On her days off, she usually slept in and might even stay in bed most of the day. She was not a big drinker and might have a couple of drinks with her friends when she went out, but that was not often. She did smoke cigarettes and smoked marijuana; she felt that the pot was the only thing that helped her to sleep, so she smoked almost every evening.

At Mary's last doctor's appointment, for her annual physical, she got the lecture about her weight and smoking, but she had expected that. However, she did not expect that she would be given a depression screening test, but she took it; she knew that she was not depressed, but who could blame her for not being in a good mood. Her doctor told her that she had scored in the moderately depressed range on the screening test and that he recommended that she start taking an antidepressant that he would prescribe. Mary was surprised because she did not think that she felt depressed, but she did not want to disagree with her doctor, so she agreed to try the medication. He also told her that she had to stop smoking pot, that they needed to stabilize her sleep pattern, and that the antidepressant would help with that, but the pot was becoming a problem and was not going to help her feel better.

Mary started taking the antidepressant, and she even stopped smoking pot; she felt that she would probably start that up again in the future but would cooperate with the doctor's advice for now. Although she did not notice much difference for a while, after about a month she could see that she was more physically active and did not stay in bed as much when she was not working. However, she still did not feel much better, and the things that bothered her were still annoying her, so the pills helped but they really did not fix anything. When she told this to her doctor, he suggested that she continue taking the antidepressant but that he wanted her to make an appointment with a psychologist, and he gave her several names of people he thought could help her.

Humanistic Psychotherapy

Mary was not happy about making an appointment with a psychologist; they would just want to talk about her failed marriage, nag her about being healthy, and lecture her about her lifestyle choices. When she met the therapist, Dr. Esalen, she seemed pleasant and was interested in Mary's history and some of the things she was doing. For example, she wanted to know a lot about why Mary had chosen her profession, how she had been trained, and what her job was like. She did ask about her marriage and a little bit about her estranged husband but did not spend much time on that.

Dr. Esalen was interested in how Mary felt and how she spent her time. They also talked quite a bit about Mary's family and her friends and what they were like. One of the things that surprised Mary was how much time they spent in the therapy sessions talking about Mary's values and goals and the things that were important to her personally, professionally, and socially. After a few sessions talking about these issues, the therapist pointed out that using Mary's own description of what kinds of things were important to her and how she spent her time, it was obvious that Mary spent most of her time on things that were not what she said were the most important elements of her life. When she asked Mary what she thought were the best things about her as a person, Mary was embarrassed to have to tell her that she really could not thing of anything positive that she could say about herself.

Mary's therapist suggested that Mary had more positive things about her than she was aware of, and they needed to explore that further. The therapist then said that there were several positive things that she saw in Mary even after only knowing her for a short time. Mary was surprised at how well the therapist seemed to know Mary, and the things that she pointed out were those that Mary could see but just did not feel like they were that important. Dr. Esalen then suggested that Mary pick a couple of people that she really trusted and ask to talk to them. She would tell them that Mary had an assignment from her therapist to find out what kinds of things others thought about her. She asked them to name three things that were her best qualities and three things they think she could improve.

At their next session, Mary's therapist pointed out some of the similarities of things that her friends (and the therapist) said were her best qualities; if more than one person saw these things, then they must be real. They also took the things that she listed as "needs for improvement"; the therapist asked if Mary agreed with these things, and she did, and then these became therapeutic goals—things that she could work on to improve even more.

As therapy progressed, Mary gained even more trust and respect for her therapist, whom she believed really valued Mary as a person. She could also see some of the positive qualities that others could see in her, and she now looked at her "faults" as targets for improvement and things to work on. After several months of working on these issues, Mary was clearly feeling better and was more physically and socially active. Since one of her goals was to be more physically active and healthier, she had started working out and even joined a kickboxing group with one of her friends. She stopped smoking and had even started eating healthier and losing weight. Her therapist pointed out that now that her thoughts and actions were more consistent with her ideal self-image (what she really wanted to be like), she would be healthier, happier, and a person she could be proud of.

Cognitive Psychotherapy

When Mary had her first appointment with her psychotherapist, Dr. Ellis, he asked her quite a few questions about her background and history, what was going on with her life, her reasons for getting into psychotherapy, and what her goals were for treatment. He took some notes, but mainly he just listened and asked some questions to clarify issues. He was interested in the fact that Mary had not been treated for depression before although she did admit to having several periods in her life when some difficult things happened and she got a little "down in the dumps," but it never lasted long, and she usually just came out of it. The therapist asked her why she was still not feeling great and had been down for quite a while. She thought about it and said she thought her current state of mind started when she and her husband started talking about separating. They seemed to have a good marriage at the beginning, but as time progressed it was clear that they were both a little unhappy with the marriage, and it did not seem like things were getting any better. Thus, they decided to try a separation and see if the distance might give them some time to think about things and hopefully try to get back together. Unfortunately, it was becoming even more clear that her husband was not interested in getting back together; he had a new girlfriend, and he still was not interested in having kids, which was important to Mary.

The therapist said that he was sorry that the marriage seemed to be heading for divorce and asked how Mary felt about that. She said that she was sorry and had hoped that they would reconcile, but it was past the point where this seemed realistic. When asked about why the marriage failed, she gave the "usual" answers: they had grown apart; they had different interests; they just did not love each other as they had earlier; and so on. When pushed for more specific reasons, Mary started to tear up and said that she felt she was the reason why the marriage did not work out. She believed that her husband felt that she was not pretty enough, was not successful enough, was not as "sexy" as he wanted, was overweight, and did not do many things outside of work that he liked to do (ride snowmobiles, go to bars, hang out with his friends), and he just did not seem to like or respect her. The therapist asked if she thought that if she fixed all those things he would want to come back to her; she said that it was probably too late and that he was no longer interested in being with her.

The therapist also asked Mary why she did not do more with her own friends, and she said that they were too busy and that they usually did not want to get together with Mary anyway—or at least that is what she believed. He asked why she was not working with a nutritionist and going to the gym to feel better about herself and to be healthier—she said it would not make much difference anyway so why bother. When asked why she smoked pot so much, she said it was the only thing that made her feel better and it was the only way that she could fall asleep.

After discussing these issues, Mary's therapist pointed out to her that the real problem was that Mary was basing her life on some dysfunctional beliefs that were keeping her unhappy and preventing her from getting better and having a more normal life. She was not sure what that meant, but he pointed out to her that she seemed to think that the marriage failing was entirely because of her inadequacies, but that her husband was at least as responsible as she was, and even when she tried to get him to go to counseling to try to help the relationship, he was not interested—it could not be only Mary's fault that the marriage had problems. He also pointed out that she had no way to know if her friends would be interested in doing things with her because she never called them and because she always said "no" when they called her; they stopped calling. He also suggested that if she would work with a nutritionist and started exercising, she would find out quickly that she would feel better, look better, and be healthier—her belief that it would not make a difference was a dysfunctional belief that simply allowed her to stay depressed. He also said that with exercise and improved sleep hygiene, she probably would not need pot to sleep and she should start eliminating that from her life as well.

Working with these beliefs, replacing them with more realistic and healthier ideas, and starting to act in ways more consistent with these new and healthier ways of thinking, it was not long before Mary started feeling better, started being more socially and physically active, and could see that a new and healthier lifestyle was starting to emerge. It took a few months to make much headway with these new approaches, but finally, Mary started feeling more positive and even looking forward to the future and her new life. She still felt badly about the loss of her marriage, but she no longer felt that it was solely her fault. They had grown apart, and perhaps they should never have gotten married to begin with, but she really hoped that they would both find happiness and new lives that would be better and healthier than their lives together had been.

Case 8: Personality Disorder

Marjorie was having problems; as a 29-year-old woman with two marriages and two divorces behind her, and two sons aged four and six both of whom lived with their fathers, she felt her life was a disaster, and most of her problems were caused by people like her ex-husbands who did everything they could to make her life miserable. She had graduated from high school and tried to go to college, but the parties and social life were more than she could resist; going to class and doing homework were not typically part of her routine, and so after two semesters of poor grades, the school suspended her for a year, but she never tried to go back.

Marjorie had a history of working in fast-food and retail jobs but had never had a job she felt was worthy of her; usually she did not last long on the jobs she found because either they let her go, or she quit because she hated the job and/or the people she worked with. Since she was not working and really had no way of supporting herself, she had applied for social services and was able to get food stamps, Medicaid for health care, and a small monthly welfare check that did not give her enough money to have a car or a good apartment. She smoked cigarettes and drank soda and wine, and this took up much of her money just to support her habits.

Marjorie's parents lived locally, as did her two brothers and one sister. She thought that her family had been pretty normal, with both parents working at decent jobs and her brothers and sister getting into some trouble but nothing serious; they had all done well in high school and had gone on to college: one brother completed a two-year degree; the other brother dropped out of college when he got a good job; and her sister went to college for four years, got a degree, and was working as a paralegal. Both of her brothers were married with children, and her sister was engaged. Marjorie saw her family on holidays, but she did not have much contact with them on a regular basis. She had always felt like the black sheep of the family and always felt her siblings looked down on her as a failure; her parents were so disappointed with her that they had even stopped asking how she was doing.

After Marjorie's doctor had tried to help her with antidepressant medication, she had suggested that Marjorie needed to start working with a psychotherapist to help get her life back on track. Although she agreed to do this, Marjorie felt therapy was a waste of time because most of her problems were because of other people and therapy could not fix them.

Existential Psychotherapy

Marjorie expected that therapy would largely amount to someone telling her to get a job, stop smoking and drinking, get out socially, and quit whining. Therefore, she was a little surprised when her therapist (Dr. Frank) was interested in what Marjorie thought were her problems and even listened carefully when Marjorie complained about the people in her life who were creating problems for her. Her therapist seemed concerned and interested in the problems that Marjorie faced and was even sympathetic about her concerns with other people.

After a few sessions with Marjorie talking about her history, her problems, her disappointments, and the people in her life who had treated her badly, her therapist asked Marjorie what she really wanted out of life and who she truly wanted to become. This sounded simple until she started thinking about it, and it was upsetting when she realized that she not only could not come up with any clear objectives or goals for her life but also could not even imagine "who" she might ever become. Dr. Frank noted that Marjorie had felt depressed at times, frequently felt anxious, was often angry at others, was drinking more than she should, and was simply not happy about anything in her life. Her therapist then took her back through her life and looked at some of the decisions that she had made, and she felt that most of the decisions she had made had been bad ones because they did not turn out as she hoped.

Her therapist then had her examine some of the decisions that she had made and looked at why they did not work out and why she had made the decisions that she had. Interestingly, most of her bad decisions had been made because of the expectations or pressures from other people. Dr. Frank then pointed out that decisions made to please others should not be expected to work out well for the decision maker.

After examining some of the decisions she had made in the past, the therapist also pointed out that many times her bad decisions resulted in less-than-optimal outcomes because of what other people had done. She also pointed out that even though Marjorie had often made decisions because of the influence of others, the decision was still the responsibility of Marjorie. At first, she felt that the therapist was blaming her, but then she explained that if Marjorie was responsible for making bad decisions, she could also be responsible for making good ones. They then focused on what kinds of changes Marjorie wanted to see in her life and then work toward making decisions to help reach those outcomes and act in ways to help the decisions to make a positive difference. As therapy progressed, Marjorie started feeling more in control of her life and less depressed and anxious and even looking forward to the future.

Cognitive-Behavioral Psychotherapy

Marjorie went to her first appointment with her therapist, Dr. Beck, and he was interested in the problems that she had experienced and wanted to know what her goals were for treatment and what she expected to get out of it. Although she had not thought much about it, she knew that she wanted to feel better, she wanted to feel more loved and accepted by others, and she wanted to be able to support herself and have a better life. They went over the history of her difficulties and some of the issues she had faced. He asked her if she had been told what her diagnosis was, and she said that people had told her that she was depressed and anxious, and a couple of people had told her that she was "borderline." She did not really know what this meant, but the therapist explained that this meant that she had a personality disorder that was often associated with people who had problems with relationships, who had difficulties controlling their emotions, who made the same mistakes repeatedly, and who were often impulsive and made poor decisions. Marjorie had to admit that this did sound like what she had been dealing with.

Marjorie's therapist then told her that the reason that this diagnosis was important to know was that there was a type of cognitive behavioral therapy that had been helpful with people who suffered from borderline personality disorder; this type of therapy was called dialectical behavior therapy, and he thought that might be helpful for Marjorie. He said there would be two different parts of the therapy that he would recommend for her; the first was a group that would meet once per week to discuss their lives, what they were trying to do differently, and how they might even do better. The other part would be individual treatment where Marjorie would meet individually with the therapist (also once per week), and they would start working on ways that Marjorie could become more effective in dealing with others as well as dealing better with her own emotions and impulses.

There were four elements to the treatment, and Marjorie and her therapist started off with the part on mindfulness. This was designed to help Marjorie be more aware of her experience, her feelings and thoughts, and what was going on in her own mind. The goal was to become more mindful and accepting of her thoughts, feelings, and inner life. As they got better at that, they then started to learn ways to deal more effectively with others and to enjoy and appreciate others even more. This is where the group treatment became even more important. The next thing they worked on was called "distress tolerance," and this involved not only being more aware of her feelings but also learning to confront her feelings and situations she could not control without having to avoid or minimize them (e.g., drinking alcohol to numb her feelings). Finally, and this was the hardest part, she was learning how to accept but also regulate her emotions so that they did not get so far out of control that she could not act in ways that would be most helpful and functional. This took a lot of practice, and once again, this was an area where the group treatment was even more helpful.

As Marjorie got more confident in her ability to manage herself and her feelings and behavior more effectively, the next thing that she started doing on a gradual basis was to take these new skills and start working on them in her "normal" environment and with the people in her life that she needed to deal with. This was even harder because other people did not expect her to act differently, and so this took some getting used to on their part as well. As Dr. Beck frequently pointed out to her, the most important part of therapy is what the patient does to make their life different and better *outside* of the office.

Case 9: Marital Difficulties

Kevin and Julie have been married for six years, and the past few have been difficult for both of them. Kevin is 31 and Julie is 28, and they do not have any children. They had always talked about having a family, but it just did not seem like it was ever the right time, and since the past couple of years had been problematic, the subject of children had not even been raised. Julie worked as an office manager in a small insurance office, and she liked her job and her coworkers although the job did not pay what she thought she should be earning. Kevin was a mechanic and had a good job working for a local car dealer, and he did have a good salary and benefits. They moved into their home three years ago and had to take out a mortgage to afford it.

Kevin and Julie had met at a party at one of their friend's houses, and they seemed to get along well, so they decided to start dating; after a few months they decided to save money and move into an apartment together, so they picked out one that was big enough for both of them but also within their budget. After living together for about 18 months, they decided to buy a house and start planning for a family.

As time passed, it seemed Kevin and Julie just did not have much time together, and they could both feel that they were drifting apart. They were still intimate, but the frequency of their lovemaking had declined significantly, and now it seemed like they rarely made love. Kevin did belong to a bowling league that met once a week, and he was also a volunteer firefighter that also took up some of his time. Julie would go with Kevin occasionally to firehouse functions but really did not care about bowling, and none of the other wives got involved with that either. Julie's social life usually involved going out with her girlfriends, going shopping with her mother, or visiting her parents across town.

Kevin was becoming frustrated with the lack of intimacy in their relationship and suspected that Julie was having an affair. While it was true that Julie would sometimes go out with her work colleagues, which also included a couple of men, she was not interested in cheating on Kevin, and she did not want to complicate her relationships at work; other than some "harmless" flirting, she did not have anything to do with other men. Kevin had been tempted to go out on Julie, and there were a few women in the fire department that he thought were interested in him, but he saw more problems than benefits in an affair with someone he needed to work with.

Julie confided in a couple of her friends as to what was going on in her marriage, and they were supportive. Of course, they wanted to know if Kevin was having an affair and if he had been abusive and wondered if he was drinking or drugging. Julie told them that she did not think he was having an affair but was not sure; she denied that Kevin had ever hit or threatened her; and she said that other than a few beers with his friends at bowling or in the firehouse, she did not think he was drinking that much, and she knew that he was opposed to drugs. One of her friends mentioned that she and her husband had also had some problems, that they went to a psychologist who specialized in working with couples, and that it had really helped them and probably saved their marriage. Julie got the contact information and went home to tell Kevin that she thought this might help. At first, Kevin was upset and said that he had no intention in sitting down with a "shrink" who would just blame him for everything and not do any good anyway. Julie pointed out that if things did not improve between the two of them it was not likely that the marriage would last much longer, and if he was interested in staying together, then this was something that they needed to try. With the understanding that if he did not like it, he could drop out of the therapy if he wanted to, they called the psychologist and decided to give it a try.

Marital Therapy (Cognitive-Behavioral)

At Kevin and Julie's first appointment, the therapist, Dr. Satir, asked them to tell her about their relationship and what kinds of concerns had brought them into therapy. She then asked each of them what they hoped and expected to get out of therapy and then had them agree on some goals that they both concurred with. She then set up individual appointments with each of the couple so that they could get into more depth about their histories, problems, and perceptions of the difficulties in the marriage.

After meeting with Kevin and Julie separately once, the therapist met again with the couple, and they spent the next few sessions discussing their concerns about the relationship and some of the things that they felt needed to change. After each session, the therapist gave them "homework" assignments that involved doing things together and individually that would help them start to build new patterns and ways of dealing with each other. She told them after one session that they were to come back the next time having thought about what each of them could do differently to help improve the relationship. She explained that most couples approached their problems by making "lists" of things that were wrong with the other person, but if they really wanted things to get better, they each needed to be looking at what they could and would do differently to help improve the relationship.

Another week, the therapist gave them the assignment that every other day they needed to spend 20 minutes "listening" to each other. What they were to do was that each of them would talk for 10 minutes about how they felt, what was going on with them, and what was important to them, and so on. The other person was not to talk, interrupt, answer questions or anything but just listen. Then the other person would do the same thing, but they were not to answer the points the other had made but just to talk about themselves and how they were feeling and thinking about. The next time they would do the same thing, but they would reverse the order as to who spoke first.

The couple would continue to work on communication and clarification issues, and Kevin and Julie were also told to spend time together just enjoying doing things—not solving problems or discussing issues but just doing things like having dinner together and going to movies. After working on these types of things, they would then come to therapy and have a frank discussion about how things were going, whether they felt like progress was being made and how they were progressing with their goals. The goals would be reexamined to determine if they were still important and agreed on. If it seemed like they were on the right track, then they would start tapering off sessions and working toward termination of treatment. If it looked like their goals had changed, then new goals would be established and agreed on, and treatment would proceed (or end) based on the new expectations.

Marital Therapy (Humanistic)

Kevin and Julie went to their appointment with the new therapist, Dr. Gestalt, and found him to be pleasant and easy to talk to. He asked a few questions but mainly seemed interested in listening to them and getting to know them. Toward the end of the first session, he did ask them about why they had made the appointment and what they hoped to get out of therapy. After clarifying their goals and expectations, he made an appointment to see them in about a week and suggested that they not argue about issues at home but just take care of routine tasks and save their discussions for in therapy.

The next time Kevin and Julie and the therapist met, the therapist had each of them explain what their concerns were for the relationship and how these issues made them feel. He also asked them to describe their concerns and feelings by talking directly to their spouse and let the therapist just be "a fly on the wall." Occasionally, the therapist would ask questions to help focus the discussion or clarify some issues that came up. He also asked them to talk about how they would change the relationship if they could to make it better and more rewarding.

As sessions progressed, the therapist had Julie and Kevin talk more directly with one another about their concerns and feelings and to discuss how they might be able to more effectively meet their own needs and respond to the issues brought up by their spouse. The therapist emphasized how important it was to be clear and honest about their feelings and concerns but to also be respectful of the thoughts and feelings of the other person and to remember that each of them had the right to their own ideas and feelings, and when you loved someone you must allow them to be honest and be themselves and to treat each other with respect and love.

The next phase of treatment involved discussions about love, what it meant, how it felt, and if they still felt love for one another. This also involved discussions about whether love would be enough to save this relationship and, if not, what else needed to be dealt with. These discussions continued until both parties came to the realization that they truly did love one another and that they were both willing to make changes to help save and improve the relationship. As things started getting better between the two of them, and they were both committed to staying together and pursuing a future as a couple, they began tapering down the visits and ultimately terminated treatment.

Case 10: Attention Deficit Hyperactivity Disorder (ADHD)

Billy is an eight-year-old boy who has had problems in school since preschool, and his teachers have told Billy's parents that they thought something was wrong and that Billy needed to be evaluated. The parents initially resisted this idea and just felt that Billy was an active child with a lot of energy. Billy's pediatrician told the parents that Billy did meet many of the criteria for ADHD and that they might want to try him on some medication, but the parents did not like the idea of medication for their little boy, and since his older brother and younger sister did not have any of these difficulties, the parents wanted to wait before actually trying treatment for Billy. However, complaints about Billy's behavior became more frequent and came from more sources, and many of Billy's friends were not allowed to have Billy over to play because he was so hard to manage. Finally, his parents agreed to let Billy's pediatrician try some medication, but the doctor told the parents that he would prescribe medication with the understanding that they would also make an appointment with a psychologist who specialized in ADHD, and they called and made an appointment for a consultation.

ADHD is a condition usually first diagnosed in childhood although it may be diagnosed later and even in adulthood. However, when people are diagnosed later, it is usually clear that they have suffered from this condition since childhood, but it simply was not diagnosed. This condition involves both hyperactive-impulsive behavior and problems with attention and concentration. Since many youngsters, especially boys, can be very active and impulsive, it is sometimes hard to tell the difference between a normal active child and one with ADHD. It is also true that there are some children who have the attention deficit part without the hyperactive part, and this is called attention deficit disorder.

Attention deficit hyperactivity disorder is a somewhat controversial diagnostic category because it is hard to diagnose in many instances, and treatment usually involved both medication and psychotherapy; many parents feel strongly that they do not want their child labeled and put on medication for what they feel is perfectly normal behavior. It is also frequently the case where a child is diagnosed with ADHD and put on medication but not involved with psychotherapy. This is one of those condition where medication alone is not appropriate treatment, and the psychotherapy part is also important. Children with this condition usually have problems in a variety of situations, including home, school, socially, and with peers, and thus, they usually feel different from others, have poor self-esteem, are attention seeking, and are frequently in trouble with authority figures. While medication can be beneficial for many youngsters with this condition, it only suppresses the symptoms and does not help the child learn new ways to deal with situations and other people, nor does the medication help them work on their self-image and self-control.

Children with ADHD are usually hard to manage, do not follow directions well, do not pay attention, forget things easily, do not like structure or rules, and are impulsive and sometimes aggressive as well. When dealing with a child like this in psychotherapy, the usual strategy is to focus on active kinds of things like interactive games, role-playing, and physical challenges (e.g., exercise and balance activities). As the child starts to make progress, more cognitive and learning activities are incorporated into the therapy. Usually, there is a parental counseling/family therapy component part of psychotherapy as well. Not only does the child have to learn to do things differently, but the family must learn to interact with the child differently as well. Often parents will blame themselves for not doing a better job of raising the ADHD child, but it is usually the case that the family will have other children who do not have ADHD, so the message to parents is that if it were simply a parenting issue, all of their children would have the same problem. Therefore, what is clear is that the ADHD child does not and will not respond to the same parenting techniques as the other children will, and while this makes parenting more complicated, it is also necessary if progress is to be made.

Existential Psychotherapy

For their first appointment, Billy and his parents met with the psychologist, Dr. Camus, who spent some time asking questions and getting to know them better. She then asked the parents why they had made the appointment, and they reported that Billy seemed to get into trouble very frequently, was not doing well in school, and had been diagnosed with ADHD by his pediatrician and that they needed help in knowing how to deal with Billy more effectively. When the therapist asked Billy why he thought that they had made the appointment, he said that the doctor told them to because he was having problems at school. She asked him if he agreed that he was having problems at school, and he said that his teachers were kind of mean and yelled at him a lot. She also asked if he thought that he got into trouble more than others in his class, and he reluctantly admitted that he did get into trouble more frequently. On further questioning, it became clear that Billy was having trouble not only at school but at home, at friends' houses, and other places as well. His therapist then suggested that she and Billy get together a few times and then they would meet again with his parents.

When Billy came for his first appointment alone, Dr. Camus welcomed him into the office and asked him how things were going, and he replied that not much had changed. When asked about the medication, he said that he could not tell a difference, but when pressed, he did say that he was not getting into trouble as much at school. She asked him how it made him feel when he got into trouble, and he said that it made him mad but also kind of sad because he really did not want to get into trouble. She then asked him to draw a picture of his family, and he drew his parents and his brother and sister, and then he drew a picture of himself over to the side of the page. She asked why he was over to the side, and he was not able to explain why, but that is where he thought he should be. Then his therapist asked him to tell her what the best things were about every member of the family and then tell her what some of the things about his family members were that he did not like. Finally, she asked him to say what he thought were the best things about him, and he had trouble thinking of good things, but with some encouragement, he said that he was a fast runner, that he liked animals, that he was nice (most of the time), and that he liked sports (although he did not excel in them and was not able to be on any teams). When asked what he did not like about himself, he had no trouble coming up with things that were wrong with him, and he listed the following: being dumb, not having many friends, being short and skinny, being messy, people thought he was bad, and he could not really do anything very well.

The existential therapist then spent time helping Billy learn more about himself, his strengths and weaknesses, and tried to help him think differently about himself and how he dealt with other people. She also worked with his parents to help them find ways to talk to and reprimand Billy that were not as negative and judgmental. Dr. Camus did explain why rules were important and why structure was important for children and especially those with ADHD. She also helped Billy learn about and understand boundaries and why it is important to respect others' boundaries and develop his own boundaries as well. The final part of his therapy involved his starting to work on making better decisions, taking responsibility for his actions including his successes and failures, and how to build on these decisions and consequences to be happier and get along better with other people. As he started making improvements, his parents were managing him more effectively, and he was getting into trouble much less frequently, they started tapering off the sessions and finally terminated treatment with the understanding that they could come back at any time for additional help.

Behavioral Psychotherapy

When Billy and his parents first met with Dr. Tolman, the new therapist, he was nice and wanted to know more about them and what brought them into treatment. Billy's parents said that they were concerned that Billy seemed to get into trouble a lot and in many different situations and that he was frequently punished and rarely seemed happy or content. Billy just said that he came because his parents said he had to, and he did not think there was really anything wrong but that people just seemed to be meaner to him than his siblings and classmates. The therapist then wanted to know what they wanted to accomplish with therapy, and his parents said that they wanted Billy to be happy, do better in school, and get into trouble less frequently. When asked, Billy said that these goals were okay with him and that he agreed with them.

The therapist then suggested an approach where he would meet with Billy individually for two sessions and then meet with the parents to discuss strategies. From that point forward, most of the treatment would involve meeting with Billy alone and then meeting with the parents occasionally to update them and to discuss strategies for dealing with Billy at home. He also asked for permission to talk with Billy's teacher and counselor at school so he could update them and give them suggestions as well.

When he met with Billy, they played several different games that Billy enjoyed, but all involved activities that required attention and concentration and depended on Billy following directions and behaving in certain ways. The therapist also got a weekly report from the parents and the school regarding Billy's behavior and any problems that they were having. He also had Billy make a list of things and activities that he liked, and these ranged from pieces of candy to a new bike, going swimming, playing video games, going fishing with his father, going hiking, and playing with friends.

As the therapist was helping Billy learn how to focus and pay attention better, and to be less impulsive in the therapy activities Billy would earn points that they kept on a chart, and they also used the chart to keep track of how Billy was doing at home and school as well. When he met his weekly behavioral goals in therapy and in the other sessions, Billy would get to choose a treat or activity that he would get to have for meeting his goals. The therapist was also working with Billy's parents to teach them how to structure his activities, to be clear in their expectations, and to be consistent in their consequences. Although his weekly "prizes" were not very big, it was one way to help Billy understand the relationship between his behavior and the consequences he received.

As Billy and his parents were doing better with the challenges they were confronting, the therapy was tapered off and eventually terminated with the understanding that they would check in with the therapist occasionally and if they needed some refresher sessions that would be included as part of the treatment as well.

Case 11: School Phobia

Occasionally, most schools will face a problem where a child will not/cannot go to school. This is usually first seen in grade school but can affect youngsters of any age. Sometimes this is because of bullying or some traumatic event at school, but other times it may simply be an intense fear that no one seems to understand or know why it emerged. Since this is an anxiety-based, intense, and irrational fear, it is usually called school phobia and can be debilitating and seriously impair a child's education and social development.

Sally is a shy and quiet youngster, who has never been a behavioral problem but has usually had fears and anxiety about things and seemed to worry more than her siblings or peers. When she started in preschool, she would get so upset when her mother dropped her off at school and left her that frequently the school would call her mother and insist that she come and pick Sally up because she was so upset it was a distraction for all of the other children and it was upsetting them as well. After this happened several times, Sally's parents finally decided that she was not ready for preschool and would just take her out of it. When they tried it again the next year, the same thing happened, and they took her out of preschool again.

The following year, Sally was supposed to start kindergarten, and she had been much better with babysitters although she would never go to sleep until her parents came home, so they never stayed out very late. When they first went to school to look at it and meet her teacher, Sally's parents were clear about the fact that Sally had to go to school, and it was required by law; they also told her it was only for a few hours since it was a half-day kindergarten. Although she usually cried when her mother or father dropped her off at school and walked her to the door, she usually quieted down and was able to stay in class until she was picked up before lunch.

When Sally started first grade, the problem became much more severe. First, the school day was a whole day with lunch at school; second, the classes were bigger; third, the children were more active and louder. Sally hated going to school and had a major tantrum each time her parents took her. When they dropped her at the school and walked her to the door, Sally would not stay with the teacher and chased her parents; when school personnel restrained her to allow the parents to leave, Sally would sometimes break away and chase her parents' car down the street. Finally, the school said that they did not have the resources to keep Sally safe at school and letting her stay sobbing and screaming in the nurse's office did not seem like a reasonable strategy either. Sally was taken out of school and referred to her PCP, who referred Sally and her parents to a psychologist to help with the problem.

Cognitive Psychotherapy

While cognitive therapy typically deals with thoughts, ideas, beliefs, perceptions, and so on, this is not easy to do with children who often respond more to active therapies than "talk" therapy. However, when Sally and her parents went to their first appointment, the therapist, Dr. Seeley, was friendly and welcomed them into his office. He talked with them for a few minutes and then asked why they had called for an appointment, and the parents told him that Sally was so afraid to go to school that it was impossible for her to go and stay at school without getting terribly upset. The therapist looked at Sally and told her that he understood how scary that must be and that he was not just going to talk her into going to school but that they were going to find some ways to help make it less scary, and he promised that they would not do anything that would frighten or upset her. He then asked Sally if he could talk to her alone for a few minutes and her parents would be right outside the door and would come back in as soon as Sally wanted them to. She reluctantly agreed, and her parents went outside.

While Sally was obviously not comfortable with this situation, the therapist asked her if she would like to see pictures of his dogs, and she said that she did. He got out some pictures of his cute little dogs and showed them to her. She wanted to know their names and asked questions about them. After a few minutes, the therapist asked her if she was feeling scared and she said, "no." He then said that all people get scared when they do not know what is going to happen to them, but sometimes they find that what happens is not as scary as they thought it would be. He then asked if it was okay to have her parents come back in the room, and she agreed. When they came back in, he said that he would like them to contact the school and ask permission to have Sally's school work brought to their house and have an in-home teacher come by a couple of times a week to keep Sally up to date with her school work. He then asked Sally if that was okay with her, and she said it was. He also said that the goal was to help Sally get back to school with her friends, but they would take their time and make sure she was ready to go back.

Dr. Seeley started off his treatment of Sally with short weekly sessions and gradually got to having weekly 45-minute appointments with her. They played games but also talked about some of the things that Sally was frightened of at school. As they identified and clarified the fears, it became obvious, even to Sally, that many of her fears were never going to happen. For example, one fear was that her parents would drop her off and never come back to get her—that would never happen. She was also afraid that someone at school would hurt her. They then discussed all the things that she could do to keep herself safe and all the things that the school did to keep all the children safe. She was also afraid that children would make fun of her, but they talked about the fact that this fear was not based on anything that had ever happened, but they also talked about what she could do if it did happen. The goal was to reduce her fears to ideas, perceptions, and beliefs and then show either how these things would never happen or, if they did, that Sally had ways to deal with it.

As Sally started feeling more secure about school, they arranged for her to visit the school for a few minutes, just to see how it felt, and the therapist used their weekly session to come to school with her and her mother. Much to Sally's surprise, when she got to school, several of her friends saw her and ran up to her excited to see her and anxious to find out when she would be coming back. After a few visits and a week's worth of half-days, Sally was finally ready to get back to school, and she kept her weekly appointments with her therapist for a month after starting back to school just to make sure that everything was working well. With Sally back to school and performing well, her therapy visits were terminated.

Cognitive-Behavioral Psychotherapy

When Sally and her parents came into the waiting room at their new psychologist's office, Sally was nervous because she did not know what to expect. After a few minutes, a door opened, and a young woman came into the room and introduced herself as Dr. Smith and shook everyone's hand. She seemed nice, and Sally went with her parents into Dr. Smith's office. When they sat down, Dr. Smith explained that she was a psychologist and that Sally's regular doctor had suggested that Sally needed some help getting to school. Dr. Smith asked the parents first to describe the problem, and then she asked Sally why she thought that it was so hard for her to go to school. Sally felt nervous because she did not know how to answer the question, and she just sat there. Dr. Smith smiled warmly and said, "That was a little unfair; if you knew what the problem was you would have already figured it out." Sally felt relieved and smiled. Her psychologist went on to explain that she was going to work with Sally and her parents to find ways to make going to school easier and more fun. She also explained that she was not going to ask Sally to do anything that she did not feel she could do. Dr. Smith said that they would take it nice and easy and have some fun learning new ways to do things.

At their next meeting Dr. Smith asked Sally about what she had done the past week and how her school work was coming. They talked for a while, and then Dr. Smith asked Sally what was so bad about going to school, but all Sally could think of was that it was scary and when she went, she got upset. Then Dr. Smith told Sally to use her imagination and think of going to school and doing something fun. At first this was hard, but Sally could do this, and Dr. Smith pointed out that by just thinking about school and imagining something fun, it was not nearly as scary. They then went on to play some games and talk about friends and family.

Each week Dr. Smith had Sally imagine more things about going to school but also had her doing fun things while she was thinking about it. After a while it became much easier to think about school. Then Dr. Smith and Sally got into Sally's car, with either her mother or father driving, and they would just drive around the neighborhood for a few minutes. Next, they drove to the part of town where the school was, and Sally tried to think about fun things she liked to do. Each week they would drive closer to school, and each time they would go only as far as Sally felt that she could, but she was getting more confident and not as scared. Gradually, they visited the school and started going to school for a few minutes each day, and each week they stayed longer until Sally was able to stay at school for a half-day and then a full day. Dr. Smith did not need to go with Sally to school at this point, but one of her parents would take her. Sally continued to see her psychologist, who helped her learn new ways to deal with situations that used to make her scared. Finally, she was back to school in her own classroom on a full-time basis, and she was able to say goodbye to Dr. Smith because Sally could now do this on her own.

Case 12: Post-Traumatic Stress Disorder (PTSD)

Post-traumatic stress disorder (PTSD) has been called many things over the years but became recognized as a legitimate mental health condition in the 1970s. At first, this condition was recognized in combat soldiers, but it quickly became obvious that anyone who experienced serious trauma was at risk for developing PTSD. Of course, not all people who experience trauma develop PTSD, and it appears to be an interaction between the traumatic event and the personality of the individual experiencing it. To get PTSD one must first experience something traumatic, and this can vary considerably because of individual differences with respect to what is traumatic for each individual. However, the person must experience, observe, hear about, or know someone who has faced a traumatic situation that made the person fear for their life, health, and/or well-being and had a sense of horror and fear. The person must also experience symptoms of hyperarousal, avoidance, cognitive and mood changes, and reexperiencing (dreams or nightmares, flashbacks, obsessive thinking, etc.). If a person has these types of symptoms within a month, it is not called PTSD but rather acute stress disorder. Since these symptoms will sometimes just go away on their own, PTSD is not diagnosed until the person has the symptoms for at least a month.

John was a college student who lived in an apartment a few blocks from campus, and he shared the apartment with two of his friends. They were all juniors in college and were starting to think about jobs after graduation, so they were getting a little more serious about their studies. John had been working late in the library doing research for a paper he was writing, and he was walking home at about 11:00 P.M.; the streets were almost empty, and it was quiet. Suddenly, he heard someone behind him, and he walked faster, but the person caught up with him and he felt something in his back that felt like a gun. The man who was behind him told him in a rough voice that he wanted John's money and his computer or he would shoot him. John did not turn around and was afraid to look at the man for fear that he would get shot. He gave the man his money (only about $20) and his computer. The man told him to count to 100 before he looked around or started walking, and John did exactly what he was told. When he got back to the apartment, he told his roommates what had happened, and they wanted to call the police, but John said "no." He had not seen the man, could not describe him, and had no idea what to tell the police, so he just said to forget it.

Understandably, John had trouble sleeping that night and drank quite a few beers just to fall asleep. He was too tired and hung over to go to class the next day, so he stayed home. Over the next few months John became less social, did not do many things with his friends, missed class frequently, and was not doing well in school; he had trouble sleeping and frequently had nightmares about being killed; he could not walk down the same street anymore and often had to walk several blocks out of his way just to avoid that street.

Finally, John's roommates got worried about him and called his parents who lived about an hour away, and they came to see John and to see if they could help. John did not want to talk about it and was angry that people were invading his privacy. However, his parents made an appointment with the dean of students and took John (reluctantly) with them. They told the dean what was happening, and he was supportive and told John that they could work with the professors to get him back on track academically. He also referred John to a psychologist friend of his who was experienced in dealing with PTSD. Although he was not happy about it, John made an appointment and went to see the psychologist.

Humanistic Psychotherapy

John went to his first appointment with his new psychotherapist and found him to be a pleasant older man, and John was not sure if he would be able to relate to this man easily. When they first met, the psychologist introduced himself and asked John to tell him a little about himself and why he had made the appointment. John told him about school and his courses and then mentioned the "mugging." Dr. Jones, the psychologist, was interested and sympathetic about the robbery and was concerned about John's health and whether he was injured or not. John assured him that other than being frightened, he was fine.

John then told Dr. Jones that he had been having problems sleeping since the mugging and often had nightmares—sometimes about the robbery and sometimes just scary dreams. He also mentioned that his parents were concerned about his not doing as well in school and that they felt that he was drinking more than usual. John told Dr. Jones that he was a little behind in his school work but did not think he would have any trouble getting back on track. He also told him that he was not really drinking more than most of his friends and did not think that was a problem.

Dr. Jones was interested in how John felt about the situation and how he thought it had affected him. John really appreciated that his therapist was not telling him what to do or how to feel, but he seemed genuinely concerned and accepting of John's feelings and beliefs. Rather than giving him instructions, Dr. Jones seemed to help John come up with his own solutions, and he supported what John wanted to do to help himself. For example, John decided that he was drinking too much and that his drinking was blunting his feelings, but it was not helping him get over the trauma. Dr. Jones pointed out that by blunting the feelings John was not allowing himself to experience the reality of his trauma and then to accept and move beyond it.

Dr. Jones and John also discussed different things that John could do to get his life back on track socially and academically, and he found that by normalizing his life the trauma did not seem to be as big a concern. Of course, the fears and pain were still there, but they did not seem to be as big an issue for him. As time passed, John did not need to see his therapist as often, and eventually he was able to discontinue his visits and found that all the things that he and Dr. Jones had discussed were still with him, and he could remember their discussions when the trauma started to bother him again; he still used what he learned in therapy, but now he could do it on his own.

Cognitive-Behavioral Psychotherapy

John went to visit his new therapist, Dr. Billings, and when he met her, he was a little surprised because she was a young woman who was nice but did not seem old enough to be a doctor. However, when they began talking, it became clear that she knew what she was doing and was professional. She asked questions about his history, the trauma, his school, and his social/family life. They discussed how the trauma had affected his life and how it continued to bother him even though it had happened many months ago.

Dr. Billings told John that they were going to start his treatment by doing things that would make it easier to manage the trauma, and while John did not see how this was going to help, he decided that he would do what she suggested. The first thing that she suggested was to stop drinking alcohol; she told him that he would be able to drink moderately and socially in the future, but right now his drinking was making it difficult for him to get past the effects of the trauma. John was not quite sure that he agreed with this, but he cooperated anyway. She also wanted him to start exercising four times a week by going to the gym or doing aerobic activities like running, walking, or biking. Finally, she wanted him to start gradually getting back into a normal social life with his friends but that he would need to avoid alcohol and he could just tell his friends that his doctor told him not to drink for a while. She also wanted him to start doing some relaxation/meditation activities daily, and she gave him some instructions as to what she wanted him to do.

After a few weeks, John could see that he was feeling better and thought that they were making progress, and he asked if their treatment was almost over. His therapist explained that this was the first part, and they would now start working on the next part that would involve working directly on the trauma and related issues. She asked John to think about what it was about the trauma that made it so difficult to deal with. The two things that John came up with were that it was the closest he had ever come to dying and that what had happened was completely out of his control. They then started working on these issues, and she helped him see that in terms of relative risk, his walking in the neighborhood was almost always safe and he had done it hundreds of times without any problem. By taking care not to walk alone at night, he could be more confident that he was being safe and careful. She also pointed out that by being more physically and socially active, he was taking control of the things that would make him more confident and safer. As they continued to work on these issues, John found that he was feeling much better, the trauma did not bother him as much, he was doing better in school, and he was starting to have fun with his family and friends again. He was able to discontinue treatment, but he continued doing the things that he had learned in therapy to keep himself healthy and happy.

Case 13: Bipolar Disorder

Bipolar disorder has been described as a mental health condition for a very long time although it has only recently used this name. In the past, it was called manic-depressive disease but was basically the same. This disorder is not just about having changing moods, and several different mental health conditions involved frequent and significant mood changes. Bipolar disorder involves a person experiencing the symptoms of major depression and having manic or hypomanic (not quite as severe) episodes. These episodes usually involve mood changes that last weeks or months although the changes can occur more frequently in some patients. It is also true that for most people with bipolar disorder there may be periods between these episodes where the person acts normally.

Joan is a pleasant woman who is married and has two children, a son in high school and a daughter in middle school. Her husband is a salesperson who works selling insurance for a local agency. Joan is a stay-at-home mom most of the time but also works part-time in a local woman's clothing store. She has always been an emotional person, and sometimes it is hard for her to control her emotions. In the past few years, however, there have been times when she was so depressed that it was hard for her to get out of bed during the day; she was not able to go to work, and she even neglected her responsibilities at home. Fortunately, these episodes usually just went away on their own, but her friends and family were concerned about her. Recently, she found that she had a lot more energy and did not need to sleep as much and even enjoyed getting up at night and doing chores like cleaning the house or washing clothes. This annoyed her husband, but she did not understand why he would be upset if she was feeling so good that she wanted to work around the house. She also was really enjoying shopping and would go out during the day and buy many clothes and particularly enjoyed picking out new things for her children and husband. He was concerned that she was spending too much money, but she got so much pleasure out of it that she continued doing it. When she maxed out their credit cards, her husband took her cards away from her and told her that she needed to go to her doctor and see what was wrong. She did go to her PCP who referred her to a psychiatrist, who diagnosed her with bipolar disorder and started her on medication. She also referred Joan to a psychologist to help her deal with her condition.

Psychodynamic Psychotherapy

When Joan met her new psychotherapist, Dr. Brown, he asked her many questions about her family and background and wanted to know details about her condition and how it affected her. Most of their sessions involved her talking about her background and relationships with important people in her life, including her parents, siblings, her husband and children, and her friends. He also asked about others in her family who may have had similar problems, and as it turned out, she remembered that she had a maternal aunt who had been hospitalized for manic-depressive disease when Joan was a child.

Dr. Brown was a good listener and seemed to be helpful in explaining to Joan how her relationships had affected her and how her parents and others had influenced her and how she dealt with others. It became increasingly clear to Joan that her depressions were related to losses that she had experienced throughout her life and that the hypomanic episodes seemed to be a way for her to deal with her depression and give her a sense of control over her life.

As her therapy progressed, they focused more on things that Joan could do differently when she started feeling depressed and when she started noticing symptoms of hypomania. Since she had started taking her medications, she did not have as many problems with depression or hypomania, but her therapist wanted her to understand the origins of these feelings and things that she could do to help deal with them besides just taking medicine. While he agreed that the medication was an important part of her treatment, he also wanted her to understand that she had a role in managing her symptoms as well.

It became increasingly clear to Joan that while she might have inherited a predisposition for bipolar disorder, that at least in part, her symptoms emerged because of her history and family dynamics. As she understood how her relationships had affected her, this also gave her the opportunity to work on these relationships to help make them healthier and more positive. As she gained more confidence in her ability to deal with her issues and her relationships, she began having fewer problems with her symptoms, and while she continued taking her medications, they were able to reduce the medicine and she did not need to take as large a dose. Eventually, she and Dr. Brown terminated treatment with the understanding that she could come back to therapy anytime she thought it would be helpful.

Existential Psychotherapy

Joan made an appointment with her new psychologist, Dr. Green, who was highly recommended by her psychiatrist and by a friend of hers who had seen Dr. Green in the past. During her first visit, they discussed her history and how her bipolar disorder had affected her. Dr. Green was a nice woman who seemed genuinely interested in Joan and what she was dealing with. They spent quite a bit of time talking about Joan's values and what was important to her. One thing that became increasingly clear was that Joan was concerned about others' opinions of her, and she seemed to always feel the need to do what people thought she should do. Much of her life seemed to be involved with meeting the expectations of others in her life—particularly her parents.

Joan had never really thought about the fact that most of the important decisions in her life (e.g., where she went to college, what she studied, whom she married) were based on what she thought she was "supposed to do." In fact, when this was pointed out to her, she was surprised to realize that she was not sure if she had ever made a really important decision for her own reasons. They then spent many sessions looking at the relationship between Joan's values and the decisions she made in life, and it turned out that her values were not usually the basis of her decisions as much as it was the values of others who were important to her.

Joan and Dr. Green then discussed issues involving assertiveness, and it became clear to Joan that it was hard for her to stand up for herself because of her fear of upsetting someone else if she did the "wrong" thing. This was not an easy thing for Joan to deal with, but her therapist pointed out to her that in our culture it was particularly difficult for women to be assertive without being perceived as being pushy or aggressive. However, being assertive did not mean that you were selfish or did not care for others but rather that you also cared for yourself and what was important to you.

Most of the remainder of her therapy involved Joan understanding herself, her needs, her values, and what was important to her as a person. With this knowledge, Joan was starting to approach her life and her decisions with the understanding of the importance of keeping her own needs and values at the forefront of her decisions and choices in life. Interestingly, as she continued to work on these issues, she found that depression was not as big an issue for her, and her hypomanic episodes were no longer a problem. She continued taking her medication, but she was getting to the point where she and her psychiatrist were considering lowering some of the doses. When she got to the point that she no longer felt like she had to please everyone else rather than take care of herself, and that she could care for and be nice to others without sacrificing the things that were important to her, she and Dr. Green decided that it was time to terminate therapy and for Joan to take control of her life on her own.

Case 14: Eating Disorder

There are several different types of eating disorders, but the most common are anorexia nervosa, where a person is obsessed with keeping weight off and sustains their weight at unhealthy levels (e.g., more than 15% lower than a healthy body weight), and bulimia nervosa. Bulimia nervosa is when someone will eat too much or binge eat (eat an excessive amount of food in a short time) and then do something to get rid of the food (e.g., induce vomiting, take laxatives, or similar actions). Non-bulimic binge eating disorder is when the person will eat way too much in a very short time and then feel terrible about it, but they do not induce vomiting or take laxatives or other forms of purging.

Julie is a 17-year-old senior in high school who is popular and a good student but has always been "chubby," and even with dieting, she has never been able to attain and keep a normal weight. Although active in school activities and with many girlfriends, she has never had a regular boyfriend although she would very much like to. It seemed like she was always the "good friend" to many boys in school, but none of them ever asked her out for a date or treated her like they treated other girls.

For the past year or so, Julie has tried to lose weight but without any success, and she started making herself throw up after she ate and particularly when she ate more than she intended. She was embarrassed about this and did not tell anyone that she was doing it. However, even with the frequent vomiting, Julie did not lose any weight and she was starting to get depressed about this. She planned to start college after high school graduation but really wanted to have a boyfriend before she went away to school.

When Julie had her regular dentist visit, her dentist mentioned that he noticed that her teeth were showing evidence of "dental erosion," and it looked like acid was eating into her teeth. He asked her if she was bulimic, and she started crying and begged her dentist not to say anything. However, he said that this was a potentially serious condition and that he would need to tell her parents and her primary care doctor.

Of course, Julie's parents were upset and wanted to know why she would do such a thing and why had she not told them about it. Her doctor was concerned but suggested that her parents should take her to see a psychologist who specialized in the treatment of eating disorders and get this under control before it became a real problem. At this point, Julie was embarrassed and angry, but she agreed to see this person, although she told her parents and her doctor that she would never do this again. However, the doctor told her that this was a complex problem and that even though she felt like she could control it, she would need to work with a professional to make sure that it was taken care of properly.

Behavioral Psychotherapy

When Julie and her parents met the psychologist, Dr. Blue, she seemed nice enough and had quite a few questions about Julie's health, her school activities, her friends, and her difficulties with food. Although Julie really did not like talking about these kinds of things, she answered the psychologist's questions somewhat briefly. At her next visit, Dr. Blue wanted to talk with

Julie alone, and she found that this was easier than talking about these problems in front of her parents.

Dr. Blue wanted to make sure that Julie understood why the bulimia was such a medically important issue and how it would affect her health in the future. Although she really did not want to hear about all of this "stuff," it was also true that she had not really listened to what others had told her because she just wanted people to leave her alone and forget about it. However, when she heard about all the problems that could occur, she did feel a little frightened. Dr. Blue quickly pointed out that Julie was lucky to have addressed this so quickly and that there was every reason to believe that she would get past all of this. She also told Julie about the many other youngsters whom she had treated for this problem and that every one of them who wanted to be helped got a lot better.

After discussing all the medical issues, Dr. Blue told Julie that she wanted to refer her to a nutritionist who would help Julie develop some new strategies for meal planning and eating. She said that dieting was not really the plan but rather coming up with ideas that would be a healthy strategy for eating for the rest of her life and would involve being able to eat "fun" stuff as well and as have sweets occasionally. Dr. Blue also told her that they would be starting to work together to develop better and healthier habits about food and eating.

At their next visit, Dr. Blue wanted to know the kinds of things that Julie was most likely to binge on and the kinds of foods that seemed to cause the most problems for her. Of course, like many people, Julie ate way too many simple carbohydrates like sugar and white flour, did not eat enough protein, and had too much fat and salty foods as well. She also tended to overeat when she was stressed out or bored, and she could see that under those circumstances, she would usually eat things that she knew were not good for her.

The next thing that Dr. Blue and Julie did was to invite Julie's parents to come in for part of an appointment and talk about limiting access to some of the high-risk foods that no one really needed to eat (junk food) and starting to make healthier food and snack options available. She pointed out that if the parents wanted to really help Julie, they needed to be good role models and work with her to have better nutrition and less unhealthy foods and snacks. Since both of her parents were a little overweight, they could see that this would be a challenge for the whole family, but it was the right thing to do.

Dr. Blue also wanted Julie to start working on an exercise program and to even get involved with recreational sports with her friends; these were activities that Julie really wanted to do and looked forward to it. She also started Julie doing some daily meditation and relaxation activities to help her deal more effectively with stress. One of the things that she wanted Julie to start was a food diary and record everything that she ate and drank every day. While she knew that this would be a pain at first, she told Julie that she wanted her to gain more awareness of her eating and to make better decisions about what she ate, when she ate, how much she ate, and how she felt while and after eating. She would not have to do this forever, but she wanted Julie to use the food diary until she was able to manage her nutrition on her own.

As Julie started working on all these activities, she found that she was feeling better, was looking healthier, had more energy, and was less stressed out, and people were telling her how great she looked. Gradually, she just checked in with Dr. Blue occasionally, and then she was able to terminate her visits. She was proud of herself; she was not vomiting anymore at all, was making better food choices, was never binging, was more physically active, had lost quite a bit of weight, and was feeling good.

Humanistic Psychotherapy

Julie and her parents went to see her new psychologist who was nice and seemed anxious to help her. After visiting for a few minutes with Julie and her parents, Dr. Simon asked to talk to Julie alone, and her parents went into the other room. After they left, Dr. Simon told Julie that she was certainly aware of her parents' concerns, but she was more interested in what Julie thought and felt and how she might be able to help her.

Julie told her that she was tired of being overweight, loved to eat, and just wanted to do something to feel better about herself. Dr. Simon seemed to really understand, but she was a pleasant-looking woman who was not skinny but was thin and stylish looking—what would she know about being overweight. Although Julie did not actually say this, Dr. Simon seemed to sense that Julie was not connecting with her message, and she said that it must be difficult to have people who do not know what she is dealing with, give her advice, and try to act as if they understood her. Julie did not answer this, but it was exactly what she was thinking. Dr. Simon went on to tell her that as an adolescent she had been overweight—more than Julie was—and that she too had dealt with bulimia. Julie was shocked that the doctor would tell her this and did not know what to say. Dr. Simon went on to say that she told her only because she wanted Julie to know that she did understand and that she was living proof that this was a problem that could be conquered.

In their next few sessions, they talked about Julie's goals, hopes, and dreams and how she wanted to pursue them. Since being healthy, normal weight, and physically and socially active were all part of how Julie wanted to be, they talked about things that Julie could do to start living up to what she thought was important for her—not what anyone else thought was important but what Julie truly wanted for herself.

What Julie learned in therapy was that although Dr. Simon did not always agree with her, she always respected and accepted Julie's thoughts and feelings. She was never judgmental or demanding and seemed to really understand and know Julie for who she was and what she wanted to become. As therapy progressed, Julie started feeling much better about herself, was making much better decisions about her life and health, was no longer binging or vomiting, was active in school, and was even getting involved in sports and fun activities with her friends. When she and Dr. Simon had their last visit, it felt like she was saying goodbye to a friend rather than a doctor, but she felt good about that because it also meant that she no longer needed Dr. Simon to be a healthy and happy person.

Case 15: Intimate Partner Violence

Intimate partner violence is an extremely important issue that affects and harms many people, and what is even more concerning is that we know that more of these crimes are unreported than are acknowledged. From a psychological perspective, the perpetrator of domestic violence has some personal/emotional issues that need to be addressed, but the victims are the ones who deserve the most attention and support, and often they are ignored or blamed for their problems. Frequently, the victims of domestic violence do not report their injuries or problems because they are afraid to, are too embarrassed, or fear that they will not be believed.

Jeanine is a 23-year-old woman who has been married for two years and has a job working as a clerk in a local bank. She enjoys her job and has several friends who work with her. She also has some girlfriends from school whom she occasionally sees. Her husband was her high school sweetheart, and they have gone together since they were 16. Both of their parents live locally, and they usually see them on weekends and during holidays. Her husband, Ted, was a popular athlete in high school, and it was assumed that he would get a scholarship to play basketball in college, but he never got a scholarship offer, so he played for one year in the local community college, and he did not do well in school and eventually dropped out. He had trouble finding a job and finally took a position working for a landscaping business and mostly mowed lawns and trimmed bushes and would plow snow in the winter.

Ted had occasionally gotten angry and yelled at Jeanine, and once or twice he had shoved her but had never actually hurt her. In the past two years, however, he started drinking more, and when he would get angry, he would take it out on Jeanine telling her that she was the cause of all of his difficulties, and if it were not for her he probably would have gotten to play basketball at the college level, and his getting tied down to her had ruined his life. He was verbally abusive, and he started getting more physical with her, pushing her down and even slapping her face when he was angry.

Jeanine was starting to get scared of Ted, but she did not know what to do about it and was afraid to tell anyone for fear of what Ted would do when he found out. One day he was very angry and pushed her very hard that she fell and broke her arm. He was drunk, but she called a friend who took her to the hospital where they set her arm and gave her a cast. The nurse and the doctor both questioned her about the injury and how it happened and even asked if she was safe at home. She just said that she had tripped on the rug and fell, which broke her arm.

When she got home, Ted was passed out on the couch, so she just went to bed. The next morning, he was upset and sorry for what had happened, and he promised that he would never touch her again. For a few days he was nice, but when he came home later in the week, he had clearly been drinking and he was furious. He had been fired at work because he lost his temper and swore at his boss, who immediately told him to leave and never come back. Jeanine was upset and said they would not have enough money to pay the rent and the car payments and did not know what to do. Ted got so angry at her that he punched her in the face with a closed fist and almost knocked her out. She ran out of the house, got into her car, and drove to the hospital; she was afraid her jaw was broken, but it was just badly bruised, and she could barely open her mouth to talk. This time, the doctor called the police and said that he suspected domestic violence. They kept her in the hospital until a woman from the police department came in and talked to Jeanine. Although she tried to keep from talking about Ted, it was obvious that Jeanine had not just bumped into a door and hurt herself. Finally, she admitted what had happened, and they convinced her to file charges on Ted so that she could be safe, and he could get the help he needed. She was then referred to a women's shelter where she could stay and be protected. They also referred her to a psychologist who specialized in domestic violence issues.

Cognitive-Behavioral Psychotherapy (CBT)

Jeanine was a little nervous about meeting her psychologist because she knew that he was a man, and she thought it might be difficult for her to trust him. She was also worried about her husband learning where she was and that he might try to find her. When she met the psychologist, she found him to be supportive and sympathetic, and he was a good listener who really seemed to understand what she was dealing with.

After listening to Jeanine and starting to understand her situation, Dr. Brady pointed out to Jeanine that she seemed to feel that she was unable to act in a way that would keep her safe and that she had allowed herself to feel helpless when confronting her husband's anger. While she understood this, she explained that given her husband's size, anger, and history, she really did not feel that there was anything she could have done. Dr. Brady assured her that her situation was completely understandable and that they would be working on finding ways for her to gain more of a sense of control over her own safety and to learn more about abuse and abusers so that she understood more of what she was dealing with.

Dr. Brady wanted to meet with her weekly but also wanted her to attend a women's support group at her shelter so that she could see what other women were dealing with and how they were handling their issues. He said that he wanted her to start gaining more of a sense of control over her life, and so he wanted her to contact her employer and see if she could get a medical leave of absence for about a month; she found her employer very helpful and concerned about her and agreed that they would touch base in a few weeks and see when she was able to return. In addition, he wanted her to start exercising daily, and this would give her another thing over which she had total control. Finally, he put her in touch with an attorney, who helped her file an order of protection with the local court so that her husband would be forbidden to contact her or to be around her at all.

As Jeanine started being more active with her daily activities, Dr. Brady was also working with her on "assertiveness" to help her stand up for herself and to make decisions based on her own needs and interests rather than just trying to please everyone else. As time progressed, he also wanted her to start being more socially active and to start seeing friends and family on a limited basis.

As Jeanine was becoming more physically and socially active, she was feeling better, and then she found that her husband was contacting her friends and family and wanted to see her and to apologize to her. Although it was difficult for her, she reported him to the police, and they told him that he had to avoid her and to stop trying to contact her or he would be arrested. Although he did not like this, he did understand that he had to respect it, and he stopped trying to get in touch with her.

As Jeanine started becoming more assertive and less fearful, she started working with a social worker as well as Dr. Brady, and the social worker started helping her get involved with her work and friends and helped her find a new place to live. Gradually, her life started getting back to a new "normal," and she felt that with all the help, she finally had her life back.

Psychodynamic Psychotherapy

When Jeanine met her new psychologist, she found her to be concerned and anxious to help Jeanine get her life back to normal. Dr. Grady encouraged her to take advantage of the legal and social opportunities at the shelter and to be involved with those activities as well as her therapy. She was interested in Jeanine's family history and wanted to know about any issues of abuse or substance use issues in her family. Although Jeanine said that her father had a temper, he was not a big drinker, and she had never known him to be physically or verbally abusive to her or her mother. She did report that she understood that her paternal grandfather had been abusive and even whipped her father with a belt occasionally.

Dr. Grady explored Jeanine's relationships with both of her parents and found that they were very loving and supportive but were also very strict and did not allow her to have many of the freedoms that most of her friends enjoyed. For example, she was not allowed to have a boyfriend until she was 16, and even then, she was not permitted to go with her dates in cars and had to meet them at their activities. When she met the boy, who would become her husband, she found that in order to have any kind of normal relationship with him she had to lie and sneak around or her parents would not have permitted it. When they got more serious and started talking about marriage, Jeanine could hardly wait to get out of the house and to have a life of her own.

Over the many sessions of therapy, Dr. Grady helped Jeanine see that she had never allowed herself to have a "voice" when dealing with authority figures, particularly males. She could not imagine ever standing up to her father and openly disobeying him; clearly, this pattern also continued into her marriage as well. Most of the therapy that Jeanine was involved with was to help her learn to see herself as an independent person who loved and cared for her parents and friends but who had needs and goals that were her own as well. Learning to be independent of her parents and others in relationships was difficult, but eventually Jeanine could see the gains and could also see herself becoming an adult who was in control of her own life. She was able to move beyond her relationship with her husband, to divorce him, and to move on with her life and career.

Glossary

Adjunctive therapy
A treatment that is used with the primary treatment with the expectation that it will help the primary treatment be more effective.

Alienist
A term used in the 19th and early 20th centuries to describe a person who specialized in diagnosing and treating patients with mental illness. Alienists were often used as expert witnesses in court trials.

Anima
Carl Jung's term to describe the feminine part of the male personality.

Animus
Carl Jung's term to describe the masculine part of the female personality.

Antianxiety (anxiolytic) medication
Drugs that are used to reduce the anxiety that a patient is experiencing.

Anticonvulsant medications
Medications that are used to control seizures in people with epilepsy; sometimes used as mood stabilizers and may also be used for certain pain disorders.

Antidepressant medication
Medicines that are used to treat and help manage depression. Some may sometimes be used to treat anxiety disorders, and some may be used to treat insomnia and pain disorders.

Antipsychotic medications
Medicines that are used to treat serious mental conditions like schizophrenia. They are sometimes used to treat other conditions such as anxiety, insomnia, bipolar disorder, and depression.

Art therapy
A form of treatment involving the free self-expression using painting, drawing, or modeling; it may also be used as a remedial activity or to aid in diagnosis.

Atypical antidepressants
A class of antidepressants that do not fall into the categories of monoamine oxidase inhibitors, tricyclics, selective serotonin reuptake inhibitors, or serotonin/norepinephrine reuptake inhibitors.

Battle fatigue
A term used in World War II to describe a mental/emotional condition experienced by some military personnel in combat; today the term used for this condition is "post-traumatic stress disorder."

Behavior modification
A group of techniques based on learning theory and research that are used to change maladaptive behavior. Historically, this referred primarily to techniques based on operant conditioning, but today it is used more generically and may be used interchangeably with "behavior therapy."

Behavior therapy
A group of techniques based on learning theory and research that are used to change maladaptive behavior. Historically, this referred primarily to techniques based on classical/Pavlovian conditioning, but today it is used more generically and may be used interchangeably with "behavior modification."

Behavioral activation therapy
This form of treatment seeks to increase the patient's contact with sources of reward by helping them be more active and, thus, improve their quality of life. This approach uses primarily behavioral techniques and does not rely on cognitive forms of treatment.

Behaviorism
An approach and group of theories in psychology that focuses primarily on overt behavior and does not rely on nonobservable and nonmeasurable types of data (e.g., unconscious materials, thoughts).

Bloodletting (bleeding)
A medical approach to treatment used in past centuries and was sometimes used with patients suffering from mental illness. This "treatment" was based on the idea that there was something in the person's blood that was causing their difficulties or that they may have had an imbalance where they had too much blood in their system. It was later proven to be ineffective as a medical/mental health treatment.

Brief behavioral activation therapy for depression
A behavioral form of treatment for depression that is directive and has specific goals and techniques and has a short and specific time frame.

Catharsis
The process of releasing, and thus providing relief from, strong or repressed emotions.

Chronic conditions
Medical or mental health conditions that are not expected to improve over time and may get worse.

Classical conditioning
May also be called Pavlovian or respondent conditioning, where a specific stimulus (unconditioned stimulus) always results in a specific response (unconditioned response). When a previously neutral stimulus (conditioned stimulus) that did not evoke a response is paired with the "unconditioned stimulus," the unconditioned response will still occur. After this pairing, the conditioned stimulus alone will now produce the new response (conditioned response).

Client-centered psychotherapy
A type of psychotherapy linked primarily with Carl Rogers, where the therapist does not direct the client but supports them, understanding and arriving at their own insights and conclusions; it may also be called "nondirective psychotherapy."

Clinical psychology
A branch of psychology that is based on the assessment, diagnosis, treatment, and research regarding people who experience psychological/emotional/ cognitive difficulties or who suffer from a form of mental illness.

Cognitive behavioral therapy
A form of psychotherapy that utilizes behavioral and cognitive processes and techniques.

Cognitive processes
Mental processes involving thinking, memory, perception, learning, and other similar mental processes.

Cognitive psychology
The branch of psychology that studies and does research on cognitive processes.

Collective unconscious
From Carl Jung's theory; this refers to the part of the unconscious mind that is derived from ancestral memory and experience and is common to all humankind, as distinct from the individual's personal unconscious.

Conditioned response
A response that is learned through conditioning techniques like operant or classical conditioning.

Conditioned stimulus
See "classical conditioning."

Conditions of worth
From the theory of Carl Rogers; this refers to the situation where a person feels good about themselves only if they believe that others value them positively.

Consciousness
The state or quality of awareness or of being aware of an external object or something within oneself.

Counseling
The provision of assistance and guidance in resolving personal, social, or psychological problems and difficulties. Although informal counseling can be provided by anyone, it is expected that professional counseling be provided by a trained and licensed professional.

Countertransference
This refers to feelings that a mental health professional may have toward a client or patient that relates to how the professional would feel about another person with whom they were not professionally involved.

Dance and movement therapy
Dance and movement therapy (DMT) is defined by the American Dance Therapy Association (ADTA) as the psychotherapeutic use of movement to promote emotional, social, cognitive, and physical integration of the individual for the purpose of improving health and well-being.

Deep brain stimulation
This involves implanting electrodes within certain areas of the brain. These electrodes produce electrical impulses that regulate abnormal processes. The electrical impulses can affect certain cells and chemicals within the brain, and this treatment is used for certain medical and mental health conditions.

Denial
A psychological defense where a person denies certain memories, events, or feelings that may be too threatening for them to experience consciously.

Depression
Depression is a mood disorder that causes a persistent feeling of sadness and loss of interest; it affects how you feel, think, and behave and can lead to a variety of emotional and physical problems. A person may have trouble doing normal day-to-day activities and sometimes may feel as if life isn't worth living. This condition must have significant symptoms and last for more than just a few days.

Depth psychology
Any psychological theory that examines and studies psychological factors below the conscious level (e.g., subconscious or unconscious materials).

D-Groups
Therapy groups that are called Development (or D) Groups and use techniques to help people understand and accept themselves and to grow to become more complete and healthy individuals. This was more commonly used in the 1960s and 1970s.

DO
This is a medical degree (doctor of osteopathy) that allows a person to be licensed and practice as a physician. This is like the MD degree, but there are some subtle differences in the training.

Double-blind study
A type of research study (often used in medical research) where a treatment is provided to a group of subjects, and another group receives a "dummy" or noneffective type of treatment (e.g., a new drug for the experimental group and a "sugar pill" for the control group). In a double-blind study, neither the subject nor the experimenter knows which group is getting the real treatment, and only the person in charge of the study knows who is getting which drug.

Drama therapy
Drama therapy is the intentional use of drama and/or theater processes to achieve therapeutic goals. This approach can provide the context for participants to tell their stories, set goals and solve problems, express feelings, or achieve catharsis.

Dream analysis
This is a therapeutic tool that may be used with several different types of psychotherapy but is more typical of the psychodynamic types of treatment. This involves a patient keeping track of and reporting their dreams to the psychotherapist who will then analyze and interpret the dreams to help the patient gain insight into their subconscious activities.

EdD
This degree is doctor of education, and depending on the course of study that the person elects, this degree can prepare a person to provide psychological services, including psychotherapy.

Ego
Originally from Freud's theory, the ego is the adaptive organ of personality that helps the individual cope with their unconscious instincts and impulses, their consciousness, and the constraints of reality. Other theorists have conceptualized the ego as the core of personality as well.

Electroconvulsive shock therapy (ECT)
A procedure, done under general anesthesia, in which small electric currents are passed through the brain, intentionally triggering a brief seizure. ECT seems to cause changes in brain chemistry that can often reverse symptoms of certain mental health conditions like depression.

Existentialism
A philosophical theory that emphasizes the existence of the individual as a free and responsible agent determining their own development through acts of the will.

Extinction
A concept from learning and conditioning theory that explains how behaviors are sustained by reinforcement, and when the reinforcers are eliminated, the learned behavior will die out for lack of reinforcement—they will extinguish.

Eye movement desensitization and reprogramming (EMDR)
A controversial form of treatment that is used for various mental health conditions, including post-traumatic stress disorder. By using eye movements and other techniques, this approach claims to eliminate or improve various conditions. The research evidence has not been as supportive as many had hoped.

Family systems theory
A theoretical approach to understanding family dynamics that is based on psychodynamic principles and techniques and focuses heavily on communication patterns in families.

Family therapy
An approach to psychotherapy that works with family units to try to identify and correct dysfunctional patterns in family dynamics.

Free association
A technique first used by Freud where the patient just talks about anything that comes to their mind without trying to edit or plan what they say. Freud felt that by reducing conscious control over what a person says, there is a better chance of some materials coming to consciousness from the subconscious, even if in symbolic or distorted form.

Gestalt therapy
"Gestalt" in German refers to the "whole" of something without breaking it down into its subparts. Gestalt therapy was founded by Fritz Perls, who tried to help people understand, accept, and integrate their personality to become a whole, healthy, honest, and complete person.

Group therapy
Psychotherapy conducted with groups of people with one or sometimes two therapists. Group sizes are usually in the four- to seven-person range, although some therapy groups could be bigger than that. Group therapy can be used with just about any type of psychotherapeutic modality.

Gymnasium
A school in many European countries that prepares students for university.

HIPAA
The Health Insurance Portability and Accountability Act was passed to help protect people's health information and access to care. Patient privacy and ability to receive care when changing insurance carriers were the bases of this legislation although it does many other things as well.

Holism
Originally discussed by Adler, this refers to the importance of seeing each individual as a whole and complete person and not just a collection of instincts, memories, and learned behaviors.

Humanism
A philosophical approach that stresses the potential value and goodness of human beings, emphasizes common human needs, and seeks solely rational ways of solving human problems. It avoids divine or supernatural explanations and solutions for human issues.

Hypnosis
This is a state of highly focused attention or concentration, often associated with relaxation and heightened suggestibility.

Hypnotics
Medication used for inducing sleep.

Hypnotism
A trance-like state of relaxed hypersuggestibility.

Hysteria
A psychological disorder (now not used as a diagnostic category) whose symptoms include conversion of psychological stress into physical symptoms, selective amnesia, shallow volatile emotions, and overdramatic or attention-seeking behavior. The term has a controversial history, and, in the past, it was regarded as a disease specific to women.

Id
From Freud's theory, this is the basic "organ" of personality that all people are born with and is the repository of all the sexual and aggressive instincts. It operates on the "pleasure principle" and demands immediate fulfillment.

Identity crisis
Originally from Erikson's psychosocial theory, this represents that crisis faced by adolescents where they struggle to establish themselves as an independent and responsible individual.

Intrapsychic
From the psychodynamic theories, this refers to conflicts, impulses, needs, and so on that occur within the psyche or mind.

Law of effect
Thorndike's original theory of learning that specified that "actions followed by pleasurable outcomes tend to be 'stamped in,' and actions followed by unpleasant outcomes tend to be 'stamped out.'"

Lay analyst
A trained psychoanalyst who did not come from a medical background.

Light therapy
A form of treatment for people suffering from seasonal affective disorder where they sit in front of a light box for several hours per day. Some research finds it helpful for mild to moderate depression in some patients.

Lobotomy
Brain surgery for severely mentally ill patients where some of the connections between the frontal lobes in the brain and some of the more primitive emotional centers in the brain are severed. This was used for several decades in the early 20th century but was discontinued because there were many complications and very few positive outcomes.

Logotherapy
A type of psychotherapy started by Viktor Frankl, a neurologist and psychiatrist, who as a Jew was incarcerated in a concentration camp by the Nazis in World War II. He was one of the primary practitioners of logotherapy, which was a type of existential psychotherapy.

Magnetic seizure therapy
An experimental form of treatment that uses strong magnetic fields to induce seizures. It is currently being investigated for the treatment of treatment-resistant depression, schizophrenia, and obsessive-compulsive disorder.

Maintenance treatment
This is treatment of chronic conditions where a cure may not be possible or likely, and the goal is to help the patient maintain whatever gains their treatment has produced. The goal is to help the patient maintain as high a level of functioning of which they are capable.

MD
A doctor of medicine degree holder who after being licensed can practice medicine.

Mesmerism
Started by Mesmer who used what he called "animal magnetism" to induce a trance in his patients and hopefully some relief of their symptoms. Today it is called "hypnotism" (see hypnotism).

Monoamine oxidase inhibitor
A type of antidepressant medications that was discovered in the 1950s and found to be effective in managing depressive symptoms by inhibiting monoamine oxidase and keeping some of the neurotransmitters in the brain at more normal levels. These drugs are rarely used because they have some unpleasant and dangerous side effects.

Mood stabilizers
Medications that are used to help control and stabilize the mood of patients suffering from bipolar disorder or other mood disorders. Lithium is the most

frequently used drug although some antiseizure medications and a few antipsychotic drugs can be used as well.

Moral treatment
In past centuries, mental patients were often incarcerated and treated cruelly and without any real form of therapy. In France, Dr. Phillippe Pinel and some of his colleagues practiced "moral therapy," where mental patients were given more freedom, better conditions, healthy nutrition, and pleasant activities. This was a major breakthrough in the treatment of mental illness.

Negative reinforcement
The probability of a response occurring is increased by the removal of an aversive stimulus.

Neo-Freudian
This refers to theories and analysts who came after Freud and departed from some of his ideas venturing into some different areas.

Neurolinguistic programming (NLP)
This is an approach to communication, personal development, and psychotherapy created by Richard Bandler and John Grinder in California in the 1970s. NLP's creators claim that there is a connection between neurological processes (*neuro-*), language (*linguistic*), and behavioral patterns learned through experience (*programming*) and that these can be changed to achieve specific goals in life. This approach has not been supported by research and is not considered by most practitioners to be a valid treatment.

Neurology
The branch of medicine concerned with the study and treatment of disorders of the nervous system.

Neuropsychology
The study and characterization of the psychological and behavioral changes that follow a neurological trauma or condition. It is both an experimental and clinical field of psychology that aims to understand how behavior and cognition are influenced by brain functioning and is concerned with the diagnosis and treatment of behavioral and cognitive effects of neurological disorders.

Neurosis
A class of functional mental disorders involving chronic distress but involves neither delusions nor hallucinations. The term is no longer used by the professional community in the United States.

Nurse practitioners
These practitioners have a nursing degree (usually an RN) and then do graduate work to expand the range of medical services that they provide in collaboration with a physician. A psychiatric nurse practitioner (NPP) can prescribe psychotropic medications.

Obstetrics/gynecology
The medical specialty that encompasses the two subspecialties of obstetrics (covering pregnancy, childbirth, and the postpartum period) and gynecology (covering the health of the female reproductive system—vagina, uterus, ovaries, and breasts).

Operant conditioning
A model of learning where behavior is shaped by its consequences. The principle concept is reinforcement (see "reinforcement").

Organizational behavior modification
The use of operant conditioning techniques to modify the behavior of people within an organization.

Pavlovian conditioning
See "classical conditioning."

Pediatrics
The branch of medicine that involves the medical care of infants, children, and adolescents.

Personal construct psychology
The approach to personality theory that is associated with the work of George Kelly.

Personal unconscious
From the theory of Carl Jung; this refers to the individual and unique unconscious that each person has. This concept is similar to Freud's use of the term "unconscious."

PhD
Doctor of philosophy is a graduate degree that can apply to any field in the arts and sciences. Most psychologists have PhD degree.

Phrenology
Primarily associated with the work of Franz Josef Gall; this is the study of the conformation of the skull based on the belief that it is indicative of mental faculties and character. It was found to be incorrect in its basic assumptions and beliefs and is no longer considered to be a valid theory.

Physician's assistants
A person who has a graduate degree (usually a master's degree) in medically related subjects that permits them to provide certain medical services under the supervision of a physician.

Physiognomy
The practice of assessing a person's character or personality from their outer appearance—especially the face.

Positive psychology
The scientific study of human flourishing; an applied approach to optimal functioning. It focuses on the strengths and virtues that enable individuals, communities, and organizations to thrive.

Positive reinforcement
When a positive outcome is presented following a specific behavior, this increases the probability of that behavior occurring again.

Preconscious
From Freud's theory, this refers to the part of consciousness that is not immediately conscious but can be brought into consciousness by focusing attention on it.

Primary care physician (PCP)
One's "regular" doctor that one would go to for routine physicals and for most health concerns.

Psyche
From the Greek; this refers to the mind, soul, or spirit of an individual.

Psychiatric residency
Following the completion of the MD or DO degree, a physician can enter a psychiatric residency where for two or three years they will focus their training and experience on psychiatric practice; this is done under supervision and in a medical school or training setting.

Psychiatry
The branch of medicine focused on the diagnosis, treatment, and prevention of mental, emotional, and behavioral disorders.

Psychoanalysis
A system of psychological theory and therapy that treats mental disorders by investigating the interaction of conscious and unconscious elements in the mind and bringing repressed fears and conflicts into consciousness by techniques such as dream interpretation and free association.

Psychodrama
This is a form of group psychotherapy, in which clients use spontaneous dramatization, role-playing, and dramatic self-presentation to investigate and gain insight into their lives and hopefully to find better ways to manage their issues.

Psychodynamics
An approach to psychology that emphasizes systematic study of the psychological forces that underlie human behavior, feelings, and emotions and how they might relate to early experience.

Psychological defenses
Originally discussed by Freud, these are psychological strategies that are unconsciously used to protect a person from anxiety arising from unacceptable thoughts, feelings, memories, or instincts/impulses.

Psychologist
A person who has completed the required education and training to be licensed to practice psychology. Psychologists must have a doctoral degree in a psychologically related field that is recognized by the appropriate state and professional organizations and must also have two years of supervised experience (one of which can be an internship that is completed before the doctoral degree is granted).

Psychopathology
The scientific study of mental disorders, including efforts to understand their genetic, biological, psychological, and social causes. This also involves the development of classification schemes that can improve treatment planning and outcomes. It also studies the course of psychiatric illnesses across all stages of development and investigates and utilizes potentially effective treatments.

Psychopharmacology
The scientific study of the effects various drugs have on mood, sensation, thinking, and behavior. It also involves the investigation of drugs as a means of treating psychological disorders.

Psychosexual development
From Freud's theory this is a central element of the psychoanalytic sexual drive theory, that human beings, from birth, possess an instinctual libido (sexual energy) that develops in five stages: the oral, the anal, the phallic, the latency, and the genital. Each stage has an erogenous zone and a conflict (except for the latency stage) that is relevant to the child's development.

Psychosocial development
Erik Erikson maintained that personality develops in a predetermined order through eight stages of psychosocial development, from infancy to adulthood. During each stage, the person experiences a psychosocial crisis that could have a positive or negative outcome for personality development.

Psychosurgery
Brain surgery, such as lobotomy, that is used to treat mental disorder. Lobotomies are controversial and rarely used anymore; some newer techniques are being used experimentally for specific mental health problems, but these are still in early stages of development.

Psychotherapy
According to John Norcross, "Psychotherapy is the informed and intentional application of clinical methods and interpersonal stances derived from established psychological principles for assisting people to modify their

behaviors, cognitions, emotions, and/or other personal characteristics in directions that the participants deem desirable" (Campbell, Norcross, Vasquez, and Kaslow, 2013).

Psychotropic medications
Medications used to treat psychological symptoms and psychiatric disorders.

PsyD
A doctor of psychology degree that focuses more on applied practice and less on research than the PhD.

Punishment
The application of an aversive stimulus or the removal of a positive outcome for the purpose of decreasing the frequency of a specific behavior.

Rapid transcranial magnetic stimulation
Rapid transcranial magnetic stimulation (rTMS) is a noninvasive procedure that uses repetitive magnetic fields to stimulate nerve cells in the brain to improve symptoms of depression. rTMS is typically used when other depression treatments haven't been effective.

Rational emotive behavior therapy
Originally developed by Albert Ellis and first called "rational emotive therapy," this approach works with dysfunctional thoughts, feelings, and behaviors and tries to help the patient explore and adopt healthier and more functional ways of thinking, feeling, and acting.

Reinforcement
Any consequence of behavior that increases the probability of that behavior being repeated in the future.

Repression
A psychological defense, originally discussed by Freud, where unwanted thoughts, feelings, memories, instincts, or impulses are pushed from the conscious mind to the subconscious and kept there to reduce the anxiety created by the unwanted mental materials.

Resistance
Originally discussed by Freud, this is a psychological defense where someone resists dealing with a troubling situation or mental event, by finding ways to avoid talking about or confronting it (e.g., changing the topic each time it comes up, forgetting appointments).

Respondent conditioning
See "classical conditioning."

Scientist-Practitioner model
The training model adopted for clinical psychology where the person is scientifically trained in theory and research but is also trained to provide professional services.

Scope of practice
This is the range of professional services that are permitted within a professional license (e.g., medical, psychological, nursing, social work).

Selective serotonin reuptake inhibitors
This is a class of antidepressant medications that selectively work on the serotonin neurotransmitter system and keeps more of the serotonin available in the system, which helps control the symptoms of depression and anxiety.

Self
An individual's essential being that distinguishes them from all others, especially considered as the object of introspection or reflexive action. It is often thought of as the core of personality.

Self-actualization
A concept used by many of the humanistic psychologists to describe a human need to become the best that each person is capable of becoming.

Serotonin and norepinephrine reuptake inhibitors
A class of antidepressant medications that work on the serotonin and norepinephrine neurotransmitter systems to keep more of those substances available in the system; this helps control the symptoms of depression and anxiety.

Shadow
From Jungian psychology, this is an aspect of personality that represents hidden or unconscious aspects of oneself, both good and bad, which the ego has either repressed or never recognized.

Shaman
A person regarded as having access to, and influence in, the world of good and evil spirits, especially among some peoples of northern Asia and North America. Typically, such people enter a trance state during a ritual and practice divination and healing.

Shaping
When conditioning a person to help them learn a complex behavior, the therapist will break the behavior down into component parts teaching the person each small part and then "shape" the behavior to accomplish learning the more complex action.

Sliding scales
When a person providing professional services charges for the services based on the patient's/client's ability to pay.

Social work
Social work is a practice-based profession and an academic discipline that promotes social change and development, social cohesion, and the empowerment

and liberation of people. Principles of social justice, human rights, collective responsibility, and respect for diversities are central to social work.

Stimulants
Drugs that stimulate a person and increase their arousal level.

Stoicism
A systematic philosophy dating back to about 300 BCE that held the principles of rational thought to reflect cosmic reason that is found and supported in nature.

Subconscious
A part of the "mind" or "psyche" that is below the level of consciousness and is not directly accessible by the conscious mind.

Sublimation
According to Freud, this is a psychological defense where unwanted instinctual urges or impulses are converted to socially acceptive needs or motives and expressed indirectly in ways that are appropriate in a social context.

Superego
From Freud's theory, this is the organ of personality that emerges as the child starts to identify with parenting figures and accepts the values and morals that they are exposed to. The superego functions as the conscience and makes people feel guilty.

Superego ideal
The superego also includes the "superego ideal," which is the highest manifestation of a person's personality that they will try to fulfill and become.

Talking cure
One of Josef Breuer's (Freud's mentor) patients referred to this early form of psychotherapy where Breuer found that some patients obtained symptomatic relief by discussing their symptoms and problems.

Teletherapy
Psychotherapy that is provided remotely through telephone or teleconferencing or when computer-mediated communication is used to make a therapeutic connection between a patient/client and a psychotherapist.

T-Groups
Discovered by Kurt Lewin, T-Groups, or Training Groups, were groups that would discuss problems and then would analyze and discuss the group processes to better understand the group functioning and performance.

Transference
Originally discussed by Freud but is widely described as an element of psychotherapy where the patient reacts to the therapist in ways similar to how

they would respond to another person (e.g., a parent). Transference would be recognized and analyzed as part of the psychotherapeutic process.

Trephination
A prehistoric surgical procedure where a hole was cut or drilled in the skull. The assumption is that this procedure was used to treat medical/mental health/ spiritual issues that affected people. Although we do not know exactly why this was done, we do know that some patients clearly survived the surgical process and lived long enough for the surgical "injury" to thoroughly heal.

Tricyclic antidepressant
A type of antidepressant medication first identified in the 1950s that is composed of three chemical rings. These drugs are used to treat depression, anxiety, insomnia, migraine headaches, and certain pain conditions.

Unconditional positive regard
A concept first discussed by Carl Rogers; he described this as a necessary condition for effective psychotherapy. Thus, the therapist should always show the client that even if the therapist did not approve or support specific behavior that the client would manifest, they would still value them as a person and show an unqualified and unconditional regard for them.

Unconditioned response
A concept from classical conditioning that refers to a response that consistently follows a specific stimulus that is already part of the person's behavioral repertoire and does not have to be learned.

Unconditioned stimulus
A concept from classical conditioning that refers to a stimulus that consistently evokes a specific response that is already a part of the person's behavioral repertoire and does not have to be learned.

Unconscious
A part of the mind or psyche that is not part of the consciousness. Also see "subconscious."

Vagus nerve stimulation
A medical procedure where depressive symptoms are treated by using an implanted device to stimulate the vagus nerve. This is still experimental but has shown some promising results.

Witch doctor
See "shaman."

Worried well
A term that is used to describe patients who enter psychotherapy and who do not have a clinically relevant mental health diagnosis but have problems or issues that worry them and that they would like to have help dealing with.

Additional Resources

Websites

Academy of Cognitive Therapy: http://www.academyofct.org/
The Albert Ellis Institute: http://www.albertellisinstitute.org/
American Art Therapy Association: http://www.americanarttherapyasso ciation.org/
American Dance Therapy Association: http://www.adta.org/
American Humanist Association: http://www.americanhumanist.org/
American Psychiatric Association: https://www.psychiatry.org
American Psychological Association: https://www.apa.org
Beck Institute for Cognitive Therapy and Research: http://www.beckin stitute.org
International Association for Jungian Studies: https://www.jungianstud ies.org/
International Association of Analytical Psychology: http://www.iaap.org/
International Association of Cognitive Psychotherapy: http://www.the-iacp.com/
International Karen Horney Society: http://www.karenhorney.byethost7 .com/ikhs/index.html
National Association of Social Workers: https://www.socialworkers.org
North American Drama Therapy Association: http://www.nadta.org/
North American Society of Adlerian Psychology: http://www.alfredadler .org/
The Positive Psychology Center: https://ppc.sas.upenn.edu/
Viktor Frankl Institute of Logotherapy: http://www.logotherapyinstitute .org/
World Alliance of Dramatherapy: https://www.worldallianceofdramathe rapy.com/
World Council for Psychotherapy: http://www.worldpsyche.org/

Relevant Books and Articles

Beck, A. (1996). The past and future of cognitive therapy. *Journal of Psychotherapy Practice and Research,* 6(4), 276–284.

Chapman, A. H. (1996). *Harry Stack Sullivan—His Life and Work.* New York: G.P. Putnam's Sons.

Cretaz, E., Brunoni, A. R., and Lafer, B. (2015). Magnetic seizure therapy for unipolar and bipolar depression: A systematic review. *Neural Plasticity.* https://www.ncbi.nih.gov/pmc/articles/PMC4444586/.

Eagle, M. (1997). Contributions of Erik Erikson. *Psychoanalytic Review,* 84(3), 337–347.

Einspruch, E. L., and Forman, B. D. (1985). Observations concerning research literature on neurolinguistic programming. *Journal of Counseling Psychology,* 32(4), 589–596.

Ellis, A. (2004). *Rational Emotive Behavior Therapy: It Works for Me—It Can Work for You.* Amherst, NY: Prometheus Books.

Funk, R. (2000). *Erich Fromm: His Life and Ideas, an Illustrated Biography.* New York: Continuum.

Goldstein, S. (2012). The benefits of psychotherapy. https://www.psychologytoday.com/blog/raising-resilient-children/20129/the-benefits-psychotherapy.

Grosskurth, P. (1986). *Melanie Klein: Her World and Her Work.* New York: Alfred A. Knopf, Inc.

Hale, N. G., Jr. (1995). *Freud and the Americans: The Beginnings of Psychoanalysis in the United States.* New York and Oxford: Oxford University Press.

Hoffman, E. (1994). *The Drive for Self: Alfred Adler and the Founding of Individual Psychology.* New York: Addison-Wesley Co.

Hogan, S. (2001). *Healing Arts: The History of Art Therapy.* London: Jessica Kingsley.

Jacobi, J. (1973). *The Psychology of C.G. Jung.* New Haven, CT: Yale University Press.

Jones, E. (1953–1957). *The Life and Work of Sigmund Freud, 3 vol.* New York: Basic Books.

Kelly, G. A. (1963). *A Theory of Personality: The Psychology of Personal Constructs.* New York: W.W. Norton.

Kramer, G. P., Bernstein, D. A., and Phares, V. (2009). Behavioral and cognitive behavioral psychotherapies. *Introduction to Clinical Psychology,* 7th ed. Pp. 269–300. Upper Saddle River, NJ: Pearson Prentice Hall.

Linehan, M. (1993). *Cognitive Behavioral Treatment of Borderline Personality Disorder.* New York: Guilford Press.

Maslow, A. (2014). *Toward a Psychology of Being.* Floyd, VA: Sublime Books.

May, R. (1995). *The Psychology of Existence.* New York: McGraw-Hill.

Mayo Clinic. Deep brain stimulation (retrieved 9/15/2018). https://www.mayoclinic.org/tests-procedures/deep-brain-stimulation/about/pac-20384562.

Mayo Clinic. Electroconvulsive Therapy (ECT) (retrieved 9/15/2018). https://www.mayoclinic.ort/test-procedures/electroconvulsive-therapy/about/pac-20393894.

Mayo Clinic. Transcranial magnetic stimulation (retrieved 9/15/2018). https://www.mayclinic.org/tests-procedures/transcranial-magnetic-stimulation/about/pac-20384625.

Mayo Clinic. Vagus nerve stimulation (retrieved 9/15/2018). https://www.mayoclinic.org/tests-procedures/vagus-nerve-stimulation/about/pac-20384565.

National Institute of Mental Health. Mental Health Medications (retrieved 4/15/2018). https://www.nimh.nih.gov/health/topics/mental-health-medications/index.shtml.

Paris, B. J. (1994). *Karen Horney: A Psychoanalyst's Search for Self-understanding.* New Haven, CT: Yale University Press.

Petruska, C., and Mackewn, J. (1993). *Fritz Perls.* Thousand Oaks, CA: Sage Publications.

Pytell, T. (2015). *Viktor Frankl's Search for Meaning.* New York: Berghahn Books.

Raskin, N. (2004). *Contributions to Client-Centered Therapy and the Person-Centered Approach.* Herefordshire, Ross-on-the-Rye, UK: PCCS Books.

Seligman, M.E.P. (1975). *Helplessness: On Depression, Development, and Death.* San Francisco: W.H. Freeman.

Skinner, B. F. (1974). *Beyond Freedom and Dignity.* Harmondsworth: Penguin.

Thompson, C., Stinson, D., and Smith, A. (1990). Seasonal affective disorder and season-dependent abnormalities of melatonin suppression by light. *Lancet,* 336(8717), 703–706.

Weinstein, D. (2013). *The Pathological Family: Postwar America and the Rise of Family Therapy.* Ithaca, NY: Cornell University Press.

Whitbourne, S. K. (2011). 13 qualities to look for in an effective psychotherapist. https://www.psychologytoday.com/blog/fulfillment-any-age/201108/13-qualities-look-in-effective-psychotherapist.

Whitbourne, S. K. (2015). Psychotherapy vs. medications: The verdict is in. https://www.psychologytoday.com/blog/fulfillment-any-age/201507/psychotherapy-vs-medications-the-verdict-is-in.

Wolpe, J. (1968). Psychotherapy by reciprocal inhibition. *Conditional Reflex,* 3(4), 234–240.

Yalom, D., and Leszcz, M. (2005). *The Theory and Practice of Group Psychotherapy,* 5th ed. New York: Basic Books.

Bibliography

Chapter 1

Allessandri, M., Heiden, L., and Dunbar-Weltrer, M. (1995). History and overview. In L. Heiden and M. Hersen (eds.), *Introduction to Clinical Psychology*. New York: Plenum Press, pp. 3–21.

American Psychological Association. (2012). Recognition of psychotherapy effectiveness. http://www.apa.org/about/policy/resolutioni-psychotherapy.aspx.

Campbell, L. F., Norcross, J. C., Vasquez, M. J., and Kaslow, N. J. (March 2013). Recognition of psychotherapy effectiveness: The APA resolution. *Psychotherapy*, 50(1), 98–101.

Goldstein, S. (2012). The benefits of psychotherapy. https://www.psychologytoday.com/blog/raising-resilient-children/201209/the-benefits-psychotherapy.

Howes, R. (2008). Fundamentals of therapy #1: Who goes? https://www.psychologytoday.com/us/blog/in-therapy/200806/fundamentals-therapy-3-the-first-session.

Nydegger, R. (2008). *Understanding and Treating Depression*. Santa Barbara, CA: Praeger.

Nydegger, R. (2012). *Dealing with Anxiety and Related Disorders*. Santa Barbara, CA: Praeger.

Oxford English Dictionary. (2012). Oxford, UK: Oxford University Press.

Whitbourne, S. K. (2015). Psychotherapy vs. medications: The verdict is in. https://www.psychologytoday.com/blog/fulfillment-any-age/201507/psychotherapy-vs-medications-the-verdict-is-in.

Chapter 2

American Psychological Association. (2017). Psychotherapy: Myths versus reality. http://www.apa.org/helpcenter/psychotherapy-myths.aspx. Retrieved 2/15/18.

Glashofer, D. R. (2017). Common misconceptions about psychotherapy. https://www.verywellmind.com/comnmon-misconceptions-about-psychotherapy-4067089?print.

Howes, R. (2008). Fundamentals of therapy #1: Who goes? https://www.psychologytoday.com/blog/in-therapy/200804/fundamentals-therapy-1-who-goes. Retrieved 2/15/18.

Nydegger, R. (2008). *Understanding and Treating Depression.* Santa Barbara, CA: Praeger.

Nydegger, R. (2012). *Dealing with Anxiety and Related Disorders.* Santa Barbara, CA: Praeger.

Pedersen, P. D. (2003). Culturally biased assumptions in counseling psychology. *The Counseling Psychologist*, 31(4), 396–403.

Sue, S., Zane, N., Nagayama Hall, G. C., and Berger, L. K. (2009). The case for cultural competency in psychotherapeutic interventions. *Annual Review of Psychology*, 60, 525–548.

Chapter 3

Depression and Bipolar Support Alliance. (n.d.). Finding a mental health professional. https://www.dbsalliance.org/. Retrieved 2/17/2018.

Healthline. (2016). Types of mental health professionals. Healthline. https://www.healthline.com/health/mental-health-professionals-types.

Mayo Clinic Staff. (2014, February 18). Mental health providers: tips on finding one. mayoclinic.org/diseases-conditions/mental-illness/in-depth/mental-health-providers/art-20045530.

National Alliance on Mental Illness. (2017). Types of mental health professionals. nami.org/Learn-More/Treatment/Mental-Health-Care-Professionals.

Chapter 4

Adler, A. (1938). *Social Interest: A Challenge to Mankind.* J. Linton and R. Vaughn (Trans.). London: Faber & Faber Ltd.

Adler, A. (1956). Introduction: Individual psychology in its larger settings. In H. L. Ansbacher and R. R. Ansbacher (eds.), *The Individual Psychology of Alfred Adler.* New York: Harper Torchbooks, pp. 1–9.

Aziz, R. (1990). *C.G. Jung's Psychology of Religion and Synchronicity* (10th ed.). Albany: State University of New York Press.

Freud, S. (1976 [1900]). *The Interpretation of Dreams.* Harmondsworth: Pelican Books.

Jacobi, J. (1973). *The Psychology of C.G. Jung.* New Haven, CT, and London: Yale University Press.

Jones, E. (1949). *What Is Psychoanalysis?* London: Allen & Unwin.

Kandel, E. R. (2012). *The Age of Insight: The Quest to Understand the Unconscious in Art, Mind and Brain, from Vienna 1900 to the Present.* New York: Random House, pp. 45–46.

McKay, D. (2011). Methods and mechanisms in the efficacy of psychodynamic psychotherapy. *The American Psychologist*, 66(2), 147–148.
Sundberg, N. (2001). *Clinical Psychology: Evolving Theory, Practice, and Research*. Englewood Cliffs, NJ: Prentice Hall.

Chapter 5

Chapman, A. H. (1976). *Harry Stack Sullivan—His Life and Work*. New York: G.P. Putnam's Sons.
Erikson, E. H., and Erikson, J. M. (1998). *The Life Cycle Completed* (extended ed.). New York: W.W. Norton and Company.
Evans, F. B., III. (1996). *Harry Stack Sullivan—Interpersonal Theory and Psychotherapy*. New York: Routledge.
Funk, R. (2000). *Erich Fromm: His Life and Ideas: An Illustrated Biography*. New York: Continuum.
Grosskurth, P. (1986). *Melanie Klein: Her World and Her Work*. New York: Alfred A. Knopf, Inc.
Jensen, W. A. (2017). *Erich Fromm's Contributions to Sociological Theory*. Kalamazoo, MI: Printmill.
Paris, B. J. (1994). *Karen Horney: A Psychoanalyst's Search for Self-Understanding*. New Haven, CT: Yale University Press.
Quinn, S. (1987). *A Mind of Her Own: The Life of Karen Horney*. New York: Summit Books.
Stevens, S. (1983). *Erik Erikson: An Introduction*. New York: St. Martin's Press.
Westkott, M. (1986). *The Feminist Legacy of Karen Horney*. New Haven, CT: Yale University Press.

Chapter 6

Davies, T. (1997). *Humanism: The New Critical Idiom*. New York: Routledge.
DeCarvalho, R. J. (1991). *The Founders of Humanistic Psychology*. Santa Barbara, CA: Praeger.
Frankl, V. (2006, originally 1946). *Man's Search for Meaning: An Introduction to Logotherapy*. Boston, MA: Beacon Press.
Maslow, A. (1966). *The Psychology of Science*. New York: Harper & Row, p. 5.
Maslow, A. (1968). *Toward a Psychology of Being*. New York: John Wiley.
Maslow, A. (1971). *The Farther Reaches of Human Nature*. New York: Penguin Books.
May, R. (1969). *Love and Will*. New York: W.W. Norton.
May, R. (1981). *Freedom and Destiny*. New York: W.W. Norton.
Perls, F. (1957). Finding self through Gestalt therapy. http://www.gestalttheory.com/persons/fritzperls/publications/finding-self-through-gestalt-therapy/. A talk given at the Cooper Union by Fritz Perls.
Perls, F. (1969). *In and out of the Garbage Pail*. Lafayette, CA: Real People Press.

Rogers, C. (1957). The necessary and sufficient conditions of therapeutic personality change. *Journal of Consulting Psychology*, 21(2), 95–103.
Rogers, C. (1961). *On Becoming a Person*. New York: Houghton Mifflin.
Wahba, M. A., and Bridwell, L. G. (1976). Maslow reconsidered: A review of research and the Need Hierarchy Theory. *Organizational Behavior and Human Performance*, 15, 212–240.

Chapter 7

Beck, A. T. (2014). Advances in cognitive theory and therapy. *Annual Review of Clinical Psychology*, 10, 1–24.
Benjamin, J. (2008). George Kelly: Cognitive psychologist, humanist psychologist, or something else entirely? *History of PsySchology*, 11(4), 239–262.
Descartes, R. (1911). The Philosophical Works of Descartes, rendered into English. E. S. Haldane and G.R.T. Ross (Trans.). Cambridge: Cambridge University Press.
Ellis, A. (2004). *Rational Emotive Behavior Therapy: It Works for Me—It Can Work for You*. Amherst, NY: Prometheus Books.
Kelly, G. (1969). *Clinical Psychology and Personality: The Collected Papers of George Kelly*. New York: John Wiley and Sons.
Quinlin, P. T., and Dyson, B. (2008). *Cognitive Psychology*. Upper Saddle River, NJ: Pearson/Prentice Hall.
Robertson, D. (2010). *The Philosophy of Cognitive-Behavioral Therapy: Stoicism as Rational and Cognitive Psychotherapy*. London: Karmac.
Yankura, J., and Dryden, W. (1994). *Albert Ellis (Key Figures in Counseling and Psychotherapy Series)*. Thousand Oaks, CA: Sage Publications.

Chapter 8

Beck, A. T. (1975). *Cognitive Therapy and the Emotional Disorders*. Madison, CT: International Universities Press.
Beck, A. T. (1996). The past and future of cognitive therapy. *Journal of Psychotherapy Practice and Research*, 6(4), 276–284.
Clark, D. M., and Fairburn, C. G. (1997). *Science and Practice of Cognitive Behaviour Therapy*. Oxford: Oxford University Press.
Hopko, D. R., Robertson, S., and Lejuez, C. W. (2006). Behavioral activation for anxiety disorders. *The Behavior Analyst Today*, 7(2), 212–233.
Linehan, M. M., Comtois, K. A., Murray, A. M., Brown, M. Z., Gallop, R. J., Heard, H. L., Korslund, K. E., Tutek, D. A., Reynolds, S. K., and Lindenboim, N. (2006). Two-year randomized controlled trial and follow-up of dialectical behavior therapy vs. therapy by experts for suicidal behaviors and borderline personality disorder. *Archives of General Psychiatry*, 63(7), 757–766.
Skinner, B. F. (1974). *About Behaviorism*. New York: Random House.

Thorndike, E. L. (1905). *The Elements of Psychology*. New York: A.G. Seiler.
Wolpe, J. (1968). Psychotherapy by reciprocal inhibition. *Conditional Reflex*, 3(4), 234–240.
Wolpe, J., and Lazarus, A. (1966). *Behavior Therapy Techniques: A Guide to the Treatment of Neuroses*. Elmsford, NY: Pergamon Press.

Chapter 9

Edwards, D. (2004). *Art Therapy*. London: Sage Publications.
Landy, R. J., and Montgomery, D. T. (2012). *Theatre for Change: Education, Social Action, and Therapy*. New York: Palgrave Macmillan.
Meekums, B. (2002). *Dance Movement Therapy: A Creative Psychotherapeutic Approach*. London: Sage Publications.
Stamm, B. H. (1998). Clinical applications of telehealth in mental health care. *Professional Psychology: Research and Practice*, 29(6), 536–542.
Weinstein, D. (2013). *The Pathological Family. Postwar America and the Rise of Family Therapy*. Ithaca, NY: Cornell University Press.
Yalom, I. D., and Leszcz, M. (2005). *The Theory and Practice of Group Psychotherapy* (5th ed.). New York: Basic Books.

Chapter 10

Deep Brain Stimulation. Mayo Clinic. https://www.mayoclinic.org/tests-procedures/deep-brain-stimulation/about/pac-20384562. Retrieved 9/15/2018.
Electroconvulsive Therapy (ECT). Mayo Clinical. https://www.mayoclinic.org/tests-procedures/eclectroconvulsive-therapy/about/pac-20393894. Retrieved 9/15/2018.
Even, C., Schröder, C. M., and Gouillon, F. (2008). Efficacy of light therapy in nonseasonal depression: A systematic review. *Journal of Affective Disorders*, 108(1–2), 11–23.
Hypnotherapy. *Psychology Today*. https://www.psychologytoday.com/us/therapyu-types/hypnotherapy. Retrieved 10/4/2018.
Krauss Whitbourne, S. (2015). Psychotherapy vs. medications: The verdict is in. https://www.psychologytoday.com/blog/fulfillment-any-age/201507/psychotherapy-vs-medications-the-verdict-is-in.
Mayo Clinic. Transcranial Magnetic Stimulation. https://www.mayoclinic.org/tests-procedures/transcranial-magnetic-stimulation/about/pac-20384625. Retrieved 9/15/2018.
Mental Health Medications. The National Institute of Mental Health. https://www.nimh.nih.gov/health/topics/mental-health-medications/index.shtml. Retrieved 2/4/2019.
Schulze-Rauschenbach, S. C., Harms, U., Schlaepfer, T. E., Maier, W., Falkai, P., and Wagner, M. (2005). Distinctive neurocognitive effects of repetitive

transcranial magnetic stimulation and electroconvulsive therapy in major depression. *British Journal of Psychiatry*, 186(5), 410–416.

Seidler, G. H., and Wagner, F. E. (2006). Comparing the efficacy of EMDR and trauma-focused cognitive-behavioral therapy in the treatment of PTSD: A meta-analytic study. *Psychological Medicine*, 36(11), 1515–1522.

Vagus Nerve Stimulation. Mayo Clinic. https://www.mayoclinic.org/tests-procedures/vagus-nerve-stimulation/about/pac-20384565. Retrieved 9/15/2018.

Index

About the Author

Rudy Nydegger, PhD, ABPP, is a clinical psychologist who has taught, practiced, and done research for more than 50 years. He has numerous published articles, and this is his eighth book. His is professor emeritus at Union College and chief of psychology at Ellis Hospital in Schenectady, New York. He has been president of the Psychological Association of Northeastern New York, member of the New York State Board of Psychology, president of the New York State Psychological Association, and president of the National Register of Health Service Psychologists. He is a diplomate in the American College of Clinical Psychology, board certified in clinical psychology by the American Board of Professional Psychology, a distinguished fellow in the New York State Psychological Association, and a distinguished fellow in the National Academies of Practice.